DIVORCE
and the
Special Needs Child

of related interest

Great Answers to Difficult Questions about Divorce
What Children Need to Know
Fanny Cohen Herlem
ISBN 978 1 84310 672 2

A GUIDE FOR PARENTS

DIVORCE

and the

Special Needs Child

MARGARET "PEGI" PRICE

Jessica Kingsley Publishers
London and Philadelphia

First published in 2010
by Jessica Kingsley Publishers
116 Pentonville Road
London N1 9JB, UK
and
400 Market Street, Suite 400
Philadelphia, PA 19106, USA

www.jkp.com

Library of Congress Cataloging in Publication Data
Price, Margaret S.
    Divorce and the special needs child : a guide for parents / Margaret "Pegi" Price.
    p. cm.
    Includes bibliographical references and index.
    ISBN 978-1-84905-825-4 (alk. paper)
    1. Divorce--Law and legislation--United States--Popular works. 2. Children with disabilities--Legal status, laws, etc.--United States--Popular works. 3. Divorced parents--United States--Handbooks, manuals, etc. 4. Children of divorced parents--Services for--United States--Popular works. I. Title.
    KF535.Z9P746 2010
    346.7301'66--dc22
                                2010000570

British Library Cataloguing in Publication Data
A CIP catalogue record for this book is available from the British Library

ISBN 978 1 84905 825 4

Printed and bound in the United States by
Thomson-Shore, Inc.

This book is dedicated to my son, Sam,
who has shaped my life

Contents

Disclaimer

None of the material in this book shall be considered as rendering legal advice, generally or specifically. Readers are urged to obtain legal advice from their own lawyers. The laws vary greatly from state to state and even within states. Laws change frequently. This book discusses general legal concepts that are intended for educational and informational purposes only. This book is not a substitute for obtaining legal counsel or for hiring a lawyer.

Note

This book addresses many types of special needs. It is not focused on any one type. The majority of the author's experience is in the area of autism, but this book is not focused on autism. This book encompasses special needs generally, including developmental disabilities, hearing and visual impairments, orthopedic impairment, neuromuscular diseases, traumatic injuries, cancer, emotional disturbances, child abuse, chronic or ongoing infectious diseases, immunological disorders, as well as cardiovascular, pulmonary, gastrointestinal, nutritional, metabolic, endocrine, kidney, liver, blood, musculoskeletal, connective tissue, neurological, gynecological and obstetric disorders, and conditions usually associated with pediatrics or genetics.

If any particular disability, condition or disorder is not mentioned specifically, it is unintentional. The focus of this book is on all our families, and the unique issues we need addressed when our families are going through the family court system, through divorce, paternity and modification of existing decrees on child support, child custody, and other family court issues.

Gender has been allocated randomly throughout this book. No assumptions have been made about the gender of the caregiver, child with special needs, legal professionals, or any other person.

About the Author

Margaret "Pegi" Price, J.D., practices exclusively in the area of family law—divorce, paternity, modifications, child support, child custody, and visitation. Pegi has been a lawyer for over 20 years. She is a past Chair of the Family Law Section of the Bar Association of Metropolitan St. Louis, and is a member of the Family Law Section of the Missouri Bar; of AFCC, the Association of Family and Conciliation Courts; and of NCFR, the National Council on Family Relations. She is frequently called in as a consultant on family law cases involving children and adults with disabilities or special needs.

She has written *The Special Needs Child and Divorce: A Practical Guide to Evaluating and Handling Cases* (American Bar Association 2009) and *What You Need To Know About Divorce* (1997), as well as many legal articles. Pegi presented a paper and was a speaker at the 2006 World Autism Congress in Cape Town, South Africa, on the topic of Divorce and Children with Autism. Pegi has been a speaker on the subject of Divorce and Children with Autism at three national conferences of the Autism Society of America, and a speaker at many state bar conferences and seminars for educators and professionals in the field of special needs, on the topic of families with special needs children.

Pegi is past President of the Gateway (St. Louis) chapter of the Autism Society of America. She has testified at many state legislative committee hearings and met with numerous legislators to urge continued funding of programs for the disabled. She works with many individuals and families in the special needs community, and does extensive public speaking to increase awareness of special needs and to spread a message of hope.

Pegi's son was diagnosed with autism when he was three years old, in 1998. He underwent intensive early intervention and therapy. When her son was six years old and still functionally nonverbal, Pegi went through her own divorce, in which she wrote her first Parenting Plan for a child with serious special needs. Two years after the divorce, in March 2003, her son emerged from autism and his medical diagnosis was lifted. His story has been the focus of two television news features, in which he was called a pioneer in the field of autism, and identified as one of the first children in the United States to emerge from autism. The television features filmed him at school and while flying an airplane. He started flying airplanes when he was ten years old. He travels extensively with Pegi to conferences, including South Africa, where he toured Robben Island and visited Nelson Mandela's actual cell. Sam is now 15 years old and in regular public high school. He does volunteer work with families whose children have autism, and provides insight on what it was like to have autism. Sam speaks at national conferences with Pegi. He aspires to be a writer and speaker to help the special needs community.

Pegi's experience has been primarily in the area of autism, but she has been involved in many types of special needs throughout her life. Her younger sister is developmentally disabled, and received hours of daily physical therapy for years. The therapy was done by the family in the home. Pegi has done extensive volunteer work with disabled children and adults, teaching fine art to blind children and adults and working with developmentally disabled persons. Her passion is to help families with disabilities and special needs.

Preface

Being the parent of a special needs or disabled child is a blessing, but it is also stressful. Some families pull together and become stronger in this situation, but unfortunately many do not. There are conflicting studies on how high the divorce rates are in families with a special needs or disabled child, but whether the divorce rate is 50, 75 or 90 percent does not matter to the individual family. What matters to each family is whether they will weather the storm, or get divorced. Statistics are irrelevant to the individual.

When a family with a special needs or disabled child goes through divorce, they need special attention paid to their unique needs. (For purposes of simplicity, the terms "special needs" and "disability" will be used interchangeably throughout the text. When one term is used, it is not intended to exclude the other.) When you have a child with a disability, you need specialized information when going through divorce, to make sure that your child's unique needs are properly handled. This book is intended to be your guidebook to help you through this difficult time.

The author has lived through this experience in her own life, as she went through divorce when her son was six years old and nonverbal with autism. She brings the type of insights that can only be achieved through experience.

CHAPTER 1

Your Child's Special Needs

You are the parent of a child with a disability or with special needs. Your life is not turning out the way you had imagined years ago when you dreamed of getting married and having a family. At some point, your life changed. You may have found out during the pregnancy, at the time your child was born or at some later point. Regardless of when it happened, life as you knew it is changed forever.

You go through the typical stages of disbelief, anger, shock, rage, and denial. You may also experience sadness, even depression. Perhaps you try to make a deal with God. You look for reasons, causes, answers. Why did this happen? What did I do wrong? If only I had done this differently or that differently, perhaps my child would be healthy and strong. You may blame yourself. You may blame your spouse, your genetics, or your doctor. After playing the blame game for a while you realize the futility of it, as that doesn't help your child. Then you settle in for the long haul.

First you educate yourself on your child's condition. Then you make the necessary changes to your lifestyle to accommodate your child's needs. As time passes, depending on the type and severity of your child's condition, you may find yourself somewhat isolated from many of your previous friends and social activities. Now your friends might be other parents in the waiting rooms at therapy sessions.

Over time you may become physically and emotionally exhausted. Raising a special needs child often means that you are never "off duty." In a healthy, strong marriage both parents pull together and work as a team to create the best possible life for the child and their family. Some of the strongest marriages are those in which there is a disabled or special needs child in the family.

This is not, however, always the case. We live in a society in which half of all marriages result in divorce. Courts are overwhelmed by the sheer numbers of divorce cases going through the court systems every day. In order to try to keep up with the massive volume of divorce cases, most courts have devised certain standard forms to be used. Often these forms improve the process of going through divorce, by streamlining cases and moving cases through the court system more quickly, less expensively and with more uniform and predictable results.

Many things can contribute to a marriage ending in divorce. Financial stress is frequently a factor, even when there is not a special needs child in the family, but it can be much more expensive to raise a disabled child than to raise a child without a disability.

In addition to the financial strain, raising a child with serious health problems causes great stress on marriages and other romantic relationships. The entire dynamic of the relationship changes. You go from being lovers to being round-the-clock home healthcare providers. One day you are going out with friends, living life to the fullest, and basking in the glow of your relationship. Then you get a diagnosis and you find yourself filling out insurance forms, scheduling doctor and therapy appointments, managing medication schedules, and battling school districts. Countless times you sit up through the night taking care of a sick child. Countless more times you sit up through the night worrying about your child's future. Will your child live through the year? Will you somehow find enough money to pay for the medicine and treatment your child needs? Will the insurance company cancel your coverage? Will your child live to adulthood? How will you take care of your child when you get old? If taking care of your child means you can't work full time and save for retirement, are you going to live in poverty in your old age? And does anyone care?

Not surprisingly, many marriages do not survive this onslaught. It doesn't have to be that way. A strong marriage can become even stronger through facing challenges together. But the reality is that many of these marriages fail. These failed marriages tend to fall into one or more of several scenarios.

One such scenario is that one parent may simply refuse to give up life as they knew it, and abandon the child and other parent. They turn their backs, and "go on with their lives."

Another scenario is that when one parent is in denial, the lion's share of the child's care falls to the other parent. The caregiver parent becomes physically and emotionally exhausted, and has nothing left at the end of the day to give to the marital relationship. The caregiver parent eventually may become resentful about the lack of help, while the other parent bemoans the lack of attention they are receiving from their spouse. The caregiver parent may not have the time or energy to take care of themselves as they used to, so the parent who is in denial may feel less attraction toward them. They grow apart, with each feeling justified in their feelings and position.

A third common scenario is that one parent may become completely devoted to the child's care, which is, of course, a good thing, unless they cross over the line and refuse to let the other parent participate. The caregiver parent may feel justified, as the other parent may not have as much training or experience in the child's care and treatment as the caregiver parent. The other parent may feel frustrated and shut out. If they cannot work this out, with the caregiver parent realizing that they did not learn everything overnight and the other parent truly getting appropriate training and experience, this tug-of-war situation is likely to result in divorce.

Regardless of what leads to the demise of the relationship, in order to obtain a divorce in the United States and in many other countries one must go through the courts. These courts are already trying to handle a huge number of divorce cases. As discussed, they have developed certain forms and procedures in order to streamline the process and achieve more uniform and efficient results.

Think of the divorce court process as an assembly line in a factory. Now think of the assembly line becoming jammed because someone threw a wrench in the machinery. This is what can happen when a divorce case involving a child with disability hits the current court system. The lawyers and judges may realize that *something* needs to be done in order to protect the best interests of the child, but they usually have no idea *what* needs to be done.

Unless they have experienced raising a special needs child, there will be many things they simply do not know. Think back to what you knew before your child's disability. How much have you learned since then? How many things have you learned through day-to-day experience, by educating yourself, through receiving training, reading books, doing research, asking questions, and attending conferences? Assume the judges and lawyers in your case do not know any of those things.

How can the judges and lawyers possibly achieve a result that is in the best interests of the disabled child? They are trying to make their way through a landmine field while wearing a blindfold. This can have several results.

One result is that the standard "cookie cutter" approach will be utilized by the court, even though it does not address the unique needs of the child or of the family. Unfortunately, this is the typical result. This is understandable, considering the realities of our legal system.

If a judge takes a risk and makes a decision that is "outside the box," it might get reversed on appeal. Since disability and divorce is a new issue for the divorce courts, the judges cannot rely upon previous decisions by other judges to justify a decision that is different from the standard way in which regular divorces are handled. No matter how much the judge might want to help your family achieve the best possible outcome, he or she is supposed to rely upon some type of authority in doing so.

It is also risky for lawyers to step outside the bounds of common practice. A lawyer can risk being sued for malpractice or receiving a bar complaint if they do not follow the usual approach to handling divorce cases. It is far easier to defend your actions if you handled a divorce case the way any of your competent peers would have handled it than when you did not use the standard forms.

Even when the judges and lawyers want to do the right thing and may have some ideas about how to do so, the inherent pressures within our legal system may cause them to think twice. Clearly, it is an uphill battle to prevent our cases from being handled in the standard, "cookie-cutter" manner.

Thankfully, the "cookie cutter" approach is not the only option. If you educate your divorce lawyer on your child's unique situation and on workable options to be incorporated into your documents, and that information is properly presented to the court, it is possible to achieve a much better result for your child and for your family. This book discusses how to work with your lawyer and how to present the relevant information to the court in order to get the best result possible.

Keep in mind that this is a new area of law, and you will have to work hard to get these results. No matter how well you present your case, some courts will be hesitant at first to step outside of their comfort zone. You may not get everything you want or need, but you should get a better result over time than if these important issues had not been presented to the court. Just because something is difficult does not mean you should give up or not even try. You have grown and become stronger through your experiences as the parent of a disabled or special needs child. You can do this.

TYPES OF SPECIAL NEEDS AND DISABILITIES

What are special needs and disabilities? We live in a society in which labels are thrown around like candy. After a while, we become desensitized to the labels, and begin just to view them as categories or stacks in which to sort people. The disability or special need itself loses meaning due to the current trend to try to make everything appear to be a syndrome or disorder. This overuse of labels and diagnoses can cause those in the legal profession to disregard the importance of special needs and disability in divorce cases. If nearly everyone you know has some label or diagnosis, it can make the labels seem irrelevant. The clear problem with this is the reality that certain special needs and diagnoses are highly relevant when going through the courts for divorce, paternity, or other family law matters.

While studies vary, some estimate the divorce rate in families with special healthcare needs is higher than that of the general population. Kraus (2005) discussed rates between 85 and 90 percent in families with special needs children. Those of us who have experienced raising a disabled or special needs child already know the stress levels are high. We have seen many people in our special community go through divorce. We have also seen many people stay in a troubled marriage out of sheer desperation and fear of being unable to make it on their own with their disabled child.

This issue impacts a huge number of families. Sneed, May and Stencel (2000) estimated that nearly 20 million children in the United States have special health needs and that 30 percent of these children have two or more special health needs. When you combine the large number of families going through divorce with the children in the United States who have special health needs, you get millions of children who are at risk when their families are going through the divorce process.

Clearly, not all special needs are relevant when the family is going through divorce; they may be very mild and not affected by such things as a visitation schedule or the amount of child support paid. Some special health needs are, however, highly relevant when the family is going through divorce, because the outcome of the divorce case will impact the child's well-being.

How do you know which special needs or disabilities are relevant when going through divorce? This must be decided on a case-by-case basis. The unique needs of each child must be evaluated. The entire family dynamic must be evaluated. Only then can you apply the true standard which should be applied to every family law case involving any child, whether disabled or not: if it is in the best interest of the child for their disability or special needs to be considered during the divorce, then they should be. *The best interest of the child* is the ultimate bottom line.

Family Court judges and lawyers are facing the issue of special needs in more of their cases than ever before. They need to be able to identify or recognize special needs. They cannot properly handle an issue if they are unaware of the issue. Since "little to nothing [has been] published on this topic in the professional literature as guidance, divorce professionals have been at a loss as to how to accurately and effectively identify and manage these cases" (Saposnek 2005, p.563). As the number of special needs children is increasing, it is more important than ever that lawyers, judges, and other Family Court professionals become well educated on this subject and learn how to recognize and handle special needs. From 1994 to 2004 the number of autistic children who receive special education services grew from 20,000 to 140,000. There are many more examples of the increasing numbers of special needs children. During the last 20 years the rate of illness in children in the United States has increased. About 30 percent of children under age 18 have some type of chronic illness. The United States Census Bureau reported there were 49.7 million Americans with some form of disability in the year 2000. This means that one person in five is handicapped. People with disabilities are expected to live longer than they used to, because of medical advancements.

Not all illnesses or medical conditions amount to special needs that should be addressed in the family courts but it is important to recognize relevant special needs, and to tell them from everyday situations. Your lawyer might not know that someone in your family has a disability or special need. You must *tell them*. I never cease to be amazed at how many times my divorce client does not mention a serious disability to me until I ask and, even then, I sometimes have to drag it out of them. Many people do not make the connection between their child's disability and their divorce—but if the disability issues are not handled properly in the divorce, the family will suffer greatly.

When you are talking with your lawyer, tell the lawyer about any physical, mental or emotional disability, learning disability, behavior or mood disorder, or any other issue that might require special consideration in the divorce, for purposes of medication or medical treatment, visitation, child support, or maintenance.

Tell your lawyer if any of the children receive special assistance at school, or have an IEP (Individualized Education Plan) or 504 Plan at school. Tell your lawyer if any of the children are on medication or are in counseling, physical therapy, behavior therapy, or psychological counseling. And by all means tell your lawyer if any of the children have a diagnosed medical condition, psychiatric condition, or learning disability.

If any of the children have a diagnosed medical condition, psychiatric condition, or learning disability, you need to provide additional information to your lawyer. The lawyer will need to understand much more in order to handle the situation appropriately.

For every diagnosed medical condition, psychiatric condition, or learning disability, provide (preferably typewritten) the following information:

- the official diagnosis
- the person who made the official diagnosis
- when the condition was diagnosed
- when the symptoms first appeared

- all testing that was done to evaluate the condition, including testing that ruled out other conditions
- what made the parents or others think the child needed to be evaluated
- all other professionals who have confirmed or agreed with the diagnosis
- all follow-up appointments since the initial diagnosis
- all treatment done since the initial diagnosis.

Once this information has been collected, your lawyer will need to know details about your child's current condition and prognosis. Diagnosis is merely the starting point in the lawyer's evaluation of how your child's disability needs to be addressed in the divorce. Your lawyer also needs to know what your child's current condition is and your child's prognosis, which is your child's expected outcome. Is your child's condition curable—can they make it go away permanently? Is your child's condition treatable, meaning they can't make it go away but they can make it better or perhaps make things not get any worse? Or is your child's condition terminal, or fatal? Clearly your lawyer needs to know all these things in order to assess the special needs issues of your case properly.

Your lawyer also needs to know how this condition will impact the child, any siblings and both parents. This should be explored thoroughly with your lawyer. Put together information that in plain language explains what your child's life expectancy is. Also discuss how your child's condition affects your child's life now and how it is expected to affect it in the future. Discuss how your child's condition affects the lives of your other children now and how it is expected to impact their lives in the future and how the child's condition affects your life and your spouse's life now and how it is expected to affect your lives in the future.

Your information for your lawyer should include a statement of who is the primary caregiver of your disabled or special needs child. This might be you or your spouse, a grandparent, or some other person.

You then need to discuss with your lawyer who, of the child's parents, provides the most time and care to the child. Break it down so your lawyer clearly understands which parent provides the most care and attention to the special needs or disability and which parent provides the most time and care of the child's typical needs.

Another area you should discuss is the impact of your child's disability on your career and your spouse's career. Explain to your lawyer how it has impacted both of your careers now and how it is expected to affect your careers in the future. Collect tax returns from a period of several years to show the impact it has had on the income of each parent. Collect end-of-the-year pension and retirement account statements for a period of years to show how it has impacted contributions to these accounts. Provide detailed information for your lawyer as to how the child's condition is expected to impact both parents' career advancement and retirement plan contributions in the future. ·

Your lawyer has a critical need for this information, including the details and the document backup, such as tax returns, end-of-the-year statements, and so on. The lawyer must be prepared to ask and answer detailed questions concerning the child's specific special needs. To do this, the lawyer must know the questions to ask the family in order to have this information in the client file. This information should be first gathered, and then read and thoroughly understood. Your lawyer may need to conduct additional research or hire a medical professional to explain the terminology and concepts relevant to your child in order to understand the material you provide him.

One of the best things you can do for your lawyer is to create a well-organized, thorough file of medical records and special needs information. Keep a full copy of this file for your own reference. Do not mark or write on any of the items in this file, as your lawyer may need to use them as exhibits for court. The items that should be in this file will vary in each case, but they should be sufficient, with written narrative from you, for the lawyer to determine certain information concerning your child's disability or special needs, such as the items discussed below. Realize that there may be additional information that is relevant and important in your case, so add to these items as appropriate.

With the information from the file you make, your lawyer should be able to easily find the names, addresses, telephone numbers, and credentials of all persons whom the child currently sees for her condition. It also needs to list clearly all medications your child currently takes, including frequency, dosage, reason for the medication, the expected result of the medication, the amount of time the child is anticipated to remain on the medication, and all side effects the child has experienced from the medication.

Your file should contain information on all therapies the child currently receives, including therapies received at home and at school. For each therapy provide information on the person or organization who provides therapy, the entity who referred the child for that therapy, where the therapy is received, the type of therapy and methodology used, frequency and duration of the therapy, the length of time the therapy is expected to continue, the cost of the therapy, how the cost is paid, the amount of uncovered cost of the therapy, incidental costs of the therapy (which can include transportation, time and cost of caregiver, supplies, meals, and equipment), and the name of the person who takes the child to the therapy.

This thorough discussion needs to be provided for all types of therapy that the child has currently and is expected to have. Include this information on all waitlisted therapy, with clear notation that the child is not yet in the therapy because of the wait list, and provide if possible an estimate of the remaining time on the wait list. Provide a thorough discussion for all types of treatment a child is currently undergoing and is expected to have.

Provide complete information on the expectations regarding future therapies, treatments and medications. Also provide complete information on every waiting list the child is currently on, including therapy, program, school, or funding wait lists.

An essential component of the file you prepare for your lawyer will be an itemization of all direct and indirect costs of the child's disability, including therapy, doctors, other healthcare providers or practitioners, prescription medications, and nonprescription medications, supplements, supplies, equipment, dietary and special nutritional requirements, caregiver training, special clothing requirements, special personal care items (such as diapers, especially in someone well past the usual age of potty training), home environment modifications, vehicle modifications, modifications at school, transportation, non-parental caregiver costs, and all other costs applicable in your child's case.

A checklist of the information you need to collect for your lawyer is provided in the "Checklists" section at the end of this book. Realize this list is not exhaustive, as your case may require additional information. This is merely a starting point.

Certain items should be addressed in the pleadings in your case. In order to address these issues you must make sure the lawyer understands the information you have given her. It may be necessary for your lawyer to consult an expert in the particular field your case involves so she will be well educated on the issues inherent in your child's condition and be able to argue your case to the judge.

In the best interests of the special needs child, the issue of special needs should be raised immediately in the case. Your lawyer should not "save" this issue to spring it on the other side at trial. Properly addressing the issues raised by special needs requires much more time than a case not involving special needs. If the issue of special needs is "saved" for surprise at trial for some perceived tactical advantage, the child will suffer.

Since many things must be stated in any Petition, a statement that there are no known or suspected special needs, or a statement that there are known or suspected special needs and a brief statement of the facts concerning them should not be a big deal. It should, of course, be stated in the responsive pleading—the Answer—as well.

Raising the subject of special needs in the initial pleading and responsive pleading will cause the parties to think about the issue early on and will bring the issue to the court's attention. By addressing known or suspected special needs, the parties would be able to amend their pleadings in the event a child became diagnosed during the pendency of the litigation. There should also be amendment of pleadings during the litigation in the event that a special need worsens during that time.

Undiagnosed disabilities or special needs

Disabilities and special needs can occur at any time in a person's life. Some special needs are obvious from birth, while others become apparent later, such as terminal illnesses and other situations. Not all disabilities or special needs may have been diagnosed when the divorce is filed. Sometimes the family is in denial or hopes that the child will grow out of it. The current doctor may not have made the diagnosis yet. The family may be aware of a problem and be going through the process of evaluation of the problem while they are going through the divorce. Whatever the reason, the lawyer or judge must be aware of certain special needs issues even when they have not yet been formally diagnosed. Your lawyer will need to decide if it is a situation that needs to be evaluated by professionals. Keep in mind that lawyers and judges do not learn medicine in law school and do not pretend to know as much as doctors. Work with your lawyer to determine if your child needs to be evaluated by a professional.

When should you send your child for professional evaluation? Some general warning signs include:

- Your child is having ongoing problems at school.
- Your child is having ongoing run-ins with law enforcement or other authority.
- You have difficulty "handling" your child.
- Your child is frequently sick or misses school.
- You or others are concerned that your child is not performing up to your child's abilities—i.e. your child is underachieving.
- Your child is not developing with his peers—including physical, emotional, academic, and skills development.
- You, your lawyer, your child's teacher or a significant caregiver express concern that "something is not quite right."

If you see these warning signs, talk with your lawyer. It would be best to bring up this concern at your initial interview with the lawyer.

If you decide your child needs evaluation by a professional, you need to determine what type of professional would be most appropriate. Just as you would not send someone with a brain tumor to an orthodontist, you need to seek the advice of the appropriate medical professional for your child's needs. The material below is by no means exhaustive or complete, but it should get you started on the path to "special needs triage."

Clearly, I am not a physician and I do not pretend to be one. I have included a discussion of the diagnostic criteria for autism, deaf/blindness, emotional disturbance, hearing impairment and deafness, intellectual disability, multiple disabilities, orthopedic impairments, other health impaired, specific learning disability, speech or language impairment, traumatic brain injury, visual impairment including blindness, and developmental delay, to get you started in the evaluation of your child's disability or special need.

It is easy for parents to become overwhelmed by divorce and want to wait until after the divorce to deal with the issue of evaluations, but that is a huge mistake. In order to advocate properly for your child's disability or special need, it needs to be properly diagnosed and documented.

Be aware that this discussion does not include every possible disability or special need that can affect a child. This is merely a factor of space limitations. There was no intent to ignore or minimize any particular condition or category. It would take several thousand pages to discuss every disability or special need. This information is intended to give general guidelines. If you have any reasonable concern that your child should be evaluated by a medical professional, get it done.

Autism

Autism incidence is increasing at an alarming rate. Some think a portion of this is due to increased awareness of autism, with the cause of autism still unknown. Most of you know someone in your family or circle of friends whose life has been touched by autism. Although there are many attempts to treat autism, the current success rates are so low that many children with autism will be institutionalized by age 12. Autism is a severe neurological condition that can impact every aspect of a child's life and can turn the family upside down. Children with autism frequently have sensory issues. This means that light, movement, sound, clothing, water, anything touching the skin, particular noises, types and textures of food and drink and so on can be excruciating, painful, and confusing to the child with sensory issues.

Children with autism can be extremely oversensitive to some things and extremely undersensitive to others. One example of this is having a very high pain threshold.

Guardians-ad-Litem (GAL) need to be aware that communication with a child with autism can be extremely difficult. When a GAL represents a child with autism, the GAL may need to use a professional or para-professional to help the GAL communicate with the child. Some children with autism are nonverbal. Even when a child with autism is verbal, the speech can be unusual—it can be high-pitched, sing-songy, and echolalic (the child repeats what is said to her, instead of using typical responsive speech). When dealing with a high-functioning child with autism who communicates well, there are often remaining aspects of language impairment, and the child may speak their native language as though it were a second language, not their native language. They might not use slang, idioms, or contractions, and speak in a "little professor" tone.

Children with autism often struggle with socialization. In severe cases the child is so withdrawn they do not interact with anyone. If you attempt to bring the child into group play or activities they might withdraw, shriek or throw a tantrum. Social development is often delayed or impaired. Sometimes they are seen as "robotic" by their peers. They are often shunned, avoided, even taunted and bullied. They often get along better with adults and much younger children than with children their own age.

Autism has a broad spectrum of severity, from mild to severe. A child with autism might have only a few of the symptoms or many of them. It can be difficult for professionals to diagnose autism. Pediatric neurologists are well educated in autism and usually do an excellent job properly diagnosing it. Sometimes speech therapists, occupational therapists, physical therapists, and special education specialists make the diagnosis, and send the child on to a neurologist. Children at the mild end of the spectrum are often not diagnosed, or are misdiagnosed with something else. Many times they don't get properly diagnosed until they get in trouble at school or with law enforcement.

Hearing deficits

All newborns should have thorough hearing evaluations. Every child should have annual hearing assessments. Despite this, hearing deficits often go undiagnosed for years. When a child has severe bilateral congenital hearing deficit, it is often recognized by the parents when the baby is only a few weeks old because the baby does not respond to voices or other sounds. Mild to moderate or unilateral hearing deficit is often not diagnosed until the child is in school. Failure to have hearing deficit properly diagnosed and treated can result in lasting developmental problems for the child, as most of a child's speech and language development takes place in the early years of life. These children often get only speech and language therapy, with the underlying hearing deficit left undiagnosed and untreated. Many children who have vestibular disturbances with abnormal motor development are misdiagnosed as having developmental disorders, including intellectual disability. Have your family practice doctor or pediatrician perform a hearing evaluation on the child, and then send the child to a specialist if necessary.

Visual deficits

All children should have regular eye exams. If your child is having difficulty with reading, art, or writing, he might have visual problems. If your child has tracking, depth perception, or other visual problems he might have trouble in gym class or recess. Often children are embarrassed by these things, so they will say they don't like art, reading, gym class, or whatever is difficult, in order to cover their disability. It may take a little detective work to discover the true problem. It is essential to get proper diagnosis and treatment, as these problems do not go away on their own, and your child may fall behind in school because of his undiagnosed impairments. Your family practice doctor or pediatrician can perform a vision test on the child, and send your child to a specialist if necessary.

Mental retardation / intellectual disability

Mental retardation is the umbrella term that was used for many years to refer to various forms of intellectual disability. Now the term "intellectual disability" is sometimes used instead of "mental retardation." Classification of mental retardation used to be based upon IQ alone, with mild MR (mental retardation) meaning an IQ of 52 to 68; moderate MR meaning an IQ of 36 to 51, severe MR meaning an IQ of 20 to 35; and profound MR meaning an IQ of less than 20. Now the definition of mental retardation/intellectual disability reflects the child's adaptation to the environment and interaction with others in addition to the child's limited intellectual function.

A child with mental retardation or intellectual disability usually has limitations in social, language, and self-help adaptive skills. Seizures, psychiatric disorders, and behavioral disorders can also occur with mental retardation or intellectual disability. A child with mental retardation or an intellectual disability may develop behavioral problems from his social rejection by other students or from realizing that others see him as different and deficient. The behavioral disorders may include explosive outbursts, temper tantrums, and physically aggressive behavior reacting to what would be considered normal stress. Your family practice doctor or pediatrician can evaluate your child, and refer your child to any necessary specialists.

Learning disabilities

Learning disabilities are being unable to get or keep specific skills or information because of problems with attention, memory, perception, or reasoning. This definition assumes the child has normal cognitive abilities. Learning disabilities can include problems in reading (such as dyslexia), arithmetic, spelling, written expression or handwriting, and in the use or understanding of verbal abilities and nonverbal abilities. Attention Deficit Disorder is usually considered related to but separate from learning disabilities.

Children with physical abnormalities and communication problems are generally diagnosed early in life. Mild to moderate disorders are often not diagnosed until the child goes to school.

Behavioral problems are found frequently in children with learning disorders and can include difficulty with impulse control, discipline problems, withdrawal, avoidance, shyness, excessive fears, and aggressiveness. Cognitive problems are problems in thinking, reasoning, and problem solving. Reasoning disabilities can include problems in conceptualizing, abstracting, generalizing, and organizing and planning information for problem solving.

Children with visual perception and auditory processing problems often have difficulty with spatial cognition and orientation, such as spatial memory, awareness of position and place, and object localization. They can have problems with visual attention and memory, and problems with being able to distinguish and analyze sounds.

Memory function is another area of difficulty for these children, both short-term and long-term memory. They may also have a hard time with verbal recall or retrieval.

A thorough evaluation and assessment should be performed if these or any other learning disabilities are suspected. Usually the child's school is the best place to have this assessment. Many of today's schools have a broad range of professionals who can perform a thorough evaluation of possible learning disorders. Evaluations should include medical, intellectual, educational, linguistic, and psychological evaluations.

Attention Deficit Disorder

Attention Deficit Disorder used to be defined with focus primarily on excessive physical activity. Attention Deficit Disorder is now defined as a pattern of developmentally inappropriate inattention and impulsivity. Hyperactivity may or may not be present. Attention Deficit Disorder is now being seen as just a different kind of brain chemistry and a different approach to learning. ADD is no longer seen as a disorder or deficit.

ADD and ADHD (Attention Deficit Hyperactivity Disorder) make up approximately half of all developmental disorders which result in referrals to clinics. There is no medical test for ADD or ADHD, and it can be difficult to diagnose. I have included detailed information to help you determine if your child needs to be evaluated for ADD or ADHD.

The Diagnostic and Statistical Manual of Mental Disorders (DSM-IV) (American Psychiatric Association 2000) criteria for ADD give nine signs of inattention, six signs of hyperactivity and three signs of impulsivity. Your child does not have to have all 18 signs to be diagnosed with ADD, but her symptoms must be present in two or more settings (e.g. both at home and at school) and her symptoms must negatively affect her social or academic functioning.

There are nine DSM-IV signs of *inattention*. They are a child who:

1. does not pay attention to details

2. has a hard time with attention to work or while playing

3. does not appear to listen when spoken to

4. does not follow instructions and does not finish projects

5. has a hard time with organization

6. avoids activities that need sustained mental effort

7. loses things

8. is easily distracted, and

9. is forgetful.

There are six DSM-IV signs of *hyperactivity*. They are a child who:

1. fidgets or squirms

2. has a hard time staying in her seat

3. runs about or climbs a lot

4. has a hard time playing quietly

5. seems to be always on the go, and

6. talks a lot.

There are three DSM-IV signs of *impulsivity*. They are a child who:

1. blurts out answers before the questions are done
2. has a hard time waiting for his turn, and
3. interrupts.

A child's teacher is often the one who suggests that the child be evaluated for ADD. The evaluation can be done by the family practice doctor, pediatrician, pediatric neurologist, or by specialists within the school system.

Emotional disturbances

Many types of emotional disturbances can be disabilities or special needs. Some of the more common emotional disturbances are discussed here, but this is not complete or exhaustive of the subject. Adjustment disorder, posttraumatic stress disorder (PTSD), substance abuse disorders, conduct disorders, depression, bipolar disorder (manic-depressive psychosis), and schizophrenia will be discussed.

If you think your child has any of these emotional disorders, prompt evaluation by a professional is critical. These disorders do not just go away on their own. Your child will not grow out of it. If you ignore the situation it will probably get worse. Your child's doctor may refer your child to a specialist for further evaluation and treatment.

Adjustment disorder is an extreme reaction to environmental stress with symptoms that let up as stress decreases. Divorce and geographical relocation are environmental stressors that can cause an adjustment disorder.

Posttraumatic stress disorder (PTSD) can occur in otherwise stable children and adolescents after major traumatic events. PTSD can occur immediately or after several weeks, months, or even years have passed. PTSD is a more severe condition than adjustment disorder.

Substance abuse disorders are occurring in younger children than ever before, even in preadolescents. *Misuse* means the use of illegal substances. *Abuse* means repeated use with bad consequences.

Conduct disorder is a pattern of behavior of aggression toward people and animals, property destruction, lying, theft, and serious rules violation. Boys with conduct disorder tend to fight, steal, and vandalize. Girls with conduct disorder tend to lie, run away, and become prostitutes. Oppositional defiant disorder (ODD) is like conduct disorder, but without a persistent pattern of behavior. ODD sometimes develops into conduct disorder. Children with conduct disorder often have suicidal ideation, and their suicide attempts must be taken seriously.

Depression in children is now being identified by most medical professionals. A child with depression can look sad, have apathy, be withdrawn, not enjoy things, feel rejected and unloved, have headaches, abdominal pain, insomnia, may act silly, and may blame himself for everything. A child with chronic depression can have anorexia, lose weight, be despondent, and have suicidal ideation. Surprisingly, children with depression are sometimes overactive and have aggressive, antisocial behavior.

Bipolar disorder rarely appears before puberty. Bouts of depression, and also having stuperous or psychotic episodes should cause concern of bipolar disorder. In children the manic episode of bipolar disorder often looks like an excited psychotic attack.

A child with *childhood schizophrenia* can be withdrawn, have a flattened affect (lack of facial expression), apathy, thought disorder (blocking and perseveration), ideas of reference, hallucinations, delusions and complaints of thought control. Schizophrenia in a child looks like schizophrenia in an adult.

Orthopedic impairments

These are best evaluated by the child's treating physician and therapists. There are many types of orthopedic impairments. Congenital anomaly, such as club foot or absence of an extremity or a portion thereof; impairments caused by disease, such as poliomyelitis or bone tuberculosis; and impairments having other causes, such as cerebral palsy, amputations, fractures, or burns with contractures, are a few examples.

Multiple disabilities

When a child has more than one diagnosis, such as cerebral palsy and depression, or mental retardation and autism, they have multiple diagnoses. The combination of disabilities can create incredible challenges for the child and the family. These children need to be thoroughly and carefully evaluated.

Traumatic brain injury

Traumatic brain injury (TBI) can include either an open head injury or a closed head injury. This category does not include brain injuries from birth trauma, or congenital or degenerative brain injuries.

Head injury is the leading cause of death and disability in people under the age of 50. Head injuries cause more deaths than anything else in men and boys under age 35. Severe head injury kills almost half of the people who suffer from it, whether they receive treatment or not. Survival rates are not greatly improved by treatment.

Severe head trauma can cause residual disabilities. The most common of the residual disabilities caused by severe head trauma are neuropsychological—problems with concentration, attention, and memory, as well as mild to moderate personality changes.

For adults, most of the recovery will occur within six months of the injury. After that there is usually little improvement in adults. Children, on the other hand, tend to recover more quickly from severe head injuries, and can continue to get better for more than two years following head injury.

Other health impaired

Other health impaired is a catch-all category that can include either chronic or acute conditions, such as AIDS, allergies, asthma, cancer, diabetes, epilepsy, heart disease, kidney disease, lead poisoning, rheumatic fever, sickle cell anemia, and many other conditions. It is best to get an evaluation from your child's treating physician and therapists.

Child abuse victims will also need special consideration during divorce. The harm caused by physical, sexual, or emotional abuse must be dealt with. Often the abuser is one of the child's own relatives or friends of people in their family. This must be addressed when crafting the Parenting Plan, custody, and visitation schedule. Abused children should also receive counseling and other necessary treatment. It is often appropriate to tailor the Parenting Plan, custody and visitation schedule for abused children, often progressing in graduated steps. Graduated steps means to have shorter visiting times at first, under careful supervision, increasing the length of visits and decreasing the level of supervision as appropriate.

Children with disabilities and special needs require lawyers and judges that are more knowledgeable about their condition than typical children. You need to educate the lawyers and judges involved in your case. You need to teach them the medical issues of your child's disability or special need. You are in the best position to advocate for the best interest of your child. Your child's disability or special need must be addressed during the divorce.

WHY DOES THIS MATTER IN DIVORCE COURT?

A child's disability or special needs must be considered when going through divorce court in order to prevent harm to the child. There is federal legislation which protects people with disabilities. The existing legislation primarily applies to healthcare and education. Title V of the Social Security Act (42 USC 7, Subchapter V §§701–710 [1989]) provides access to healthcare systems. The Individuals with Disabilities Education Improvement Act (IDEA) of 1997, amended in 2004 (Pub. L. No. 108–446) protects access to free appropriate public education, with modifications for children with disabilities. Neither of these bodies of legislation apply to or protect children with disabilities or special needs when their families are going through the divorce courts.

The visitation schedule, Parenting Plan, amount of child support, property distribution, and other issues may need to be tailored to meet the child's special needs. Using the standard forms may not meet the child's needs, in fact using these forms may cause harm in some cases. The standard forms used by many family courts and divorce lawyers were not written for families who have a child with a disability, but in order to streamline the process and have some uniformity and predictability of results. Standard forms can be a very good thing when they are used in the appropriate circumstances. They are not a good thing when they are used for a purpose for which they were never intended.

Families who have a child with a disability face serious issues every day that other people don't even contemplate. If, for example, you do not have a child who is undergoing chemotherapy, you do not understand what it is like to have to juggle your work schedule, your child's school schedule, your child's hospitalizations and out-patient appointments, your child's numerous sick days, your other children's schooling and activities along with other necessary things such as cooking, cleaning, laundry, grocery shopping, and generally maintaining a roof over your heads. Clearly, a "cookie-cutter" visitation schedule would be a nightmare for this family and would not meet the medical or other needs of the children. But if the lawyers and judge do not know the details of this family's life, they cannot fashion an appropriate, workable visitation schedule. The families must work with their lawyers and judges to make sure they have the information they need. The lawyers and judges need to be open to this information and to changing their standard way of handling divorce and other family law cases when the family has a child with a disability or special need.

Although this list does not cover every situation, a child's special need or disability may be considered relevant during a divorce or other family court case when a child has a serious medical condition, a chronic developmental disorder, or serious psychological or behavioral issues. The child may be chronically or terminally ill; may be unable to care for himself at the present time; may be unlikely to be able to live independently as an adult; may need special therapy, medication, equipment, treatments or other interventions on a regular and ongoing basis; and/or may be a significant risk of harm to himself or others.

There are times when a child's condition does not fit within those categories, yet still requires special attention in the family courts. For instance, when the child's condition requires special modifications during the process of custody and visitation; when it is such that the standard amount of child support would not be appropriate; or when it causes one of the parents to reduce her hours, take a different job, have her career negatively affected, and/or have her pension or retirement negatively affected.

When a child has significant disability or special needs, it can be extremely difficult, if not impossible, for the primary caregiver parent to maintain full-time employment and provide the care the child needs. Providing and managing the care of a child with significant disabilities or special needs can be a full-time job. Frequently the primary caregiver parent must go from full-time to part-time employment in order to meet the child's needs. This will result in a marked reduction of income for the primary caregiver parent and often results in the loss of health insurance and eligibility to participate in the employer's retirement plan. In these situations, fairness requires a different approach to determining the amount of maintenance (alimony) and the distribution of retirement accounts.

It is much more expensive to raise a child with a disability than to raise a typical child. There are numerous direct and indirect costs associated with meeting the special needs of this child. The standard formulas for the calculation of child support do not meet these needs. The primary caregiver parent is usually unable to pay these extra costs without financial contribution from the other parent, especially if the primary caregiver parent has had to reduce their income in order to take care of the disabled child.

These are but a few examples of why courts need to consider the unique issues involved in handling divorce or other family court cases in a family with a disabled or special needs child. The specific issues of any particular case will be unique and will be based upon the facts of that case. Your child's disability or special need is important and needs to be part of the process when your family is going through divorce.

IMPACT OF DIVORCE ON SPECIAL
NEEDS CHILDREN

Divorce is highly stressful on all parties concerned—both adults and children. Children with disabilities or special needs are even more vulnerable during the divorce process. Children with special needs can have different reactions to divorce than typical children (Perryman 2005). The extent of their reaction can also be different than that of typical children (Ball 2002). Tanner (2002) found that parental divorce is one of the most common significant risks to the healthy development of children today.

Wertlieb (2003) stated that family stress can negatively affect a child's health. Martinez-Gonzalez *et al.* (2003) noted that divorce presents a higher psychiatric risk to children and that children whose parents are separated, divorced, or widowed have a higher rate of eating disorders than children whose parents are married. Dube *et al.* (2003) argued there was a strong relationship between divorce and the risk of drug use from early adolescence to adulthood. O'Connor *et al.* (2000) found parental divorce to be associated with a higher rate of incidents, accidents, injuries, and illness in children. In their research, Hillis *et al.* (2004) found a higher rate of teen pregnancy in children whose parents are divorced. Hagan's research (2001) led him to the conclusion that the medical issues of children are complicated and even worsened by parental divorce. Divorce has been associated with a decrease in adherence to anti-retroviral medications in children and adults with HIV infection, in research by Williams *et al.* (2006). These are the consequences divorce can have on typical children. Now consider the effect on children with disabilities or special needs. If the lawyers and judges handling the cases involving children with disabilities or special needs do not have the necessary information, all the elements have gathered to create a perfect storm.

Saposnek (2005, p.563) argued that "[c]ourt professionals [are] largely ignorant of the unique and sensitive care required to competently address the special needs of these children when formulating parenting plans." He further stated that many family lawyers and judges are handling these cases on the fly. Sneed, May and Stencel (2000) estimated that millions of American children have a disability. When you combine the millions of American children with a disability and the current divorce rates, with the harm that can come to children from divorce, you get a huge segment of our population that will be subject to a gross miscarriage of justice unless courts and lawyers become educated on the issues relevant to these cases. The families must educate the courts and lawyers on these issues. These things are not taught in law school. This is an emerging field of law. Special needs and disabled children are some of the most vulnerable people in our society. We owe them a higher duty of care.

Jennings (2005) wrote that during the divorce, a disabled child's symptoms may become worse. In their research, Johnson *et al.* (2000) found this could include withdrawal, aggression, regression, loss of academic and social skills, loss of toilet training and language ability, emotional outbursts, depression, self injury, hopelessness, suicidal ideation, running away, and worsened physical condition. After the divorce, the disabled or special needs child may experience all of those conditions on a new long-term or permanent basis, which can lead to the institutionalization or even death of the child. Jennings (2005) discovered that after divorce it is sometimes necessary for the child to enter institutional care because the primary caregiver parent becomes so exhausted and overwhelmed. These families also have the additional stress of decreased standard of living, in addition to the worsening of their existing conditions, as found by Kaufman, Halvorson and Carpenter (1999). Barham, Devlin and LaCasse (2000) established that the standard of living of all parties usually declines after divorce. When the family has a decreased standard of living, there is less money available to care properly for the disabled child.

Divorce can have a harmful effect on disabled or special needs children. These children can suffer short-term or long-term medical consequences. They can suffer financially. They can lose their treatment or therapy. If their unique needs are understood and treated properly during the divorce, these negative impacts can be reduced or eliminated.

You should now understand the important issues when going through divorce with a disabled or special needs child. You should also know why your child's disability or special need matters in divorce court. Finally, you now know the impact of divorce on disabilities and special needs. With this knowledge, you will be able to advocate better for your child when your family is going through divorce.

Chapter 2

How to Hire a Good Divorce Lawyer for Your Special Needs Case

Perhaps you've reached the point at which you realize the marriage is over. You are headed for divorce. The first thing you need to do is get a good divorce lawyer.

CHOOSING YOUR DIVORCE LAWYER

Choosing the right divorce lawyer is one of the most important decisions you'll make in the entire divorce. Changing lawyers is not like changing shoes. Changing lawyers is difficult, expensive, and sometimes flat-out prohibited by the judge—so you had better choose wisely.

Changing lawyers is difficult, because a good divorce lawyer will be cautious about taking on your case if another lawyer has been involved. They know they were not your first choice. They know you are unhappy with your previous lawyer. They know you are probably unhappy with lawyers in general at that point. And they know they will have to step into the case midstream, and not be able to handle the case the way they would have if they had been involved from the beginning.

Changing lawyers is expensive as well. The new lawyer will have to get all the documents from the previous lawyer. They will have to take the time to read and become familiar with everything in your case file. You will have to pay them for their time to do this. This means you are paying for extra work that would not be necessary if you were not switching lawyers.

Changing lawyers is sometimes prohibited by the judge. If you are close to the date of trial or some other important hearing, the judge may refuse to let you change lawyers. Changing lawyers often results in a delay in the case, in order to get a new lawyer time to come up to speed. If the judge does not want the case delayed, the judge might refuse to let you change lawyers. This may be true despite how badly both you and your original lawyer may want you to change lawyers. You may be surprised to learn that usually when a client is not happy with their lawyer, the lawyer is also not happy with their client. The lawyer may want out of the case as badly as you want them out.

FINDING GOOD CANDIDATES

Since hiring a good divorce lawyer is such an important decision, how do you do that? First, you have to find good candidates. One of the best ways to find a good lawyer is by word of mouth. Ask your friends, your relatives, neighbors, and your coworkers if they know of any good divorce lawyers.

One of the worst ways to hire a divorce lawyer is by their advertisement. Anyone can take out an ad and tell you that they're great. In fact, anyone who has to tell people they're great usually is not. In some areas of law, advertising might be necessary in order to reach clients. This is not the case in divorce law. A good divorce lawyer is busy. The nature of divorce work is such that future problems frequently arise in cases. A lawyer will often represent a client off and on over a period of years. Also, people tend to discuss their divorces with their circle of friends and relatives. When one person is going through divorce, they will remember hearing their friend rave about their great divorce lawyer. They then ask their friend for the name of that lawyer.

If you cannot find a recommendation of a good lawyer among your friends and relatives, take a day and visit your local court, where the case would be filed. Call ahead to find out which judges hear divorce cases, and the dates on which they will be having divorce court hearings. Then simply go and sit in the courtroom and observe. In juvenile cases, paternity cases and some other cases the bailiff may clear the courtroom and not allow non-parties to be present, but in many other family court matters the courtroom is open to the public. See the lawyers in action. When there is a break and the judge is no longer on the bench or the court takes a recess, ask the bailiff, the judge's clerk, or other courtroom personnel for the names of particular lawyers with whom you were impressed. Doing your own courtroom reconnaissance can be an excellent way to find a good divorce lawyer for your case.

Another option is to call your state and local bar associations and request the names of divorce specialists in your area. You can check directories of legal professionals for lawyers who specialize in divorce as well. Divorce has become quite complex, and is best done by a lawyer who specializes in family law. Legislation affecting divorce changes rapidly. In order to keep up with the constant changes in the law properly, a lawyer needs to focus on family law.

Online legal directories can be a good way to compile some names, but maintain a healthy skepticism until you verify information. Just as with anything else, people can make unsubstantiated claims on the internet. Just because a person is listed under the category of divorce or family law, do not assume that is their specialty. Some lawyers list under several, even many, different specialties hoping to get business in any of those areas. Check to see if the lawyer is listed under other categories of law within the directory. Other categories frequently listed by some lawyers include general practice, litigation, personal injury, estate planning, and workers' compensation. There is absolutely nothing wrong with any of these categories. All you are trying to find out is whether the lawyer truly specializes in family law, or has a general practice. If you wanted a doctor for your routine checkups and general health matters, you would hire a family practice or general practice doctor. If, on the other hand, you needed brain surgery, you should hire a neurosurgeon. I am not suggesting that divorce law is brain surgery; however, practicing divorce law today is complex and is best done by a specialist. Your family's divorce is compounded by the fact that you have a disabled or special needs child. You need to get the best divorce lawyer you can find and afford.

If the lawyer has a website and/or social media listing (Facebook or MySpace, for example), by all means go and check them out. This is another way to find out if the lawyer truly specializes in divorce. It is also a great way to learn about the lawyer's personality, interests, and approach. You may discover the lawyer is involved in various organizations or activities that will indicate their likelihood to be responsive to the special needs or disability issues in your case.

After you have gotten the names of several promising candidates, call their offices to set up initial consultations. Make sure you know ahead of time if there will be a charge for the initial consultation and, if so, how much the charge will be. Verify whether they accept personal checks, cash, or your particular credit card.

THE INTERVIEW

In hiring a good divorce lawyer, first impressions are indeed important. Let the lawyer know you are interviewing several attorneys. Advise the lawyer on when you will be making your decision as to which lawyer will be representing you. Be candid and forthright. Discuss your income and cash flow openly, as well as your ability to stay current on your fees throughout the case. The lawyer deserves to know if they will be paid as they do the work, or if they might have to wait many months in order to get paid. You would certainly want to know if your paychecks were going to be delayed for months on end. Find out and discuss the lawyer's office policies and requirements regarding fee deposits and payments throughout the case. Ask how much the lawyer's hourly billing rate is as well as the required fee deposit. After the initial fee deposit is exhausted, do you then have to post another fee deposit, or will you be required to keep up with expenses as they are billed on a monthly basis? What costs and expenses will you be required to pay? Does the lawyer have a minimum billing policy? This means that for every time you contact your lawyer's office you'll be charged a minimum fee, of 15 minutes worth of billing time, for example, even if the phone call was only two minutes. This can add up quickly and unexpectedly if you are not aware of this policy.

As you are speaking with the lawyer, evaluate her personality. Does she give straightforward answers, or is she always vague? Does she appear to be experienced and knowledgeable?

Have a list of questions prepared to ask the lawyer. A good lawyer will welcome a client who comes in prepared.

Tell the lawyer your expectations as to child custody, visitation, child support, maintenance (alimony), property distribution, and all other important aspects of the case. You may find that your expectations are reasonable, but you may just as easily find that your expectations are way beyond what you are likely to receive. Lawyer shows on television tend to give the general public an extremely skewed view of the legal system. A real courtroom is nothing like what you see on *Judge Judy* or on *Boston Legal*. Many lawyers hate so-called television legal shows because they create so many problems for lawyers in having to correct their clients' grossly inaccurate perceptions about the legal system. In the real world, 90 percent of the time in the courtroom is excruciatingly boring, usually spent waiting. You are waiting for 23 other cases to be handled, because they are ahead of you on the docket. You're waiting for your soon-to-be ex-spouse to show up. Your lawyer is stuck in another courtroom and the judge will not let them leave. You wait for three hours and the judge reschedules the rest of the docket (including your case) for several months down the road. You take off work, come to court, and discover that the entire docket is canceled because the judge is sick.

Find out who will be working on your case. In some offices, much of the work is done by paralegals and by less experienced lawyers, called associates, instead of the lawyer with whom you met at the consultation. You deserve to know this information ahead of time, and to know what types of tasks will be done by other people and the billing rate you will be charged for their work. Some of the work in divorce cases is time intensive, but rather routine if you have experience in the field. This type of work can be handled quite confidently by a paralegal or associate with appropriate training and supervision, and result in great financial savings for you.

Discuss with the lawyer how cooperative or uncooperative you and your spouse are in the issues relative to the divorce. Together, you and the lawyer should try to determine if the case will be contested or uncontested. You do not necessarily have to go to trial just because you're going through a divorce. Again, real life is not television. Over 90 percent of divorce cases settle without having to go to trial. If you are able to resolve or settle your case and achieve a fair result, you and your entire family win. If you are not able to settle your case, and you have to go through a full trial and have a total stranger—the judge—decide the future for you and your family, the lawyers win (much more legal fees) and you and your family lose in many ways.

Find out if the lawyer genuinely tries to settle cases to achieve a fair result. If the lawyer brags about sticking it to the other side, about making them suffer, about leaving the other side with nothing, you should consider politely standing up and ending the consultation. A special needs child will suffer greatly if the parents are at each other's throats throughout the divorce. This is not about bragging rights or about settling scores. This is yet another situation in which your primary job is to advocate for your child. Get a fair result and be done. The more money you spend on legal fees, the less money you will have to spend on your child's treatment and therapy. To drag your children and your family through a vicious divorce for your personal satisfaction is extremely selfish. Good people sometimes end up in that situation, because they get caught up in the hurt and emotion of the situation. I'm not suggesting that you be a doormat. I am suggesting that you step back, take a deep breath and think about what you are really doing. If you hire the wrong kind of lawyer, you may get sucked into a nasty divorce that rips apart your family for the rest of your lives. The damage can be permanent. High school graduations, weddings, births of grandchildren, and many other wonderful, blessed life events can be ruined for everyone by a senselessly ugly divorce. It is virtually impossible to undo this type of damage.

Find out the lawyer's expectations for the outcome of the case. Be aware that the lawyer is not a soothsayer and cannot predict the future. Sometimes when clients repeatedly press me for guarantees and detailed predictions, I smile and tell them my crystal ball is in the shop. Divorce is extremely unpredictable. Many factors go into the resolution of any particular facet of a divorce. Anything can happen at any given moment at any stage of the divorce that can completely change the direction of the case and outcome. A case may be going extremely well for one side, until the client blurts something out of court that turns everything upside down in the case. Despite all this, a lawyer should have some general expectations for any given case. If the other side already has a lawyer, an experienced divorce lawyer may well have had other cases against that lawyer or know of the lawyer's reputation, depending on how large the population is in your area. If the case has already been filed, the lawyer may know certain things about the judge, if one has been assigned. With sufficient data and information from you, the lawyer should be able to make a general assessment of the case, with the qualification that if the facts change, the results may well change.

One of the most important things you need to cover with the lawyer at the initial consultation is the fact that you have a child with a disability or special need. This may seem obvious, however, an astounding number of people do not tell the lawyer that their child has, for example, cerebral palsy, Down syndrome or cancer. This is extremely important information the lawyer needs to know from the very outset. It will affect many aspects of the case, and should be included in the very first papers the lawyer files with the court.

I ask clients if any child in the case has any special need or disability. If I am told that no one does, I then ask if any of the children have IEPs (Individualized Education Plans) at school or are in therapy or undergoing medical treatment. You would be surprised how many people tell me only then, after I had to dig for it, that one of the children has a serious medical condition. I explain to the client how important this information is, and we explore the situation in depth and collect the appropriate documentation. We then go through the same process regarding whether any of the adults has any special need or disability.

Another reason you need to discuss the special need or disability with the lawyer at the initial consultation is to determine if the lawyer feels they can handle a case of that type. Frequently lawyers will refer the case to another lawyer if the initial lawyer does not feel they have the experience or information to handle a case involving a person with a serious disability or special need. Remember, they do not teach us this stuff in law school. And there is almost no information available to teach lawyers or judges this information, neither books nor seminars. This is an emerging field of law.

The lawyer will need a great deal of information from you. In the event that you know at the initial interview that this is the right lawyer for you, do not waste the consultation time and fee. Have the information the lawyer will need to proceed with the case. This will vary from one jurisdiction to another, however, the following list will be very helpful for you to gather much of the information your lawyer will need. You should be prepared with as much of this information as possible when interviewing the lawyers.

Information you will need for your lawyer

- Your name and any maiden and former names you have used.
- Your current address.
- How long you have lived at this address.
- How long you have lived in your county and state.
- A secure mailing address for your lawyer to send you mail.
- A secure email address your lawyer can use to contact you.
- Do you want maiden/former name back?
- Your social security number.
- The date of this marriage.
- City, county and state where you got married.
- The date you and your spouse separated.
- Your home phone, cell phone, work phone and any other phone.
- Where can your lawyer call you, and where can she leave messages?
- Your date of birth.
- Your place of birth—city, county, state and country.
- Your years of education and your race (required for Bureau of Vital Statistics form).
- Your employer, job title, annual gross income and bonuses.
- Do you want maintenance? If so, how much?
- Have you been married before? If so, how many times? When, where and how did each previous marriage end (death, dissolution, annulment)?
- Are you on active military duty?
- Are you pregnant? If so, is it of this marriage? What is your due date?

Information your lawyer will need about your spouse

- Your spouse's name and any maiden and former names used.
- Your spouse's current address.
- How long your spouse has lived at this address.
- How long your spouse has lived in his/her county and state.
- A mailing address for your spouse.
- A secure email address for your spouse.
- Does your spouse want maiden/former name back?
- Your spouse's social security number.
- Your spouse's home phone, cell phone, work phone and any other phone.
- Your spouse's date of birth.
- Your spouse's place of birth—city, county, state and country.
- Your spouse's years of education and race (required for Bureau of Vital Statistics form).
- Your spouse's employer, job title, annual gross income and bonuses.
- Does your spouse want maintenance? If so, how much?
- Has your spouse been married before? If so, how many times? When, where and how did each previous marriage end (death, dissolution, annulment)?
- Is your spouse on active military duty?
- Is your spouse pregnant? If so, is it of this marriage? What is her due date?

Other information your lawyer will need

- What is the reason for the divorce?
- Was there a prenuptial agreement?
- Are there any pending lawsuits?
- Do either of you receive goverment support?
- Are either of you in counseling?
- Have either of you had any restraining orders?
- Has your spouse already filed for divorce?

- For all children of this marriage: name, date of birth, social security number, age and whether they have any disabilities or special needs.
- Current custody arrangements: physical custody and legal custody.
- Your wishes as to custody: physical custody and legal custody.
- Is child support being paid currently?
- If so, how much is being paid, and by whom?
- Who carries the health insurance on the children?
- Do you or your spouse have other children?
- Are either of you paying or receiving child support or maintenance not related to these parties?
- Contact person (emergency).

Special needs

If any of the children have special needs, detail:

- which child(ren)
- what type(s) of special needs
- doctors, therapists
- date of diagnosis
- types of therapy
- costs—direct and indirect
- schedule
- prognosis
- short-term and long-term plans
- regular caregiver(s)
- respite care
- educational situation including IEPs and 504 Plans
- medications
- effects on primary caregiver parent—job, stress, career, retirement savings program
- specific needs of the child(ren)

- sensory issues
- transition and adjustment issues.

Your lawyer will probably need detailed financial information from you, either at the very beginning of the case or at some point during the case. It is best to collect as much of this information as possible at the outset. Take along a recent typical paystub, because your lawyer may need to know:

- name and address of your employer
- gross wages or salary and commission each pay period
- pay period: weekly, biweekly, semimonthly, monthly
- number of dependents claimed
- payroll deductions:
    - FICA (Social Security tax)
    - federal withholding tax
    - state withholding tax
    - city earnings tax (if applicable)
    - union dues
    - other deductions
    - total deductions each pay period
    - net take home pay each pay period
- additional income from rentals, dividends and business enterprises, Social Security, A.F.D.C. V.A. benefits, pensions, annuities, bonuses, "commissions and all other sources" (give monthly average and list sources of income)
- average monthly total of additional income
- total average net monthly income
- your share of the gross income shown on last year's federal income tax return.

Your lawyer may also need information on your expenses. Be prepared to provide information on your monthly expenses for:

- rent or mortgage payments
- utilities: gas, water, electricity, telephone, trash service
- automobiles: gas, routine maintenance, taxes and license, payment on the auto loan
- insurance: life, health & accident, disability, homeowners, automobile

- total payment installments contracts
- child support paid to others for children not in your custody (excluding children of this marriage)
- maintenance or alimony (excluding your current spouse)
- church and charitable contributions
- other living expenses: food, clothing, medical care, dental care, medication, recreation, laundry and cleaning, barber shop or beauty shop, school and books
- daycare center or babysitter
- all other expenses
- special needs expenses: medical treatment, doctors, therapy, other medical expenses, equipment, supplies, training, transportation, caregiver, companion, professionals, medication, supplements, dietary modifications, household modifications, daily/personal care items, respite care, activities, meals, sensory items, other special needs items
- total special needs items.

Your lawyer will also need detailed information on the property you and your spouse own, as individuals and together. This can include detailed information on your house and all other real property, vehicles, boats, trailers, bank accounts, investment accounts, retirement and pension accounts, business interests, personal property, household goods, and many other items, depending on your jurisdiction.

When you prepare your list of property information, make sure you note which items are required for the care of your child's needs. Note which items are needed for routine care of your child's ordinary needs, and which items are required for your child's disability or special needs. With this information, you should be well prepared for the questions your lawyer may ask you. While the lawyer is asking you questions, you can evaluate the lawyer.

The lawyer's approach and personality

It is important during the interview process to assess the lawyer's approach and personality. It is not enough for the lawyer to be experienced and knowledgeable. You deserve to be treated with dignity and respect. You deserve to be spoken to politely and courteously. You have the corresponding duty to treat your lawyer with dignity and respect and to speak politely and courteously. Lawyers should not browbeat or yell at their clients. Clients should not take out their anger at their spouse on their lawyer. Both lawyer and client should treat each other as professionals.

The lawyer should explain important legal concepts to you, but should not talk down to you. The lawyer should show interest in your case. This does not mean that the lawyer should serve as your counselor or best friend. You do need a best friend and counselor when you're going through divorce, but let your lawyer focus on being your lawyer. Also be aware that if you call your lawyer's office, you are most likely going to be charged for doing so. Frequent telephone calls to your lawyer can quickly add up to large legal fees. They can also distract and prevent a lawyer from completing important work in your case. Sometimes lawyers appear to not be interested in a client's case, when in reality they are trying to prevent a situation in which the client will fall into the habit of calling the office three or four times every day.

A variation of this is the client who sends successive emails to their lawyer. Be aware that every time you send your lawyer an email, the lawyer has to stop the other work they are doing, open the email, read the email, respond to the email, print the email to put in your correspondence file, and address whatever issues you raised in the email. You probably would not consider writing your lawyer four or five regular letters per day, but since emails can be so quick to send, people often dash them off without a thought. And certainly, they can be an extremely efficient way to communicate. Just be aware of the work they create at the lawyer's office as well as the impact this can have on your legal fees.

Pay attention to your initial emotional response to the lawyer at the first consultation. If your initial impression of a lawyer is that he is a jerk, your impression is most likely correct. Then realize that the initial consultation is the "honeymoon phase" of your attorney–client relationship. If the lawyer comes across as a jerk at the initial consultation, things will probably only get worse throughout the case. Divorce is difficult enough without being saddled with a difficult lawyer. If you have a strong dislike for the lawyer at the initial consultation, for any reason or even for no reason you can identify, do not hire that lawyer. You will do yourself and the lawyer a favor to find someone else. In managing your divorce, you should hire a lawyer in whom you have confidence. You should hire a lawyer who treats you with respect. You should hire a lawyer with whom you can get along.

THE LAWYER'S CREDENTIALS

You already know the lawyer whom you hire to handle your divorce case needs to specialize in family law or divorce law. That is just the beginning of the credentials they need to have. They also need to be experienced and knowledgeable in the field. You don't want to be the first trial your lawyer handles. I know they call it the practice of law, but let them practice on someone else. Ask the lawyer how many divorce cases he has handled and how long he's been handling divorce cases. You don't want someone who's just starting to practice divorce law because they tried some other area of law and could not make a living at it.

You should choose a divorce lawyer who takes continuing legal education courses on divorce law subjects on a regular basis. How do you find out this information? It's easy. Ask them how much of their continuing legal education (CLE) is in the area of family law. If they truly specialize in family law, the vast majority of their CLE should be within that field. One of the best ways to keep up on recent changes and developments in the law is for lawyers to attend CLE in their field.

Some states have certification in family law. Contact your State Bar Association and find out if your state offers such certification. If they do, obtain a list from the State Bar Association of the lawyers in your area who have attained family law certification. It might be called something different in your state, but the Bar Association should know what you're talking about.

In your case, you need something even more than a good divorce lawyer. You need a good divorce lawyer who will be receptive to the special needs or disability issues of your case. Usually that means hiring the best divorce lawyer you can get and then hiring experts to consult with and assist the lawyer on the special needs issues. Sometimes, however, you can find a good divorce lawyer who can take on the challenge of handling the special needs or disability issues. You need to work hard to educate this lawyer on your child's unique situation and how this needs to be addressed in the divorce. This will only be effective if you have hired the right kind of lawyer.

A lawyer who does Guardian-ad-Litem (GAL) work frequently deals with "at risk" children. Lawyers who do GAL work are trained and experienced in focusing on the child's needs and best interests. They frequently have a different mindset than lawyers who only represent the husband or wife. They are often more open and receptive to addressing disability and special needs issues in divorce cases. In some jurisdictions, the courts or judges maintain lists of court-approved GALs. Call your local courthouse, ask to speak with the domestic relations department, the circuit clerk's office or the clerk for a judge who hears divorce cases. Ask about a list of GALs. When you get the names of several GALs, proceed as you would with any other candidate to handle your divorce.

EXPECTATIONS

Be candid with your lawyer as to your expectations. Ascertain what your lawyer's expectations are for the case as well. These expectations for both of you should include expectations of how much the case will cost in attorneys' fees and expenses as well as what the outcome of the case will be.

Resist the temptation to ask other divorced people how they did in their case. Every case has a unique set of facts. Just because someone down the hall at your office got $1200 per month in child support does not mean that you will. There can be 20 or 30 different factors that go into the calculation of child support. There is no way that the random acquaintance has the exact same fact pattern that you do on all those factors. It is like expecting any two random math problems to result in the same answer regardless of what the equation was.

OFFICE PROCEDURES AND PRACTICES

Find out what your lawyer's office procedures and practices are. Does the office have a call return policy? Most divorce lawyers try to return phone calls the same or next business day, unless they are in court. Phone calls can be returned either personally by the lawyer, or by the lawyer's assistant obtaining the answer from the lawyer and calling the client with information. Other lawyers do not return calls for a week or more, and some lawyers simply never return phone calls. It may be better to try to reach your lawyer by email, if they respond more promptly to emails than telephone calls. Many lawyers carry cell phones which receive emails. This can enable the lawyer to be aware of client emails and sometimes respond to the email even if out of the office at court.

Does the office charge clients for secretarial time? What about paralegal time? Will you be charged for copies, faxes, postage, supplies, couriers, or long-distance phone calls? Will the lawyer try to get some of your fees paid through an interim or temporary court order (Motion for Orders Pendente Lite, or PDL)? Does the lawyer offer payment plans or accept credit cards? Make sure you receive all of this information in writing from the lawyer so there can be no misunderstandings. Also make sure you carefully read the lawyer's fee agreement or representation agreement before hiring the lawyer.

This is probably much more work than you were anticipating just to hire your lawyer. It will be well worth the time and effort you spend. Having a good divorce lawyer can make the difference to getting a good result in your case. The result you get in your divorce can affect your life for years to come. It can also affect the lives of your children for years to come. You would not hire a lousy cook to be the chef at a five-star restaurant, and then hope for good results. It is absolutely paramount that you hire a good divorce lawyer if you want to have your child's disability or special needs properly addressed.

Chapter 3

How Does a Case Go through Divorce Court?

You cannot just hire a good lawyer and then leave everything in their hands, expecting to show up at court at the end and have everything fall into place like a television show. There are many steps in between the start of a divorce case and the trial. Also, since over 90 percent of cases settle without having to go to trial, the odds are that your case will not be going to trial. You need to know the process by which these cases navigate their way through the court system.

OVERVIEW OF FAMILY COURTS

It can be very intimidating when you are facing something new and you don't know what to expect. Your first date, your first kiss, your first child, are all events that can fill you with anxiety. You may find yourself wondering, what am I supposed to be doing? Am I doing this right? Is there something else I'm supposed to be doing? It has often been said that if life came with an instruction book things would be much easier.

Divorce is a high stress situation. Even if you have gone through divorce before, it is still stressful. It is even more stressful if you do not know what to anticipate. Your future and the future of your children are all on your shoulders. Learning what to expect can decrease some of the anxiety.

Often people speak with their friends and relatives in order to learn about divorce court. This can result in incorrect information. The fact pattern in your friend or relative's case may be quite different from yours. Their case may have been uncontested, whereas yours might be hotly contested. Their case might have been a "knock down drag out" custody battle, whereas your case might be resolved amicably. Their case may have been in a different state, in a different county, or in front of a different judge. Even if their case was heard in front of the very same judge, the laws may have changed since their case was heard. Realize that any information you obtain through the rumor mill may do you more harm than good.

In the United States, there are two main types of courts: civil and criminal. Divorces are heard in the civil court system. Some places have special courts designated for hearing divorces and other family court matters. These courts have different names around the country, including family court, matrimonial court and domestic relations court. Within these courts, the rules can be different from regular civil courts. In fact, the procedural rules and the substantive law on divorce are different in every single state in America. The rules and law can also be different from one county to another within the same state. Even within the same county, one judge may have different rules than another judge, and one judge may interpret the laws and rules in a different way than another judge down the hall. And the laws and procedural rules are constantly changing.

Often husbands and wives going through divorce get extremely upset about the laws, and feel they are unfair. Sometimes they are. It will do you no good to complain to your lawyer or to the judge about the unfairness of these laws. It will do you even less good to blame your lawyer or the judge for the unfairness of these laws.

In the United States, we have separation of powers. We have three branches of government: executive, legislative, and judicial. The legislative branch makes the laws. The judicial branch interprets and applies the law. Judges are not allowed to change the law. They are only authorized to interpret and apply the existing law.

When a lawyer is handling your divorce case, she is not acting as any branch of the government, executive, legislative, or judicial. Therefore, she cannot make the law, interpret the law, or apply the law. Her job is to advocate for you within the existing laws and rules.

Judges and lawyers who handle divorce cases every day usually do dislike some of the laws and rules. They are stuck with those laws and rules until they are changed by the legislative branch. The flipside of that is the fact that sometimes you have laws and rules that are working quite well, that get messed up by changes to the existing legislation. It can be quite frustrating.

Generally, a divorce is filed in the county where the family lives. Sometimes the parties have already separated and one spouse lives in another county. Your lawyer will need to check the laws in your state governing jurisdiction and venue to determine the appropriate place to file the divorce. In some states, divorce can be filed wherever either the husband or the wife is living. In some states, the divorce can be filed in a county where none of the parties is living, if the parties agree to filing it there. This is often done for privacy reasons. Celebrities and other public figures often file for divorce in a small rural community, especially if that rural community is more protective of their court files and requires less financial information to be filed. The divorce can be completed quietly and privately before the media even discovers where it has been filed. The court file can be sealed to further protect the privacy of the parties. In some jurisdictions it is much easier to get a court file sealed than in others.

THE FIRST DOCUMENTS FILED WITH THE COURT

You have met with your lawyer, who has determined the appropriate place to file for divorce. You will need to provide your lawyer with a massive amount of information: see Checklist C and D at the end of the book. Make sure your lawyer is fully aware of any disability or special needs situation in the family before any papers are filed with the court.

If you are the one filing for divorce, you will be called either the Petitioner or the Plaintiff. Your spouse will be called either the Respondent or the Defendant. Throughout this book, we will use the terms Petitioner and Respondent, for consistency and to avoid any confusion with criminal cases.

The Petitioner is required to file certain initial pleadings. These can vary from state to state and county to county. A pleading is a document filed with the court.

First, a Petition or Complaint is filed. We will use the term Petition. The Petition is a document in which the Petitioner makes certain statements, called allegations, about himself, his spouse, their marriage, their children, their property, and the issues of child custody, child support, visitation, maintenance (also known as alimony), property distribution, attorney fees, and costs of the lawsuit, as well as any other pertinent information.

A filing fee is required by the court in order to file the Petition. Sometimes the filing fee includes the fee for serving the Petition on the Respondent. Other times, there is a separate fee that must be paid to the sheriff or other department in order to have the Petition served on the Respondent.

There are ways to avoid the embarrassment of having the Petition served by the sheriff. The Respondent can sign a form acknowledging that she received the initial pleadings and waiving personal service. If she does this, she should be extremely careful about the waiver she signs. Some lawyers try to sneak other things into the waiver of personal service.

Another way to avoid being served by the sheriff is to have your lawyer speak with your spouse's lawyer and agree that your lawyer will accept service of the Petition and will enter his appearance in the case. Even if the Petition must be personally served on the Respondent, it can be done more discreetly with a special process server who is instructed to be discreet. The parties can agree on a time and place for the special process server to serve the documents on the Respondent.

The lawyer for the Petitioner sends a completed form to the court that will be sent to the Bureau of Vital Statistics at the end of the divorce case. The Bureau of Vital Statistics records marriages, births, deaths, and other important information.

Often the Petitioner is required to file financial information either with the Petition or soon thereafter. This financial information tells the court what the Petitioner's income is, what his expenses are, and what property he owns. This property can include the assets of both or either party, and can include a marital residence, all other real estate owned by either party, investments, bank accounts, pensions, and personal property as well as all other assets of the parties.

You will have to give your lawyer sufficient information so he can draft a Petition that contains statements about the case, including: the court's jurisdiction over the case; employer and social security information; when and where you were married; when you separated; whether either of you are on active duty military service; a statement that the marriage is irretrievably broken; marital and separate property and debts; names, dates of birth, and social security numbers of children born of the marriage; emancipation status of the children; whether the wife is pregnant; where the children have lived before the filing of the divorce Petition; any prior litigation about custody of the children; legal and physical custody of the children; child support; whether there is need for maintenance; health, dental, or vision insurance for the children; and whether wife wants her maiden or former name back.

A sample Petition is included to show you what this document can look like. There is no one universal Petition. A lawyer may have many different ways of drafting a divorce Petition, depending upon the circumstances of the case and where the case will be filed. This is merely one way that a Petition can be written. (All the information contained in the Petition and other sample documents in this book is completely fictitious.)

SAMPLE PETITION

IN THE FAMILY COURT FOR THE COUNTY OF SOMEWHERE
STATE OF YOURSTATE

PAUL JONES, Petitioner,	))) Case Number _____
v.	))
RITA JONES, Respondent.	) Division _____))

PETITION FOR DISSOLUTION OF MARRIAGE

COMES NOW Petitioner, Paul Jones, and for his Petition for Dissolution of Marriage hereby states to the Court as follows:

1. Petitioner, Paul Jones, has been a resident of the state of Yourstate for more than ninety (90) days immediately preceding the filing of this Petition, and is now residing at 123 Oak Street, Hometown, Somewhere County, Yourstate, 11111.

2. Respondent, Rita Jones, has been a resident of the state of Yourstate for more than ninety (90) days immediately preceding the filing of this Petition, and is now residing at 456 Elm Street, Hometown, Somewhere County, Yourstate, 11111.

3. Petitioner is self-employed as an accountant. His social security number is xxx-xx-xxxx.

4. Respondent is not employed, and is a homemaker. Her social security number is xxx-xx-xxxx.

5. Petitioner and Respondent were married on January 1, 1990 in Honolulu, Hawaii, and said marriage is registered in Honolulu, Hawaii.

6. Petitioner and Respondent separated on or about July 4, 2010.

7. There was one child born of the marriage, namely Brian Peter Jones, born January 1, 2000, having the social security number xxx-xx-xxxx. Said child is not emancipated.

8. To the best of Petitioner's knowledge, Respondent is not now pregnant.

9. Neither Petitioner nor Respondent are members of the armed services of the United States, and neither Petitioner nor Respondent are entitled to the protections and immunities of the Servicemembers Civil Relief Act.

10. The parties possess certain marital and separate property.

11. There is no reasonable likelihood that the marriage of the parties can be preserved, and therefore, the marriage is irretrievably broken.

12. The minor child has lived with Petitioner and Respondent at 456 Elm Street, Hometown, Somewhere County, Yourstate, 11111 continuously for a period of more than six months immediately preceding the filing of this Petition.

13. Petitioner has not participated in any capacity in any other litigation concerning the custody of the minor child in this or any other state. Petitioner does not know of any other person not a party to these proceedings who has physical custody of said minor child or who claims to have custody or visitation rights with respect to such minor child.

14. Petitioner further states that it is in the best interest of the minor child that custody and visitation be ordered pursuant to the Parenting Plan to be filed by Petitioner in this case.

WHEREFORE, Petitioner respectfully prays that the marriage of the parties be dissolved; that the Court award the care, custody and control of the parties' minor child pursuant to Petitioner's Parenting Plan; that child support be calculated using the Yourstate Supreme Court mandated child support calculation form; that the Court apportion the marital property of the parties in a fair and equitable manner; that the Court set aside to Petitioner his separate property; that the Court order Petitioner and Respondent to each pay their own attorney's fees herein; that the Court costs be split equally between the parties; and for such other and further orders as this Court shall deem just and appropriate.

> Ima Lawyer, Bar No. xxxxx
> 123 Courthouse Road
> Hometown, Yourstate 11111
> (111) 111–1111 tel
> (111) 111–1112 fax
> ima@imalawyer.com

STATE OF YOURSTATE   )
) SS
COUNTY OF SOMEWHERE   )

PAUL JONES, being first duly sworn upon his oath, of lawful age and competent to testify herein, states that he is the Petitioner above named and that the facts contained herein are true according to his best knowledge, information and belief.

_____

PAUL JONES, Petitioner

Sworn and subscribed before me, a Notary Public, this ___ day of ____, 20___.

_____

Notary Public

My commission expires:_____

Not all courts require the filing of financial forms. Many of the courts that do require that financial forms be filed have their own format which must be followed. Because there is so much variation among these forms, a sample is not included in this book.

Once the Respondent has been served with the Petition (or her lawyer entered his appearance), the Respondent has a certain amount of time, usually 30 days, within which to file an Answer. If she does not file an Answer, a default judgment can be taken against her. A default judgment means that the court gives the Petitioner everything he asked for in his Petition.

If the Petitioner and Respondent are cooperative and in agreement on the terms for settling the case, sometimes they sign a Settlement Agreement. In such a situation, sometimes the Respondent elects to not file an Answer. There is always the risk that a default judgment can be taken against the Respondent if she does this, yet there can be good reasons for not filing an Answer. In some court systems, it takes much longer to get a divorce if the Respondent files an Answer, even if there is a signed Settlement Agreement. Some courts automatically put the case on a different track and timeline if an Answer is filed. You can sometimes get a faster hearing date to complete the divorce if no Answer has been filed. But always be aware of the risk that is taken—a default judgment—if no Answer is filed. You need to discuss this issue with your divorce lawyer to determine what is best for your case.

An Answer responds to each and every statement made in the Petition. It should be done line by line, paragraph by paragraph so nothing is omitted or overlooked. If anything is not specifically denied or otherwise admitted in the Answer, the court will often construe it as being admitted.

When your lawyer has prepared your Answer, go to the office and review the Answer with her. Have a copy of the Petition on hand, and carefully make sure your Answer says everything you intended it to, admits everything you intended to, denies everything you intended to, and omits nothing. Typographical errors can occur, and they can be harmful to your case if in an Answer. Your lawyer is human, and humans make mistakes. Both you and your lawyer need to take responsibility for your Answer being 100 percent accurate.

A sample Answer is included to show you what this document can look like. There is no one universal Answer. A lawyer may have many different ways of drafting an Answer, depending upon the circumstances of the case, the allegations raised in the Petition and where the case has been filed. This is merely one way that an Answer can be written. The Respondent may also have to file additional documents, such as financial documents, with her Answer.

SAMPLE ANSWER

IN THE FAMILY COURT FOR THE COUNTY OF SOMEWHERE
STATE OF YOURSTATE

PAUL JONES,	)
Petitioner,	)
	) Case Number _____
v.	)
	) Division _____
RITA JONES,	)
Respondent.	)

ANSWER TO PETITION FOR DISSOLUTION OF MARRIAGE

COMES NOW Respondent, Rita Jones, and for her Answer to the Petition for Dissolution of Marriage hereby states to the Court as follows:

1. Respondent admits the allegations contained in paragraphs 1 through and including 13 of Petitioner's Petition for Dissolution of Marriage.

2. Respondent denies the allegations contained in paragraph 14 of the Petition. By way of further Answer, Respondent states that it would be in the best interest of the minor child that custody and visitation be ordered pursuant to the Parenting Plan to be filed by Respondent in this case.

WHEREFORE, having fully answered, Respondent respectfully prays that the marriage of the parties be dissolved; that the Court award the care, custody and control of the parties' minor child pursuant to Respondent's Parenting Plan; that child support be calculated using the Yourstate Supreme Court mandated child support calculation form; that the Court apportion the marital property of the parties in a fair and equitable manner; that the Court set aside to Respondent her separate property; that the Court order Petitioner to pay the attorney's fees of Respondent herein; that Petitioner be ordered to pay the Court costs herein; and for such other and further orders as this Court shall deem just and appropriate.

Ura Turney, Bar No. xxxxx
456 Courthouse Road
Hometown, Yourstate 11111
(111) 111–2222 tel
(111) 111–2223 fax
ura@uraturney.com

STATE OF YOURSTATE	)
	) SS
COUNTY OF SOMEWHERE	)

RITA JONES, being first duly sworn upon her oath, of lawful age and competent to testify herein, states that she is the Respondent above named and that the facts contained herein are true according to her best knowledge, information and belief.

RITA JONES, Respondent

Sworn and subscribed before me, a Notary Public, this ____ day of ____, 20___.

Notary Public

My commission expires: _____

Even if things appear to be amicable, it is the nature of divorce that things can change for the worse during the case. Face it, if things always went smoothly between you and your spouse, you would not be getting a divorce. Therefore, it is a good idea to file a Cross Petition or Counter Petition. (Some courts call it a Cross Petition, others call it a Counter Petition, and many call it either. It will be referred to as a Counter Petition throughout this book.) A Counter Petition makes all the allegations you would have to make if you were filing for divorce instead of your spouse filing.

The reason you should file a Counter Petition is to give the court a way to continue handling your case if your spouse dismisses her Petition. Sometimes people change their minds after divorce is filed, or they want to play games or try to get a better deal, or just mess with you. They can wait until the day of trial, then dismiss their Petition. You would then have to start all over and file your own Petition if you wanted to go through with the divorce. All that time and money will have been wasted. If, on the other hand, you have filed a Counter Petition, your spouse can dismiss her Petition, and you can ask the court to proceed on your Counter Petition. No delay, no game playing. You can proceed as if nothing happened.

A sample Counter Petition is included to show you what this document can look like. There is no one universal Counter Petition. A lawyer may have many different ways of drafting a divorce Counter Petition, depending upon the circumstances of the case and where the case has been filed. This is merely one way that a Counter Petition can be written.

SAMPLE COUNTER PETITION

IN THE FAMILY COURT FOR THE COUNTY OF SOMEWHERE
STATE OF YOURSTATE

PAUL JONES,	)
Petitioner/Counter Respondent,	)
	) Case Number _____
v.	)
	) Division _____
RITA JONES,	)
Respondent/Counter Petitioner.	)

COUNTER PETITION FOR DISSOLUTION OF MARRIAGE

COMES NOW Respondent/Counter Petitioner, Rita Jones, and for her Counter Petition for Dissolution of Marriage hereby states to the Court as follows:

1. Petitioner, Paul Jones, has been a resident of the state of Yourstate for more than ninety (90) days immediately preceding the filing of the original Petition, and is now residing at 123 Oak Street, Hometown, Somewhere County, Yourstate, 11111.

2. Respondent, Rita Jones, has been a resident of the state of Yourstate for more than ninety (90) days immediately preceding the filing of the original Petition, and is now residing at 456 Elm Street, Hometown, Somewhere County, Yourstate, 11111.

3. Petitioner is self-employed as an accountant. His social security number is xxx-xx-xxxx.

4. Respondent is not employed, and is a homemaker. Her social security number is xxx-xx-xxxx.

5. Petitioner and Respondent were married on January 1, 1990 in Honolulu, Hawaii, and said marriage is registered in Honolulu, Hawaii.

6. Petitioner and Respondent separated on or about July 4, 2010.

7. There was one child born of the marriage, namely Brian Peter Jones, born January 1, 2000, having the social security number xxx-xx-xxxx. Said child is not emancipated.

8. Respondent is not now pregnant.

9. Neither Petitioner nor Respondent are members of the armed services of the United States, and neither Petitioner nor Respondent are entitled to the protections and immunities of the Servicemembers Civil Relief Act.

10. The parties possess certain marital and separate property.

11. There is no reasonable likelihood that the marriage of the parties can be preserved, and therefore, the marriage is irretrievably broken.

12. The minor child has lived with Petitioner and Respondent at 456 Elm Street, Hometown, Somewhere County, Yourstate, 11111 continuously for a period of more than six months immediately preceding the filing of this Petition.

13. Respondent has not participated in any capacity in any other litigation concerning the custody of the minor child in this or any other state. Respondent does not know of any other person not a party to these proceedings who has physical custody of said minor child or who claims to have custody or visitation rights with respect to such minor child.

14. Respondent further states that it is in the best interest of the minor child that custody and visitation be ordered pursuant to the Parenting Plan to be filed by Respondent in this case.

15. Petitioner is gainfully employed and earns a substantial wage, sufficient to provide for his own living expenses, pay child support to Respondent and contribute to the living expenses of Respondent.

16. Respondent is not employed, and is a homemaker. Respondent lacks sufficient income or other financial resources to provide for her own living expenses or the living expenses of the minor child without contribution from Petitioner. Respondent lacks sufficient income or other financial resources to pay her attorney fees or costs of this action without contribution from Petitioner.

WHEREFORE, Respondent respectfully prays that the marriage of the parties be dissolved; that the Court award the care, custody and control of the parties' minor child pursuant to Respondent's Parenting Plan; that child support be calculated using the Yourstate Supreme Court mandated child support calculation form; that the Court order Petitioner to pay child support to Respondent pursuant to such calculation, retroactive to the date of filing of the original Petition; that the Court order Petitioner to pay maintenance to Respondent; that the Court apportion the marital property of the parties in a fair and equitable manner; that the Court set aside to Respondent her separate property; that the Court order Petitioner to pay the attorney's fees and litigation costs of Respondent herein; that the Court assess the court costs against Petitioner; and for such other and further orders as this Court shall deem just and appropriate.

Ura Turney, Bar No. xxxxx
456 Courthouse Road
Hometown, Yourstate 11111
(111) 111–2222 tel
(111) 111–2223 fax
ura@uraturney.com

STATE OF YOURSTATE   )
) SS
COUNTY OF SOMEWHERE   )

RITA JONES, being first duly sworn upon her oath, of lawful age and competent to testify herein, states that she is the Counter Petitioner above named and that the facts contained herein are true according to her best knowledge, information and belief.

_____
RITA JONES, Counter Petitioner

Sworn and subscribed before me, a Notary Public, this ___ day of ____, 20___.

_____
Notary Public

My commission expires: _____

Now that you are familiar with examples of a standard Petition, Answer and Counter Petition, realize that these pleadings should be modified in cases involving children with a disability or special need. Samples of "special needs versions" of a divorce Petition, Answer, and Counter Petition are included below. As with all other documents, these are only examples. Your documents will certainly need to be different based upon your local jurisdiction's requirements and the facts of your case. These samples are provided for your information. Work together with your lawyer to craft the best pleadings for your case.

You need to include these things when working with your lawyer on the Petition, if relevant to your case: a statement of the child's special needs; a statement of the need to use a different child support amount; a recital of the need to use a different Parenting Plan; a statement of the type of physical custody appropriate; a statement of the type of legal custody appropriate; a statement of the type of visitation appropriate and a statement of the need for maintenance.

SAMPLE PETITION FOR SPECIAL NEEDS CASE

IN THE FAMILY COURT FOR THE COUNTY OF SOMEWHERE
STATE OF YOURSTATE

PAUL JONES, Petitioner,	))) Case Number _____
v.	)) Division _____
RITA JONES, Respondent.	))

PETITION FOR DISSOLUTION OF MARRIAGE

COMES NOW Petitioner, Paul Jones, and for his Petition for Dissolution of Marriage hereby states to the Court as follows:

1. Petitioner, Paul Jones, has been a resident of the state of Yourstate for more than ninety (90) days immediately preceding the filing of this Petition, and is now residing at 123 Oak Street, Hometown, Somewhere County, Yourstate, 11111.

2. Respondent, Rita Jones, has been a resident of the state of Yourstate for more than ninety (90) days immediately preceding the filing of this Petition, and is now residing at 456 Elm Street, Hometown, Somewhere County, Yourstate, 11111.

3. Petitioner is self-employed as an accountant. His social security number is xxx-xx-xxxx.

4. Respondent is not employed, and is a homemaker. Her social security number is xxx-xx-xxxx.

5. Petitioner and Respondent were married on January 1, 1990 in Honolulu, Hawaii, and said marriage is registered in Honolulu, Hawaii.

6. Petitioner and Respondent separated on or about July 4, 2010.

7. There was one child born of the marriage, namely Brian Peter Jones, born January 1, 2000, having the social security number xxx-xx-xxxx. Said child is not emancipated.

8. Said minor child Brian Peter Jones has SPECIAL NEEDS in that he has been diagnosed with autism.

9. As a result of the minor child's special needs, it is necessary to deviate from the usual child support calculations.

10. As a result of the minor child's special needs, it is necessary to deviate from the standard Parenting Plan, in the areas of physical custody, legal custody and visitation, among others.

11. To the best of Petitioner's knowledge, Respondent is not now pregnant.

12. Neither Petitioner nor Respondent are members of the armed services of the United States, and neither Petitioner nor Respondent are entitled to the protections and immunities of the Servicemembers Civil Relief Act.

13. The parties possess certain marital and separate property.

14. There is no reasonable likelihood that the marriage of the parties can be preserved, and therefore, the marriage is irretrievably broken.

15. The minor child has lived with Petitioner and Respondent at 456 Elm Street, Hometown, Somewhere County, Yourstate, 11111 continuously for a period of more than six months immediately preceding the filing of this Petition.

16. Petitioner has not participated in any capacity in any other litigation concerning the custody of the minor child in this or any other state. Petitioner does not know of any other person not a party to these proceedings who has physical custody of said minor child or who claims to have custody or visitation rights with respect to such minor child.

17. Petitioner further states that it is in the best interest of the minor child that custody and visitation be ordered pursuant to the Parenting Plan to be filed by Petitioner in this case.

WHEREFORE, Petitioner respectfully prays that the marriage of the parties be dissolved; that the Court award the care, custody and control of the parties' minor child pursuant to Petitioner's Parenting Plan; that the child support calculation include additional costs as a result of the minor child's special needs; that the Court apportion the marital property of the parties in a fair and equitable manner; that the Court set aside to Petitioner his separate property; that the Court order

Petitioner and Respondent to each pay their own attorney's fees herein; that the Court costs be split equally between the parties; and for such other and further orders as this Court shall deem just and appropriate.

> Ima Lawyer, Bar No. xxxxx
> 123 Courthouse Road
> Hometown, Yourstate 11111
> (111) 111–1111 tel
> (111) 111–1112 fax
> ima@imalawyer.com

STATE OF YOURSTATE	)
	) SS
COUNTY OF SOMEWHERE	)

PAUL JONES, being first duly sworn upon his oath, of lawful age and competent to testify herein, states that he is the Petitioner above named and that the facts contained herein are true according to his best knowledge, information and belief.

_____

PAUL JONES, Petitioner

Sworn and subscribed before me, a Notary Public, this ___ day of ____, 20___.

_____

Notary Public

My commission expires: _____

SAMPLE ANSWER FOR SPECIAL NEEDS CASE

IN THE FAMILY COURT FOR THE COUNTY OF SOMEWHERE
STATE OF YOURSTATE

PAUL JONES,	)
Petitioner,	)
	) Case Number _____
v.	)
	) Division _____
RITA JONES,	)
Respondent.	)

ANSWER TO PETITION FOR DISSOLUTION OF MARRIAGE

COMES NOW Respondent, Rita Jones, and for her Answer to the Petition for Dissolution of Marriage hereby states to the Court as follows:

1. Respondent admits the allegations contained in paragraphs 1 through and including 16 of Petitioner's Petition for Dissolution of Marriage.

2. Respondent denies the allegations contained in paragraph 17 of the Petition. By way of further Answer, Respondent states that it would be in the best interest of the minor child that custody and visitation be ordered pursuant to the Parenting Plan to be filed by Respondent in this case.

3. Respondent is without sufficient resources to pay for living expenses, the living expenses of the minor child, or Respondent's attorney fees and costs of this action without contribution from Petitioner. Petitioner is gainfully employed and earns a substantial wage, sufficient to meet his own needs and contribute to the payment of Respondent's living expenses, the living expenses of the minor child, and Respondent's attorney fees and costs of this action.

WHEREFORE, having fully answered, Respondent respectfully prays that the marriage of the parties be dissolved; that the Court award the care, custody and control of the parties' minor child pursuant to Respondent's Parenting Plan; that the child support calculation include additional costs as a result of the child's special needs; that the Court apportion the marital property of the parties in a fair and equitable manner; that the Court set aside to Respondent her separate property; that the Court order Petitioner to pay a reasonable sum of maintenance to Respondent; that the Court order Petitioner to pay the attorney's fees of Respondent herein; that Petitioner be ordered to pay the Court costs herein; and for such other and further orders as this Court shall deem just and appropriate.

> Ura Turney, Bar No. xxxxx
> 456 Courthouse Road
> Hometown, Yourstate 11111
> (111) 111–2222 tel
> (111) 111–2223 fax
> ura@uraturney.com

STATE OF YOURSTATE   )
) SS
COUNTY OF SOMEWHERE   )

RITA JONES, being first duly sworn upon her oath, of lawful age and competent to testify herein, states that she is the Respondent above named and that the facts contained herein are true according to her best knowledge, information and belief.

_____

RITA JONES, Respondent

Sworn and subscribed before me, a Notary Public, this ___ day of ___, 20____.

_____

Notary Public

My commission expires: _____

When you are working with your lawyer on the Answer and Petition, consider including the following items if they are relevant in your case:

- a statement of your child's special needs, if the child's special needs have not been recited in the Petition

- a correction about your child's special needs if they have been inaccurately alleged in the Petition

- the need to use a different child support amount, if appropriate but not stated in the Petition

- the need to use a different Parenting Plan, if appropriate but not stated in the Petition

- physical custody, legal custody, visitation, and the need for maintenance.

SAMPLE COUNTER PETITION FOR SPECIAL NEEDS CASE

IN THE FAMILY COURT FOR THE COUNTY OF SOMEWHERE
STATE OF YOURSTATE

PAUL JONES,	)
Petitioner/Counter Respondent,	)
	) Case Number _____
v.	)
	) Division _____
RITA JONES,	)
Respondent/Counter Petitioner.	)

COUNTER PETITION FOR DISSOLUTION OF MARRIAGE

COMES NOW Respondent/Counter Petitioner, Rita Jones, and for her Counter Petition for Dissolution of Marriage hereby states to the Court as follows:

1. Petitioner, Paul Jones, has been a resident of the state of Yourstate for more than ninety (90) days immediately preceding the filing of the original Petition, and is now residing at 123 Oak Street, Hometown, Somewhere County, Yourstate, 11111.

2. Respondent, Rita Jones, has been a resident of the state of Yourstate for more than ninety (90) days immediately preceding the filing of the original Petition, and is now residing at 456 Elm Street, Hometown, Somewhere County, Yourstate, 11111.

3. Petitioner is self-employed as an accountant. His social security number is xxx-xx-xxxx.

4. Respondent is not employed, and is a homemaker. Her social security number is xxx-xx-xxxx.

5. Petitioner and Respondent were married on January 1, 1990 in Honolulu, Hawaii, and said marriage is registered in Honolulu, Hawaii.

6. Petitioner and Respondent separated on or about July 4, 2010.

7. There was one child born of the marriage, namely Brian Peter Jones, born January 1, 2000, having the social security number xxx-xx-xxxx. Said child is not emancipated.

8. Said minor child Brian Peter Jones has SPECIAL NEEDS in that he has been diagnosed with autism.

9. As a result of the minor child's special needs, it is necessary to deviate from the usual child support calculations.

10. As a result of the minor child's special needs, it is necessary to deviate from the standard Parenting Plan, in the areas of physical custody, legal custody and visitation, among others.

11. Respondent is not now pregnant.

12. Neither Petitioner nor Respondent are members of the armed services of the United States, and neither Petitioner nor Respondent are entitled to the protections and immunities of the Servicemembers Civil Relief Act.

13. The parties possess certain marital and separate property.

14. There is no reasonable likelihood that the marriage of the parties can be preserved, and therefore, the marriage is irretrievably broken.

15. The minor child has lived with Petitioner and Respondent at 456 Elm Street, Hometown, Somewhere County, Yourstate, 11111 continuously for a period of more than six months immediately preceding the filing of this Petition.

16. Respondent has not participated in any capacity in any other litigation concerning the custody of the minor child in this or any other state. Respondent does not know of any other person not a party to these proceedings who has physical custody of said minor child or who claims to have custody or visitation rights with respect to such minor child.

17. Respondent further states that it is in the best interest of the minor child that custody and visitation be ordered pursuant to the Parenting Plan to be filed by Respondent in this case.

18. Petitioner is gainfully employed and earns a substantial wage, sufficient to provide for his own living expenses, pay child support to Respondent and contribute to the living expenses of Respondent.

19. Respondent is not employed, and is a homemaker. Respondent lacks sufficient income or other financial resources to provide for her own living expenses or the living expenses of the minor child without contribution from Petitioner. Respondent lacks sufficient income or other financial resources to pay her attorney fees or costs of this action without contribution from Petitioner.

WHEREFORE, Respondent respectfully prays that the marriage of the parties be dissolved; that the Court award the care, custody and control of the parties' minor child pursuant to Respondent's Parenting Plan; that the child support calculation include costs caused by the minor child's special needs; that the Court order Petitioner to pay child support to Respondent pursuant to such calculation, retroactive to the date of filing of the original Petition; that the Court order Petitioner to pay maintenance to Respondent; that the Court apportion the marital property of the parties in a fair and equitable manner; that the Court set aside to Respondent her separate property; that the Court order Petitioner to pay the attorney's fees and litigation costs of Respondent herein; that the Court assess the court costs against Petitioner; and for such other and further orders as this Court shall deem just and appropriate.

> Ura Turney, Bar No. xxxxx
> 456 Courthouse Road
> Hometown, Yourstate 11111
> (111) 111–2222 tel
> (111) 111–2223 fax
> ura@uraturney.com

STATE OF YOURSTATE   )

) SS

COUNTY OF SOMEWHERE   )

RITA JONES, being first duly sworn upon her oath, of lawful age and competent to testify herein, states that she is the Counter Petitioner above named and that the facts contained herein are true according to her best knowledge, information and belief.

_____

                      RITA JONES, Counter Petitioner

Sworn and subscribed before me, a Notary Public, this ___ day of____, 20____.

_____

                              Notary Public

My commission expires: _____

ADDITIONAL DOCUMENTS FILED WITH THE COURT

Every jurisdiction has its own requirements concerning documents that must be filed with the court. Your lawyer may require additional information from you in order to complete these documents. You may have to provide such information as the educational background of husband and wife, place of birth of husband and wife, month and date of all previous marriages of either husband or wife, when and how all previous marriages were terminated (by death or divorce), as well as other information. Obtaining a divorce is seldom an easy, simple or quick process. Be prepared to have to do a lot of work over a long period of time.

TEMPORARY ORDERS AND OTHER MOTIONS

Sometimes one party may need a temporary or interim order from the court, which temporarily resolves some issues until the final divorce hearing. In this situation, they often file a Motion for Orders Pendente Lite, also known as a PDL Motion. A PDL Motion can deal with such issues as child custody, visitation, child support, maintenance, who gets to live in the marital home, who has to pay which bills, whether there will be a Guardian-ad-Litem appointed, who will pay how much for the Guardian-ad-Litem, who has to pay whose attorney fees during the divorce, as well as any other relevant issues which cannot wait until the final resolution of the entire divorce case. If the judge enters a PDL Order, the order will remain in effect until it is superseded by a later order of the court, usually the divorce decree.

ORDERS OF PROTECTION

Unfortunately, sometimes people become violent or threatening during a divorce. One party may be in fear of harm from the other. This may be due to threats of harm or from actual abuse. If this happens to you, immediately call your lawyer, unless you are in danger of immediate harm, in which case, *call the police, get help, get yourself safe, get the children safe*, then call your lawyer.

Your lawyer can tell you the procedure in your state for obtaining an Order of Protection. These are also called Restraining Orders. The court can order the person who hurt you or threatened you to stay away from you, whether at home, at work, or wherever you are. Sometimes these orders specify that the other person cannot come within a certain distance of you, for example, within 1000 feet or within 1 mile of you.

Sometimes the judge will grant you a temporary Order of Protection for a short period of time until a hearing can take place in which the other side can tell the judge his or her side of the story. At that hearing, the judge will then determine if a long-term Order of Protection is appropriate. These orders can vary in length, but are often 6 or 12 months long.

One of the most important things for you to know about Orders of Protection is that they are merely pieces of paper. The police cannot follow you around night and day. If you are in a situation in which you needed an Order of Protection in the first place, you need to be very careful to keep yourself safe. Sometimes people obtain an Order of Protection and then behave in a carefree manner, as though the other person would not dare to violate the order. Orders of Protection are pieces of paper that allow the police to keep someone away from you, if the police happen to be where you are. Pieces of paper do not stop bullets. If you are in fear that someone may try to hurt you, you must keep yourself safe.

COURT MEETINGS OR CONFERENCES

There are often several informal conferences at court before a case goes to trial. These will vary based upon your local court's procedure. Often these informal conferences result in the entire case or major portions of it being settled. It can be very helpful to meet with your lawyer prior to these conferences. You might be required to update some of your information prior to these conferences, such as financial information.

Although many people do not realize it, you show your respect for the court or your lack of respect for the court by what you wear to court. Do not wear shorts, sandals, tank tops, T-shirts, jeans, anything camouflage, anything showing the midriff, or other casual clothing to court. Courts have dress codes, and people can be sent home if they are dressed inappropriately. What you would wear to a house of worship is usually appropriate to wear to court, although what people wear to a house of worship has changed vastly in recent decades. For men, nice pants (khakis, twill, but not blue jeans) with a button-down shirt and tie are fine. At trial a suit is best. For women, dresses are best, or blouse and skirt, for all court appearances.

Another way you show your respect or lack thereof for the court is by how you speak to the judge and others in the courtroom. Just as being disrespectful to a police officer at a routine traffic stop will frequently get you one or more tickets, being disrespectful to a judge in a divorce case will not help your case. Be polite and respectful. Address the judge as "Your Honor," and always say "sir" or "ma'am." Speak in a respectful tone of voice and do not ever be sarcastic to a judge. Rolling your eyes in court is frankly immature and stupid. You might be upset with your spouse and even disagree with how the judge rules in your case, but do not ever show a bad attitude with the judge. The judge represents our entire system of justice in the United States. Our justice system is not perfect, but is one of the best, if not the best in the world. Be grateful for what we have, for others have far less justice.

Sometimes when you are at an informal court conference or hearing, the hearing will be handled "in chambers." It means the judge will meet with the lawyers in the judge's office, known as chambers, and they will discuss the issues that are in dispute in your case. Each lawyer argues his or her side, then the judge will make suggestions as to how she would rule if she were to hear that testimony in the case. Efforts are made to settle as many issues as possible in the case, even to settle the entire case. Since fewer than 10 percent of divorce cases actually go to full trial, many cases are settled at or after these informal hearings.

DISCOVERY

During the divorce, parties need to find out certain information about each other. The discovery phase of a divorce is when you try to find out this information. Sometimes this is done informally and cooperatively. One lawyer may write the other lawyer and request certain documents. The lawyers may agree verbally at court to exchange certain documents. The judge might instruct the lawyers to exchange certain documents informally.

There is also more formal discovery. Interrogatories are written questions mailed from one lawyer to the other side. They must be answered in writing, under oath, and within a certain number of days.

If either parent feels any of the children has a disability or special need, written interrogatory questions can be sent to the other side, asking them what the disability or special need is, which child has it, when they first got it, and when it was diagnosed. You can ask for the name, address, and phone number of the person who diagnosed it. You can ask for information on all modifications currently used, all modifications the other side feels are necessary in addition to the current modifications, all medications, therapy and treatment the child is receiving for this disability or special need, including the location, organization, frequency, duration, and cost of such. Other areas to ask questions about can include the child's prognosis; the financial impact of the special need; public and private services and assistance currently received for this special need; breakdown of each parent's involvement in the care of this child, by percentage; the impact of this special need on daily life of the family, on the current and future career of mother, on the current and future career of father; and any other information on this special need relevant to this divorce.

Another more formal method of discovery is the deposition. One lawyer sends a notice to the other, for the other lawyer and client to come to the first lawyer's office on a certain date at a certain time, to be asked questions in person. Often the depositions of both husband and wife are taken the same day, one after the other. The court reporter will swear in the witness, and then take down on a court reporting machine everything that is said during the deposition, including questions and answers. First one lawyer will ask the witness questions. This is called direct examination. When the first lawyer is done, the other lawyer can ask questions of that witness. This is called cross examination. This continues back and forth until one of the lawyers, on his turn, declines to ask any questions. The other lawyer is not then allowed to come back and ask more questions. The deposition is over. In a divorce, both the husband and wife and their lawyers are allowed to attend all depositions in the case.

A document request is another more formal method of discovery. Your lawyer can request documents from your spouse and from her employer, schools and doctors. Many documents can be requested by subpoena or by a Request for Production of Documents. These documents can include tax returns, bank statements, canceled checks, copies of bills and credit card statements, telephone records, brokerage statements, and other documents.

In the discovery process, your lawyer needs to learn about all the disabilities and special needs of all children in the family. Sometimes there is more than one special need within a family. You need to get copies of Individualized Education Plans (IEPs) and 504 Plans from the schools. Also get copies of information on all medications, physical therapy, behavior therapy, psychological counseling, and other therapy and counseling. Your lawyer needs thorough information and documentation on your child's diagnosis, symptoms, testing, and evaluations.

You need to prove and document your child's current condition and prognosis. Get reports that say whether your child's condition is curable, treatable, or terminal and that talk about the likelihood of your child getting a high school diploma, living independently, or being employed. Your child's life expectancy may need to be determined.

You need to talk with your lawyer about the current and future impact of the special needs on your child, as well as the current and future impact on the lives of the parents and any siblings. Your lawyer needs this information to determine the amount of child support, maintenance, and property distribution, including retirement plans.

Get copies of scholarly and authoritative materials on these areas for your lawyer. Collect documentation, medical records, and proof of costs. Work with your lawyer to make sure all of these materials, documentation, records, and proof of costs are obtained in the proper way so they will be admissible in court.

Discovery summary list

Use this summary list as a starting point for things you and your lawyer may want to do during the entire discovery process, in addition to the usual discovery that can be done in cases that do not involve children with a disability or special need. This list is not complete or exhaustive. You need to add to it everything else that is relevant to your case. Determine with regard to *all* of the children whether they have any physical, mental, or emotional disability, learning disability, behavior or mood disorder. Often there will be more than one special need within a family. Ask about this subject through interrogatories and/or depositions. Follow up with Request for Production of Documents. Obtain signed and notarized releases so you can obtain medical records of all medical and therapeutic professionals and record keepers.

- Do any of your children have any physical, mental or emotional disability, learning disability, behavior or mood disorders? Sign releases so your lawyer can get records for this and all categories in this summary list.

- Do any of your children receive special assistance at school?

- Do any of your children have an IEP or 504 Plan at school? You may need to sign two releases, one for the general education program and one for the department that provides the special education/therapy at the school.

- Are any of your children on medication?

- Are any of your children in counseling, physical therapy, behavior therapy, or psychological counseling?

- What is the official diagnosis?

- Who made the diagnosis and when was it made?

- When did the first symptoms appear? You may need records from preschools, babysitters, pediatricians, emergency room personnel, law enforcement personnel, relatives of the child, Parents As Teachers, or other early childhood programs.

- What testing was done to evaluate your child's condition, and why was your child seen by the person who made the diagnosis?

- Has any other professional confirmed the diagnosis?

- Find out about your child's current condition. Do research on your child's actual condition. Get authoritative and scholarly materials on your child's particular condition.

- Find out about your child's prognosis. Get authoritative and scholarly materials on your child's particular prognosis.

- Is your child's condition curable, treatable, or terminal? Get authoritative and scholarly materials on the curability, treatment, and terminal nature of your child's particular condition.

- Find out if your child is expected ever to be able to get a high school diploma, get a college degree, live on her own, hold a regular job, live completely independently, marry, or have children. Get authoritative and scholarly materials on the lifetime implications of the child's particular condition.

- Find out about your child's life expectancy. Get authoritative and scholarly materials on the life expectancy of your child's particular condition.

- Find out about how this condition impacts your child's life now, how it is expected to impact your child's life in the future, how this condition impacts siblings' lives now and how it is expected to impact siblings' lives in the future. Get authoritative and scholarly materials on the impact of the child's particular condition.

- How does this condition impact the lives of you and your spouse now and how is it expected to impact your lives in the future? Get authoritative and scholarly materials on the future impact of the child's particular condition on parents.

- Who is the primary caregiver? Outline how the condition has impacted the careers of you and your spouse and how it is expected to impact your career advancement and retirement plan contributions in the future. Get employer and retirement account records from three time periods: prior to your child's special need; the time your child's special need occurred; and the current time. Get authoritative and scholarly materials on the impact of the child's particular condition on career advancement and retirement plan contributions of parents.

- Provide the names, addresses, telephone numbers, and credentials of all persons your child currently sees for this condition.

- List all medications your child currently takes, the frequency and dosage, the reason for the medication and the expected result from the medication.

- Detail all therapies and treatments your child currently receives, including therapies at home and at school. Get authoritative and scholarly materials on each of the child's particular treatments and therapies. Collect billing, invoices, and receipts. *For each treatment or therapy provide details about:*

- o who provides the treatment or therapy
- o who referred your child to that person or organization
- o where the treatment or therapy is received
- o the type of treatment or therapy and method used
- o the frequency and duration of treatment or therapy (for example: two times a week, one hour each time)
- o how long the treatment or therapy is expected to continue
- o cost of the treatment or therapy
- o how this is paid (private pay, insurance, grant, funding program)
- o amount of uncovered costs and incidental costs of this treatment or therapy—transportation, caregiver, supplies, meals, equipment
- o who takes your child to the therapy
- o what the expectations are for future therapies and medications.

- Is your child is on a waiting list for any therapy, program, school, or funding?

- Keep an itemization of all direct and indirect costs resulting from the child's special needs, including therapy, doctors, other practitioners, medications, supplements, equipment, supplies, caregiver training, special nutritional requirements, special clothing and personal care item requirements, home modifications, vehicle modifications, modifications at school, non-parental caregiver costs, transportation, and any other costs.

- Your lawyer's special needs discovery file should contain: medical reports, test results, diagnoses, evaluations, treatment plans, therapy plans, medication plans, child's safety plans for home, school, and away, medical bills, documentation of all costs, IEPs, 504 Plans current and previous, information on every treating professional, copies of articles or book excerpts providing information on your child's particular condition, detailed therapy and treatment schedule, and your child's detailed daily schedule.

WHAT YOU NEED TO KNOW BEFORE THE FIRST COURT DATE

Before the first court date, make sure you know what your lawyer is expecting of you. Are you supposed to bring any documents or witnesses to court? Do you need to review or update any pleadings or other documents by a certain date before court?

This seems oversimplistic, but make sure you know where the courthouse is, where you can park for several hours without getting a ticket, the security procedures at the courthouse, and the floor and room you are to go to within the courthouse. Will you be meeting your lawyer at the lawyer's office or a court? If you are meeting at court, will you meet in the first floor lobby or at the specific courtroom? Will the court date be a formal hearing or an informal conference? Are you expected to testify? Regardless of whether your lawyer expects you to testify, make sure you follow the guidelines in these materials for dressing appropriately for court. Court can be unpredictable, and you never know when you may be called on to testify. If your lawyer expects you to be stuck at court for several hours, make sure your cell phone is well charged and that you have reading or other materials to keep yourself occupied while you wait. Money for the parking meter or parking lot, money for lunch and possible coffee breaks should be on hand as well. Make arrangements for your children to be picked up from school or daycare in the event you are not able to leave at a given time.

SETTLEMENT OR TRIAL

The vast majority of divorce cases settle without having to go through a full trial. Quite a few of those cases, however, settle at court on the day of trial. Generally it is far better to settle your case, if you can achieve a fair result this way. If you go to trial, you are asking a total stranger (the judge, who doesn't know you or your family) to make decisions that will impact the rest of your lives. That is why the best result is usually achieved through settlement. In most states, divorce trials are heard by a judge only, without a jury. Some states do offer a jury for divorce trials, but there are two very good reasons to choose a judge, also known as bench, trial in your divorce case. One reason is the simple fact that many personal and highly private issues may come out in the course of the testimony. To minimize the embarrassment for all concerned, is usually advisable not to have a jury hear this testimony. This is especially true if you live in a small community. No one wants their dirty laundry to be waved about in public. The second reason to choose a bench trial for your divorce case is that it is far less expensive than a jury trial. Jury trials take much longer than bench trials. In a jury trial, your lawyer will have to prepare documents, such as jury instructions, that are not necessary in a bench trial. The additional time in court and the additional document preparation and other work required by a jury trial add up to greater legal fees to the client.

Chapter 4

What Is Different about Your Case?

Now that you understand how divorce cases go through the courts, you need to learn how your family's divorce will be different from a case that does not involve a child with a disability or special need. Some divorce cases involving children with disabilities or special needs must be handled in a different way from the general or typical divorce case. In other cases, however, after thoroughly considering and evaluating your child's disability or special need in the context of the divorce case, it may be appropriate to proceed with the usual manner of handling a divorce case. This can only be determined by a thorough consideration and evaluation of your particular case.

CHILD CUSTODY AND VISITATION

Your child's unique needs may require tailoring certain provisions of child custody and visitation. For example, if you have a 16-year-old son with cerebral palsy who requires special lifting and transfer equipment which is located only at one parent's house, a custody and visitation plan which provides for the child to live with one parent one week and the other parent the next week would be ridiculous. If your child has a life-threatening condition which has resulted in the child needing resuscitation and only one parent is trained in the resuscitation techniques, the child could be at risk with the other parent until that parent successfully completes appropriate training. A child who has great difficulty with transitions should not have a custody and visitation schedule that includes frequent transfers of the child from one parent to the other.

CHILD SUPPORT

If your local court uses a standardized child support calculation form, it is unlikely to result in a sufficient child support amount to properly meet the needs of a child with a severe disability or special need. There are many costs of raising a disabled child that are not covered by health insurance. Many health insurance companies specifically disallow coverage for certain diagnoses. Direct medical costs can include costs of doctors, hospitals, outpatient treatment, therapists, medications, supplements, specialized equipment, home environment modifications, co-pays, deductibles and all other medical costs. Make sure you maintain receipts and billing statements. Many children with special needs have to be on a special nutritional regime, which can be expensive. If your child requires orthopedic devices, include replacement costs for these as the child grows. There are many indirect costs associated with raising a child with a disability or special need. Itemize as many of these as you can and provide the data with backup to your lawyer.

ALIMONY (MAINTENANCE OR SPOUSAL SUPPORT)

Frequently one parent will quit their job or go from full-time to part-time employment in order to care for the needs of the child properly. During and after the divorce, they will need financial assistance from the other parent in order to survive. Many times the job loss or going from full-time to part-time status is not voluntary on the part of the parent. Children with a disability or special needs have on average three times as many sick days as typical children. Few employers will allow employees to miss that many days of work, so it can be difficult if not impossible for the primary caregiver parent to maintain steady full-time employment. In these cases, the issue of maintenance, also known as alimony or spousal support, should be thoroughly investigated.

PROPERTY DISTRIBUTION
AND RETIREMENT ACCOUNTS

If one parent will be able to engage in full-time employment after the divorce, and the other parent will be unemployed or employed part time in order to care properly for the disabled child, an argument should be made for other than 50/50 distribution of property. The primary caregiver parent will have far less opportunity to obtain or replace items in the future, due to their lower income. In many families, the marital home is the asset with the greatest value. If the primary caregiver parent receives the marital home as his or her property in the property distribution, but is required to somehow buy out the other parent's equity, such buyout may be a financial impossibility. When there is a child with a serious disability or special need, the award of the marital home should be viewed more in terms of an award for the needs of the child and as a dollar value in the property distribution. If the equity in the marital home equals the value of the bank and investment accounts, and the primary caregiver parent receives the marital home with equity while the other parent receives the bank and investment accounts, the primary caregiver parent will be cash poor, and with less opportunity to rebuild liquid assets due to their decreased employment income. All these factors should be considered in the property distribution in the case.

Generally, the amount of retirement accounts that were earned or accumulated during the marriage are distributed equally in the divorce. When one parent has sacrificed their career or livelihood in order to care for the disabled or special needs child, that parent will not have the same opportunity as the other parent to make future contributions toward retirement savings. One parent may spend the next 20, 30, 40 years or more laboring night and day to care for a child with a serious disability and face old age in poverty while still caring for the then adult disabled child—while the other parent may spend those same 20, 30, 40, or more years employed full time, enjoying a higher standard of living, and then retiring in comfort with a generous fully funded retirement portfolio. Clearly, this is an inequity. Taking care of your child should not have to result in spending your twilight years in poverty.

GUARDIAN-AD-LITEM

Often it is a good idea to have the judge appoint a Guardian-ad-Litem (GAL) to represent the legal interests of a disabled or special needs child when the parents are going through divorce. The GAL can explore and investigate the child's unique needs and make a recommendation to the court as to what would be in the best interests of the child. Courts frequently appoint a GAL when there are credible allegations of abuse and neglect. A GAL is a lawyer with experience in protecting the interests of children who are at risk. They already have the mindset required to protect your child's special interests. A GAL is often more receptive to implementing a plan that is not the "cookie cutter" approach, but rather a plan that meets your child's unique needs.

EXPERT WITNESSES

Expert witnesses may be necessary in order to prove to the court your child's disability or special need, as well as how those needs are relevant in the divorce case. These experts can be the child's teachers, doctors, therapists, respite care providers, and other service or care providers. When there is disagreement between the parents on the extent of the child's disability, expert witnesses can usually clarify the issue for the court.

PROVING YOUR CASE TO THE COURT

If your case is contested, you will need to prove your child's disability or special needs as well as the accommodations required in the divorce case. Discuss with your lawyer the appropriate way in which to obtain documents that will be properly admissible in court. You may need to obtain copies of doctor records, therapist notes, therapy plans, treatment plans, school records, Individualized Education Plans (IEPs), hospital records, pharmacy records, daycare provider records, service provider records, respite care provider records, test results, nutritional and dietary regimen protocols and other information. Assume that the lawyers and the judge in the case know absolutely nothing about your child's disability or special need. Plan with your lawyer how you will obtain admissible information to educate the courts and lawyers on your child's condition and how that affects daily life, both short term and long term. Sometimes this is best done through the GAL. You need to understand that courts have very specific rules that govern what evidence is admissible in court. You need to make sure that your important information is capable of being presented to the judge.

PARENTING PLAN

Many jurisdictions require that a document be filed with the court, outlining specific terms that have been agreed upon by the parties or ordered by the court concerning the children. These documents have several names, including Parenting Plan, Custody Agreement, Co-Parenting Agreement. In this book they will be referred to as Parenting Plans. The details of every Parenting Plan will vary greatly by what your local courts require as well as by the facts of your case. I have included a sample Parenting Plan to let you see what a Parenting Plan for a family with a disabled or special needs child can look like. Work with your lawyer to fashion a Parenting Plan that works for your family. Use what works from the provided sample document, disregard what does not work, and add language that is necessary to make the best plan for your family.

SAMPLE SPECIAL NEEDS PARENTING PLAN

IN THE FAMILY COURT OF THE COUNTY OF SOMEWHERE
STATE OF YOUR STATE

PAUL JONES, Petitioner, v. RITA JONES, Respondent.	))) Case Number _____)) Division _____))

CONSENT PARENTING PLAN FOR SPECIAL NEEDS

Mother and Father shall have joint legal custody and Mother shall have sole physical custody of said minor child. Mother's residence shall be designated as the primary residence of the minor child for mailing and educational purposes.

Due to the special needs of the child, the standard visitation schedule is not in the best interests of the child. The child has autism. He receives intensive therapy for many hours every week and, because of his special needs, his life is extremely structured.

The two most important aspects of this Parenting Plan are:

- the best interests of the child, and

- cooperation of the parents.

CUSTODY, VISITATION AND RESIDENTIAL TIME FOR THE CHILD WITH EACH PARENT SHALL BE AT SUCH TIMES AS THE PARTIES SHALL AGREE. The parties are strongly encouraged to work together cooperatively and flexibly to reach by amicable agreement such custody, visitation and residential times as shall be in the best interests of the child and keeping in mind his special needs. In the event the parties cannot agree, Father shall have custody, visitation or residential time as set forth below and Mother shall have all other time as her custody, visitation or residential time.

EACH PARENT IS STRONGLY ENCOURAGED TO PUT THE CHILD FIRST AND TO MAKE EVERY REASONABLE EFFORT TO MEET THE UNIQUE NEEDS OF THE SPECIAL NEEDS CHILD.

WEEKDAY VISITATION

Father may come to Mother's house to visit the child during the evenings whenever his schedule permits, as long as the parties shall so agree. In the event the parties cannot agree upon the night or nights of this visitation, Father shall visit the child at Mother's house or pick him up at Mother's house on Wednesday evenings. Father shall visit/pick up child at 6:00 pm and return him to Mother's house by 7:30 pm, when he is welcome to participate in his bedtime routine, which usually lasts until 8:30 pm. Father may extend this weekday visitation to overnight visitation. In the event the parties agree upon overnight visitation during the week, Father shall either return the child to Mother's house the next morning or take him to his morning activity, as agreed to by the parties.

WEEKENDS

The child is involved in many activities due to his special needs. These activities require great flexibility and cooperation by the parents regarding the weekend visitation. The general goal is that Father shall have the child for approximately half of the weekends, although this will often not be every other weekend. The parties shall frequently consult each other regarding the scheduled activities and arrange the weekend visitation around the schedule and best interests of the child. If the parties cannot agree, Father shall have visitation of the child every other weekend beginning at 6:00 pm on Friday through and ending at 6:00 pm on Sunday, beginning the weekend following the date of the judgment.

SUMMER

The child attends summer school for six weeks every year. This usually runs between June and August. There is usually a week or two between the regular school year letting out and the start of summer school, and there is a week or two between the end of summer school and the beginning of the next school year. During these weeks, the child usually attends a special needs summer day camp. It is important for the child to attend summer school. If he is registered for summer school but does not attend consistently, he will not be eligible to attend in subsequent years.

Father may exercise periods of summer visitation during the summer regardless of whether it is during the weeks of summer school, as long as he shall take the child to summer school if his time periods fall during those weeks. Since these arrangements must be made well in advance, Father shall notify Mother of his choice in writing by February 1st every year.

Father may have liberal summer visitation as the parties shall agree. In the event the parties cannot agree, subject to the above provisions, Father shall have three weeks each summer (to be divided into three 7 consecutive day periods) to coincide with the child's school summer vacation. Father may select the first week of this summer vacation by notifying Mother of same (each notification herein to be in writing) by February 1st of each year, one week may then be excluded by Mother by February 15th and then the next week may be selected by Father by March 1st, one more week may then be excluded by Mother by March 15th, the final week may be selected by Father by April 1st. Mother's excluded weeks shall prevail over Father's weekend and weekday periods set forth above.

HOLIDAYS AND SPECIAL DAYS

1. Holiday and special day custody shall prevail over weekend, weekday and summer vacation set forth above. Birthday periods shall not prevail when in conflict with other Holidays and Special Days.

2. Mother shall have the minor child on her birthday and on Mother's Day of each year from 9:00 am to 9:00 pm; plus "Holiday Group A" in even-numbered years and "Holiday Group B" in odd-numbered years.

3. Father shall have the minor child on his birthday and on Father's Day of each year from 9:00 am to 9:00 pm; plus "Holiday Group A" in odd-numbered years and "Holiday Group B" in even-numbered years.

4. Mother and Father are encouraged to communicate to attempt to arrange a combined event/activity for the child's birthday. In the event they cannot agree, the following provisions regarding the child's birthday shall apply.

5. Due to the serious special needs of the child, the conditions stated in the above paragraphs concerning WEEKDAY, WEEKEND and SUMMER visitation shall apply to HOLIDAY GROUPS A & B.

HOLIDAY GROUP A

1. PRESIDENT'S DAY/WASHINGTON'S BIRTHDAY (OBSERVED) weekend from 5:00 pm the Friday prior to 8:00 am the following Tuesday.

2. A period of 7 (seven) days during the child's school Spring break, the exact days to be selected and notice given in writing to the other parent by February 1.

3. INDEPENDENCE DAY If July 4 falls on a: (a) Tuesday, Wednesday or Thursday from 5:00 pm on July 3 until 9:00 am on July 5, (b) Friday or Saturday from 5:00 pm on the Thursday before until 9:00 am on the following Monday, (c) Sunday or Monday from 5:00 pm on the Friday before until 9:00 am on the following Tuesday.

4. HALLOWEEN (October 31) night from 4:00 pm until 9:00 am the following day.

5. CHRISTMAS VACATION from December 25 beginning at 10:00 am through 9:00 am on December 31.

6. The child's birthday from 9:00 am until 9:00 am the following day.

HOLIDAY GROUP B

1. MARTIN LUTHER KING weekend from 5:00 pm the Friday prior through 8:00 am the following Tuesday.

2. MEMORIAL DAY weekend from 5:00 pm the Friday prior through 8:00 am the following Tuesday.

3. LABOR DAY weekend from 5:00 pm the Friday prior through 8:00 am the following Tuesday.

4. THANKSGIVING weekend from 5:00 pm the Wednesday prior through 8:00 am the following Monday.

5. CHRISTMAS VACATION from 5:00 pm the day the child's school Christmas vacation begins through 10:00 am on December 25 and December 31 beginning at 9:00 am through 8:00 am the day the child's school Christmas vacation ends.

6. The day prior to the child's birthday beginning at 9:00 am through 9:00 am the day of the birthday.

The serious special needs of the child require that Mother and Father be far more cooperative and flexible than the parents of a child without special needs.

EXCHANGES

Exchanges of the child shall occur at the residence of Mother or at school or summer camp, unless otherwise agreed. If an exchange occurs at a location other than a parent's residence, the parent scheduled to have time with the child shall pick up and return the child to the specified location and the other parent shall be responsible for assuring the child is at the specified location for pick up, unless other arrangements are described.

TRANSPORTATION

Transportation arrangements for the child for all scheduled parenting times including weekdays, weekends, holidays and vacation times, shall be as follows:

Father shall be responsible for transportation of the child at the beginning and end of the visit.

CHANGES

The parents' schedules and commitments may require occasional changes in the parenting time schedule. Parents shall attempt to agree on any changes, but the parent receiving a request for a change shall have the final decision on whether the change shall occur. The parent making the request may make such request in person, by phone, in writing to the other parent, by text message or by email. The request for change shall be made no later than one week prior to the date of the requested change. The parent receiving the request shall respond no later than 24 hours after receiving the requested change. The response to the request may be made in person, by phone, in writing to the other parent, by text message or by email. Any parent requesting a change of schedule shall be responsible for any additional childcare or transportation costs resulting from the change. Mother and Father shall cooperate to allow the child to meet their therapeutic, school and social commitments.

ELECTRONIC CONTACTS

Each parent shall have reasonable access to the child by telephone, text message, email or social media during any period in which the child is with the other parent, unless otherwise specified.

RELOCATION

Absent exigent circumstances as determined by a Court with jurisdiction, you, as a party to this action, are ordered to notify, in writing by certified mail, return receipt requested, and at least 60 days prior to the proposed relocation, each party to this action of any proposed relocation of the principal residence of the child, including the following information: (1) The intended new residence, including the specific address and mailing address, if known, and if not known, the city; (2) The home telephone number of the new residence, if known; (3) The date of the intended move or proposed relocation; (4) A brief statement of the specific reasons for the proposed relocation of the child; and (5) A proposal for a revised schedule of custody or visitation with the child. Your obligation to provide this information to each party continues as long as you or any other party by virtue of this order is entitled to custody of a child covered by this order. Your failure to obey the order of this Court regarding the proposed relocation may result in further litigation to enforce such order, including contempt of court. In addition, your failure to notify a party of a relocation of the child may be considered in a proceeding to modify custody or visitation with the child. Reasonable costs and attorney fees shall be assessed against you if you fail to give the required notice.

LEGAL CUSTODY

Legal custody: The parties shall agree before making any final decisions on issues affecting the growth and development of the child; including, but not limited to, choice of religious upbringing, choice of childcare provider, choice of school, course of study, special tutoring, extracurricular activities, including but not limited to, music, art, dance and other cultural lessons or activities and gymnastics or other athletic activities, choice of camp or other comparable summer activity, non-emergency medical and dental treatment, psychological, psychiatric or like treatment or counseling, the choice of particular healthcare providers, the extent of any travel away from home, part or full-time employment, purchase or operation of a motor vehicle, contraception and sex education, and decisions relating to actual or potential litigation on behalf of the child. However, each parent may make decisions regarding the day-to-day care and control of the child and in emergencies affecting the health and safety of the child while the child is residing with him or her. The parents shall endeavor, whenever reasonable, to be consistent in such day-to-day decisions.

Communication: Each parent shall ensure that the other parent is provided with copies of all communications or information received from the child's school, and if a second copy of the communication is not provided by the school, shall make a copy for the other parent. Each parent shall notify the other of any activity such as school conferences, programs, sporting and other special events etc., where parents are invited to attend and each shall encourage and welcome the presence of the other.

Child not involved in court or financial communications: The parties shall not talk about adult issues, parenting matters, financial issues, and other court-related topics, when the child is present. Such discussions shall not be had during custody exchanges of the child or during electronic visits. The child shall not be used to carry such messages, written communication or child support payments between the parents.

Medical care information: Each parent shall have the authority to seek any emergency medical treatment for the child when in his or her custody. Each shall advise the other of any medical emergency or serious illness or injury suffered by the minor child as soon as possible after learning of the same, and shall give the other parent details of the emergency, injury or illness and the name and telephone numbers of all treating doctors. Each parent shall inform the other before any routine medical care, treatment or examination by a healthcare provider including said provider's name and telephone number. Each party shall direct all doctors involved in the care and treatment of the minor child to give the other parent all information regarding any injury or illness and the medical treatment or examination, if requested. For purposes of this paragraph, a serious injury or illness is one which requires the child (1) to be confined to home for more than 48 hours, or (2) to be admitted to, or treated at, a hospital or surgical facility, (3) to receive any type of general anesthesia or invasive surgical procedure or test, or (4) to miss school.

Childcare provider: If both parents will need to use a childcare provider during periods of custody or visitation they shall use the same childcare provider, unless the distances between their residences or places of employment make the use of the same childcare provider unreasonable.

Access to records: Each parent shall be entitled to immediate access from the other or from a third party to records and information pertaining to the child including, but not limited to, medical, dental, health, childcare, school or educational records; and each shall take whatever steps are necessary to ensure that the other parent has such access.

Activities to not conflict with custody or visitation: The parties shall enroll the child in activities, particularly outside of school, which, to the extent possible, are scheduled at times and places which avoid interruption and disruption of the custody or visitation time of the other party unless consented to by that parent. The special needs of the child requires far greater cooperation and flexibility by the parents than is required of the parents of a child without special needs.

Resolution of disputes: If the parties fail to agree on the interpretation of the Parenting Plan, or are unable to agree upon a final decision on issues affecting the growth and development or health and safety of the child, they shall submit the dispute to a mutually agreed-upon Special Needs Coordinator who shall hear and arbitrate the issue. In the event they are not able to agree on a Special Needs Coordinator they shall each select a Special Needs Coordinator from the list of approved Special Needs Coordinators maintained by the Somewhere County Family Court and the two Special Needs Coordinators shall determine who shall mediate the case. The Special Needs Coordinator shall be a quick and informal tribunal to arbitrate issues which may arise in the future, including but not limited to: increasing or decreasing child support, changes in therapy, treatment, education, custody and/or visitation, and issues relating to expenses.

CHILD SUPPORT AND OTHER EXPENSES

Due to the special needs of the child, the application of Standard Child Support Guidelines would be inappropriate and/or unjust. The initial amount of child support shall be $_____ per month, payable by Father to Mother. This amount shall be modifiable. This is the base amount, which DOES include the current amount for nutritional supplements/regimens, and DOES NOT include additional support for therapy, activities, camps, or other expenses necessitated by the child's special needs. Parents shall pay for these additional items based upon their proportional share of income. Parents acknowledge that future nutritional supplements/regimens may involve an increased cost, and parents agree to pay such increased cost based upon their proportional income.

The Parties recognize that due to the special needs of the minor child, child support may not terminate at age 18 or at any particular age and may continue if the child is physically or mentally incapacitated from supporting himself and insolvent and unmarried as per § _____ [Statutes of state of Yourstate].

In addition, each party will continue to contribute to child support as long as they are able to provide child support.

The child support shall be paid 50% on the first and 50% on the 15th day of each month.

HEALTHCARE COSTS

The child is currently covered by medical insurance through Father's employer. Both parents shall cooperate to keep the child covered under this insurance or under another plan. In the event it becomes appropriate to obtain other health insurance for the child, the parents shall pay the expense of such coverage based upon their proportionate share of income. Both parents shall cooperate to provide insurance ID cards to the other parent as applicable, and to complete all forms required by the coverage.

Unless both parties have agreed to use a healthcare provider that is not covered by the health benefit plan, if a parent incurs an expense to a healthcare provider that is not covered by the health benefit plan that would have been covered, or covered at a more favorable rate, if a provider included in the plan had been used, then that parent shall pay seventy-five percent (75%) and the other parent shall pay twenty-five percent (25%) of the uncovered expenses.

"Health expenses" shall be defined in accordance with Internal Revenue Code (1987) §213 "Medical, Dental, etc., Expenses" or any other section enacted in replacement, in addition or in substitution thereof, and/or any Internal Revenue Regulation including, but not limited to, §1.213–1 or any relevant Regulation enacted in replacement, in addition or in substitution thereof, or any relevant

Treasury Decision, Regulation or any Revenue Ruling defining those types or kinds of medical costs that are deductible under the Internal Revenue Code, and shall also include orthodontic and optical care (including, but not limited to, prescription eyeglasses or contact lenses and eye examinations conducted by an optician, optometrist or ophthalmologist), treatment and appliances. Psychological and counseling expenses shall be paid as the parties agree, or absent agreement to the extent they are included as "Health Expenses" defined above or are determined by the child's case manager to be in the best interests of the child.

All health expenses incurred on behalf of the child and not paid by the health benefit plan shall be paid based upon each parent's proportionate share of income. The health expenses covered by this paragraph are not limited to just the usual medical, dental, orthodontic, optical and psychological expenses of the child without special needs. Due to the special needs of the child, they have and are expected to continue to have extraordinary medical, therapeutic and other expenses, which shall be paid by the parents based upon proportionate share of income, in addition to the base amount of child support.

The Parties recognize that due to the special needs of the child, the duty to provide health insurance and to pay medical and dental expenses may not terminate at age 18 or at any particular age and may continue if the child is physically or mentally incapacitated from supporting himself and insolvent and unmarried as per § _____ [Statutes of state of Yourstate].

In addition, each party will continue to contribute to healthcare as long as they are able to provide healthcare.

AN EXHIBIT SHALL BE ATTACHED CONTAINING A SUMMARY OF:

[ ] Child's diagnosis

[ ] Doctors, therapists and other professionals

[ ] Child's current daily schedule and routine

[ ] Child's current therapy plan

[ ] How special needs affect the child's daily life

[ ] Itemization & explanation of the costs involved in or caused by the special needs

[ ] Who the primary caregiver of the child is

[ ] Primary caregiver's daily schedule

[ ] Statement as to the impact of transitions and schedule changes on the child

[ ] List of equipment and special items needed by the child and the location of such items

[ ] Suggested physical custody arrangement

[ ] Suggested legal custody arrangement

[ ] Suggested visitation—daily, weekly, weekends, holidays, summers & special days

EDUCATION AND EXTRAORDINARY EXPENSES

Due to the special needs of the child, he currently incurs and is expected to continue to incur extraordinary educational and other expenses. These shall be paid by the parties based upon their proportionate share of income. If the parties cannot agree on the extraordinary expenses for education, therapy, activities, equipment, supplements and/or other items, the parties agree to pay (based upon their proportionate share of income) for the items determined by the child's Special Needs Coordinator to be in the best interest of the child.

_____   _____
       Petitioner   Respondent

_____   _____
  Attorney for Petitioner   Attorney for Respondent

(Adapted from Special Needs Parenting Plan co-written with Kieran Coyne, attorney in St. Louis, Missouri.)

SETTLEMENT AGREEMENT

If you are able to settle your case and not have to go to trial, you will need to have a document that contains the terms of the settlement. This document provides a reference of what was agreed to, so each party knows what they are supposed to do. It also provides a legally enforceable document that can be used in court if either party does not do what they are supposed to do. A sample Settlement Agreement for a case involving a disabled or special needs child is included for your information. Every Settlement Agreement is different. Your Settlement Agreement will be different, because of the laws of your local jurisdiction and the facts of your case.

SAMPLE SETTLEMENT AGREEMENT

IN THE FAMILY COURT OF THE COUNTY OF SOMEWHERE
STATE OF YOUR STATE

PAUL JONES,   )
Petitioner,   )
) Case Number _____
v.   )
) Division _____
RITA JONES,   )
Respondent.   )

MARITAL SETTLEMENT AGREEMENT

This Marital Separation Agreement (hereinafter the "Agreement") is made on the _____ day of _____, 20___, between _____ (hereinafter the "Wife"), and _____ (hereinafter the "Husband"), and collectively referred to as the "Parties."

WHEREAS, the Parties to this Agreement were married on the 1st day of January, 1990, and because of irreconcilable differences which have arisen between them, which render it impossible for them to live together as husband and wife, and

WHEREAS, the Parties believe there is no reasonable likelihood that the marriage of the Parties can be preserved, and that the marriage is irretrievably broken, and

WHEREAS, there was one child born of the marriage, namely: Brian Peter Jones, born January 1, 2000 (hereinafter the "Minor Child"), and

WHEREAS, there is now pending an action in the Family Court of the County of Somewhere, State of Yourstate praying that the marriage of the Parties be dissolved, and

WHEREAS, the Parties hereby desire to fully and finally settle all property rights, and claims between them and make provisions regarding the disposition of their property, maintenance, child support, child custody, attorneys' fees and the costs of these proceedings;

NOW, THEREFORE, for valuable consideration, each received by the other and for mutual promises herein contained, it is agreed as follows:

I. AGREEMENT CONTINGENT UPON COURT REVIEW

All of the stipulations, conditions and Agreements hereinafter contained are contingent upon the Family Court of the County of Somewhere, State of Yourstate, entering an order and judgment dissolving the marriage of the Parties and are contingent upon the Court's determination that this Agreement is not unconscionable.

II. CHILD CUSTODY AND SUPPORT MATTERS

The Parties agree that the provisions of the Parenting Plan (hereinafter the "Plan") attached as Exhibit "A" shall govern the terms of the Minor Child's custody, visitation, and support arrangements. The Parties agree that they will abide by the terms of the Plan. (Father shall pay Mother the sum of $_____ per month in child support.)

III. DIVISION OF PROPERTY

A. NON-MARITAL PROPERTY

The Parties agree that there is non-marital property to be set apart by the Court, which property is divided as indicated on Exhibit "B" attached.

B. MARITAL PROPERTY

1. PERSONAL PROPERTY

a) Division of personal property

The Parties make specific reference to the division of personal property identified on Exhibit "B" attached, with the property being awarded to the Party indicated. Any household goods and personal effects not identified on said exhibit or awarded by this Agreement are awarded to the party who has possession or control of such unidentified goods or personal effects. Each Party is to be responsible for the payment of personal property taxes, if any, that are due for the personal property they are awarded by this agreement.

Vehicles

The Parties agree that Husband is awarded the _____ as his sole and separate property. Further, Husband shall pay and be responsible for any loan or obligation secured by said vehicle, any personal property tax obligations for said vehicle, any leases for said vehicle, and the cost of insuring and operating said vehicle and shall indemnify and hold harmless Wife for such debts.

The Parties agree that Wife is awarded the _____ as her sole and separate property. Further, Wife shall pay and be responsible for any loan or obligation secured by said vehicle, any personal property tax obligations for said vehicle, any leases for said vehicle, and the cost of insuring and operating said vehicle and shall indemnify and hold harmless Husband for such debts.

Joint bank account

The Parties agree that the parties will close this account and share the proceeds from this account equally.

Individual bank accounts

The Parties agree that Husband is awarded all checking and savings accounts in his name as his sole and separate property.

The Parties agree that Wife is awarded all checking and savings accounts in her name as her sole and separate property.

Pensions and IRAs

The Parties acknowledge that Wife is currently receiving retirement and/or disability benefits as a result of her military service. The Parties agree that Wife shall be awarded 100% of her own retirement/pension/disability benefits as her respective property. The Parties agree that Husband and Wife shall each receive 50% or one-half of the retirement/pension/disability benefits in the name of Husband. Husband is awarded the IRA in his name as his property. Wife is the primary caregiver for the Minor Child, who has Special Needs, and thus is unable to work to her otherwise full ability, thereby decreasing the amount she is able to contribute to a retirement plan for her future benefit; therefore the parties agree that this is a fair and equitable distribution of the pensions, retirement accounts and IRAs.

Life insurance

The Parties are each awarded the life insurance policies in their respective names (on their respective lives) as their property. The Parties agree that they will continue to maintain their child as the sole beneficiary on the existing life insurance policies until the child is actually emancipated as defined within the Parenting Plan. Further, each Party shall provide the other Party documentation regarding the terms of the Policy and its current status, upon the other Party's request. Further, the Parties consent to the insurance company issuing, and/or managing, such Policy providing to the Other Party such information about the Policy that is reasonably necessary to determine the existence, terms, beneficiaries, and status of the Policy.

Additionally, the Parties agree that there is a life insurance policy insuring their child, and the Parties agree to maintain such insurance Policy and to each pay one-half of the insurance premiums for said Policy until the insured minor child is emancipated. The Parties further agree that they will each be designated as equal co-beneficiaries on such Policy, and in the event of the death of the insured minor child, the insurance proceeds will be used to satisfy the burial costs of the child, the child's outstanding uninsured medical bills, if any, the child's outstanding educational expenses, and thereafter such remaining proceeds shall be shared equally between the Parties.

b) Titles and papers

Each Party shall promptly deliver to the other all property or documents evidencing ownership of property which by the terms of this Agreement is to remain or become the property of the other. Each Party shall execute and deliver to the other Party such Affidavits of Gift and Limited Powers of Attorney that are reasonably required to transfer each Party's interest in the cars, automobiles, and vehicles awarded the other Party and to permit the other Party to act as attorney in fact for the sole purpose of transferring title of the car, automobile or vehicle awarded by this Agreement.

Further, each party agrees to keep all property, and documents evidencing ownership of property, which by the terms of this Agreement is to remain or become the property of the other in good condition, normal wear and tear excepted, until such time as delivery of such property and documentation to the other Party has occurred. The Parties agree that neither Party shall be obligated to store or keep the property or documentation of ownership of such property, which by the terms of this Agreement, is to remain or become the property of the other, for more than 30 days after written notice of a request to pick up such property and documentation has been mailed by certified mail, return receipt requested, to the Party to whom such property and documentation is awarded by this Agreement. (Such notice to pick up property shall be addressed to the last known mailing address of the recipient Party and shall specify a date, time and place, where the property and documentation in question is to be picked up, which date and time shall be reasonable, and not sooner than five days from the date of mailing of such notice.)

2. REAL PROPERTY

a) Identification of real property

The Parties acknowledge that they now own or have a marital interest in the following real property:

i) 123 Oak Street, Hometown, located in the County of Somewhere, State of Your-State, with the legal description contained on Exhibit ___ attached (hereinafter the "Marital Residence") which real property is security for an obligation, evidenced by a Deed of Trust, in favor of XYZ Bank (hereinafter the "Mortgagee for Marital Residence").

b) Division of real property

The Parties agree that the real property in which they have a marital interest shall be disposed of as follows:

i) Marital residence

The Parties agree that the Marital Residence is awarded to Wife as her sole and exclusive property.

Wife shall assume and pay the unpaid balance of approximately $_____, owing on the Marital Residence. Wife shall also assume and pay the unpaid balance of any other obligation or line of credit that is secured by the Marital Residence and shall indemnify and hold Husband harmless for such other obligations, if any.

Wife shall indemnify and hold Husband harmless should the Mortgagee for the Marital Residence, or its assigns or successors, proceed against Husband upon Wife's failure to assume or pay the obligation owed to the Mortgagee for the Marital Residence, or upon Wife's default under any provision of the loan instruments, promissory notes, or Deed of Trust evidencing or securing the obligation to the Mortgagee for the Marital Residence.

Wife shall also be responsible for any obligation for taxes, subdivision dues, insurance costs, repair costs and utility costs, and any other costs, associated with the ownership, possession or use of the Marital Residence. Wife shall indemnify and hold Husband harmless on such costs.

Wife agrees to take such reasonable action as is necessary to remove Husband's name from the obligation to the Mortgagee for the Marital Residence, including but not limited to, refinancing the obligation. Husband's name shall be removed from the obligation within six months of the date of a Judgment of Dissolution of Marriage between the parties.

Husband shall deliver a Quitclaim Deed, transferring his interest in the Marital Residence to Wife concurrently with the removal of his name from the mortgage obligation.

Husband does herewith assign, transfer and set over to the Wife all of interest in the Escrow fund, if any, held on the Marital Residence and further the Husband assigns, transfers and sets over to the Wife all of Husband's interest in all existing insurance on the Marital Residence.

Husband waives any interest in any deposit previously paid to any utility service providers, whether for phone, water, trash, electric, gas, and sewer service, for service to the Marital Residence. Husband agrees to cooperate with Wife and to do all things reasonably necessary to have the water, phone, electric, gas, sewer, and trash utilities for the Marital Residence put in the name of the Wife.

c) Other real property

The Parties each acknowledge and represent to the other that neither party has any interest in any real property in the State of YourState or elsewhere, whether in their names alone or with others, except as identified above.

3. NATURE OF PROPERTY DIVIDED

The Parties agree that all of the property divided by Section B above is marital property (except for property listed on Petitioner's Statement of Property filed with the Court as being separate/non-marital property). The transfers represent fair and equitable divisions of property after consideration of the other financial provisions of this Agreement.

4. TRANSFERS OF PROPERTY INTEREST

The Parties stipulate and agree that the transfers of property interests, which take place in order to satisfy the terms of this Agreement, shall be transfers pursuant to Section 1041 of the Internal Revenue Code, and the Parties agree to execute any forms or other documents as might be necessary to establish this intent.

IV. MAINTENANCE

The Parties agree, after examining all relevant factors, including the factors specified under Section _____ (statutes of state of _____), that Husband shall pay to Wife the sum of $_____ per month as and for maintenance, such payments are due on the first day of each month, beginning on first of _____, 20___. The Parties agree that this provision as to maintenance shall be modifiable. Maintenance shall automatically terminate upon the first of the following to occur: Husband's death, Wife's death, Wife's remarriage. The Parties agree that no wage withholding orders are required at this time, although the Parties understand that in the event maintenance or child support is not paid in a timely fashion, then a wage withholding order may be applied for by Wife.

V. DEBTS

a) Assumption of debts and liabilities: From and after the date the Petition in this cause was filed, each Party will be solely liable for the debts acquired by him or her.

b) Terms of payments: The Parties' debts and liabilities will be assumed and paid as provided on the exhibits attached hereto (i.e. Exhibit "B") and incorporated herein by reference. Each Party is responsible for any debt or obligation that is incurred in connection with the ownership, possession or use of an asset of property, whether real or personal, unless specifically indicated otherwise in this Agreement.

c) Indemnification: The Parties agree to indemnify and hold harmless each other and defend the other from and against all claims and liabilities and will reimburse the other for any and all expenses made or incurred by the other, either directly or indirectly, including reasonable attorney's fees, as a result of his or her failure to pay or otherwise satisfy the debts and liabilities assumed by each in this Agreement.

d) No undisclosed debts: The Parties warrant to each other that he or she has not incurred any debt or obligation which is either (1) an obligation on or for which the other Party is or may become personally liable, or (2) an obligation that could be enforced at any time against an asset held or to be received under this Agreement by the other Party, except as disclosed on attached Exhibit "B". Each Party covenants not to incur any such obligations or debts on or after the execution of this Agreement.

VI. INCORPORATION IN DECREE

It is the intent of the Parties that the terms of this Agreement be incorporated and fully set forth in any Decree of Dissolution of Marriage entered by the Court, and the Parties shall be ordered to perform the terms thereof.

VII. SEVERABILITY OF PROVISIONS

In the event that any provision of the Agreement is unenforceable when incorporated as part of the Court's judgment, it shall be considered severable and enforceable by an action based on contractual obligation, and it shall not invalidate the remainder of this Agreement as incorporated in any Decree.

VIII. PROVISIONS FOR FAILURE TO PERFORM
WITH NOTICE REQUIRED

In the event that either Party brings an action for failure to perform any of the obligations imposed by the Agreement due him or her, or for enforcement or clarification of the Agreement, the prevailing Party in such action shall have the right to recover his or her reasonable attorney's fees and litigation costs reasonably expended in prosecuting or defending the action. However, no attorney fees shall be so recovered by a Party filing an action unless the Party seeking to recover said attorney fees and costs shall have mailed to the other Party written notice of the alleged failure to perform and said alleged failure was not cured within ten (10) days after the date of mailing of said notice by certified mail to the alleged breaching Party's residential address. Provided further, that no such notice shall be necessary as to any periodic child support obligation which Petitioner has failed to perform in a timely fashion in accordance with this Agreement on more than two occasions. Provided further, that no such notice shall be necessary as to any periodic maintenance obligation which Wife has failed to perform in a timely fashion in accordance with this Agreement on more than two occasions.

No fees or costs authorized by this paragraph shall be recovered except as determined and awarded by the Court in an action brought for enforcement, breach or clarification of the Agreement.

IX. MODIFICATION AND APPROVAL

The terms of this Agreement shall be subject to modification or change only by a mutual agreement of the Parties in writing. It is understood that this provision is not applicable to the terms of the Agreement dealing with child custody, visitation, and child support. The Parties recognize that the provisions relating to custody, visitation, and child support are subject to the approval of the Court, and may be modified by the Court regardless of this paragraph.

X. MUTUAL RELEASE

Subject to the provisions of the Agreement, each Party has remised, released and forever discharged and, by these presents, does himself or herself and his or her heirs, legal representatives, executors, administrators and assigns remise, release and forever discharge the other Party, and the other Party's family, employees, agents and attorneys, of and from all cause or causes of action, claims, rights or demands whatsoever in law or equity, which either Party hereto ever had or now has against the other, except any and all cause or causes of action for dissolution of marriage or rights arising from this Agreement or subsequent Court Order.

XI. MUTUAL WAIVER OF RIGHTS IN ESTATES

Except as otherwise provided in this Agreement, each Party shall have the right to dispose of his or her property of whatsoever nature, real or personal, and each Party, for himself or herself, respectively, and for their respective heirs, legal representatives, executors, administrators, personal representatives and assigns, hereby waives any right of election which he or she may have or hereafter acquire regarding the estate of the other or to take against any Last Will and Testament of the other or any codicil thereto, whether heretofore or hereafter executed, as provided for in any law now or hereinafter effective of this state or any other state or territory of the United States or any foreign country and renounces and releases all interest, right or claim of distributive share or interstate succession or dower or courtesy, or community property or statutory exemption or allowance or otherwise, that he or she now has or might otherwise have against the other or the estate of the other, or the property of whatsoever nature, real or personal, of the other Party under or by virtue of the laws of any state or country. Nothing contained in this particular paragraph, however, shall affect any obligation undertaken in the other paragraphs of the Agreement by either Party.

XII. DISPOSAL OF PROPERTY

Except as set forth in this agreement, each of the Parties shall, from the date of the execution of this Agreement, have the right to dispose of his or her property by *intervivos* conveyance, gift, Last Will or otherwise, as though a single person.

XIII. EXECUTION OF PAPERS

The Parties agree that they shall take any and all steps to execute, acknowledge and deliver to the other any and all instruments, assurances and affidavits that the other Party may reasonably require or find convenient, expedient or businesslike for the purpose of giving full force and effect to the provisions of this Agreement.

XIV. PERFORMANCE OF ACTS REQUIRED IN AGREEMENT

Where acts and things are required to be performed under the terms of this Agreement and no time is specified for their performance, they shall be done as soon as practical after a Judgment of Dissolution of marriage is entered between the Parties, or within 15 days of the date the Judgment of Dissolution of marriage is entered between the Parties, whichever is sooner.

XV. VOLUNTARY AGREEMENT AND INVESTIGATION AND DISCLOSURE

Each of the Parties hereby affirms that they each are entering into this Agreement freely and voluntarily; that they have ascertained and weighed all the facts and circumstances likely to influence his or her judgment herein; that they have given due consideration to such provisions in question; that they have sought independent advice of counsel in regard to all details and particulars of the Agreement (or, they had an opportunity to seek independent advice of counsel) and the underlying facts; and that they clearly understand and assent to all the provisions hereof.

Each Party further warrants that they have each disclosed to the other the full extent of their respective properties and income, either on the Statements of Property and/ or Statements of Income and Expenses filed with the Court, or on the attachments to this Agreement. Each Party further warrants that they have not secreted, hidden, transferred, or disposed of any assets that either Party may have an interest in. Each Party warrants that neither Party has since the ___ day of _____, 20___ withdrawn, consumed or borrowed, except for ordinary, regular and normal living expenses, funds from the bank accounts, stock holdings, retirement plans, 401k plans, pension plans, and Thrift Savings Plans, in their respective names or control. Each Party warrants that the equity values or balances of the bank accounts, stock holdings, retirement plans, 401k plans, pension plans, and Thrift Savings Plans, except as values fluctuate with the market or accounts are subject to third party charges, are as disclosed on each Party's Statements of Property filed with the Court, or as disclosed on the account statements or documentation provided the other Party in response to Requests for the Production of Documents, whichever documentation contains the most current information.

Each Party agrees that in the event property, assets or interests are discovered that have not been disclosed on their Statements of Property or on attachments to this Agreement, and which property, assets or interests were acquired in whole or in part during the marriage and not by way of inheritance or gift or in exchange for non-marital property, that such property, assets or interests shall be divided equally between the Parties promptly after the discovery of the same.

XVI. WAIVER OF DISCOVERY

Each party acknowledges that he or she has had the opportunity to complete the discovery each as Interrogatories, Request for Production of Documents, appraisals, real estate and other property, and depositions, and has chosen not to do same. Each party acknowledges the risks of proceeding without completion of such discovery. Each party has, nevertheless, directed his or her attorneys to proceed without completion of such discovery. Each party acknowledges that without such completed discovery, his or her counsel has not conducted any investigation or analysis that would permit his or her counsel to determine the full extent and value of the parties' marital property, debts, income and expenses, and whether there is any marital component in any non-marital property. The settlement has been based on the personal knowledge of each party, and the review of limited documents exchanged between the parties and Statement of Income and Expenses and Statement of Property filed by each party herein.

XVII. RIGHTS TO TRIAL

Both Parties understand they have a right to trial. The Parties agree and stipulate, having been fully advised by their respective attorneys of the consequences and considerations that could result if fully litigated and that trying the case could be more favorable or could be less favorable than the terms of this Property Settlement and Separation Agreement. Nevertheless, the Parties have agreed it is in their respective best interests to waive any trial of this matter and settle the case.

XVIII. LIVING APART

The Parties shall continue to live separate and apart and from the date of the execution of this Agreement, free from any interference by the other, as if fully unmarried, and further, neither will molest, malign, annoy or trouble the other in any manner.

XIX. JOINT INCOME TAX RETURNS

The Parties agree to file joint income tax returns for the tax year ending December 31, 20 ___, and each shall be entitled to one-half (1/2) of any refund on any joint returns filed for said tax year and will likewise be responsible for one-half (1/2) of any taxes, interest and penalties on returns which are jointly filed.

The Parties agree that in the event any jointly filed income tax return is audited by the appropriate taxing authorities, they will cooperate with each other and their respective attorneys, and accountants, to investigate, respond to or comply with such audit. Any non-cooperating Party shall indemnify and hold harmless the other Party for failure to perform any reasonable request to assist the attorney/ accountants in investigating, responding to or complying with said audit.

The Parties agree that in the event either Party receives any notice or documentation from the Internal Revenue Service, or any state taxing authority, that references or involves an income tax return that was filed by either Party, or the Parties jointly, during the course of the marriage, they shall promptly forward a copy of such notice or documentation to the other Party at their last known mailing address. In the event a Party fails to promptly forward a copy of such notice or documentation to the other Party and additional taxes, interest or penalties are assessed against the other Party after the date of receipt of such notice or documentation by the non-forwarding Party, then the non-forwarding Party shall indemnify and hold harmless the other Party for such additional taxes, interest and penalties.

XX. PAYMENT OF ATTORNEY'S FEES

The Parties agree that Husband shall pay his own respective attorney fees and costs incurred in this cause, and that Husband shall pay $5,000.00 to Wife's attorney as and for her attorney fees incurred in this cause.

XXI. PAYMENT OF COURT COSTS

The Parties agree that the court costs, excluding deposition costs, of this proceeding shall be equally shared between the Parties. Any deposition costs shall be borne solely by the Party taking the deposition. In the event the Court orders court costs paid from any deposits already on hand with the Court, then the Respondent shall indemnify, hold harmless, and reimburse Petitioner for Respondent's share of court costs as agreed to in this paragraph.

XXII. BINDING EFFECT

This Agreement shall be binding on the heirs, representatives and assigns of the Parties hereto except as to the specific paragraphs which contain provisions for termination of obligations on the death of one or both of the Parties.

XXIII. EXECUTION

Each Party hereto acknowledges that each of them is making this Agreement of his or her own free will and volition and acknowledges that no coercion, force, pressure or undue influence has been used against either Party in the making of this Agreement or by any other person or persons.

XXIV. STATUTORY COMPLIANCE

The validity and construction of this Agreement shall be determined in accordance with the laws of the State of YourState.

XXV. SIGNATURES

IN WITNESS WHEREOF, the Parties set their signatures to this document here-after.

STATE OF _____   )
) SS
COUNTY OF _____   )

_____, of lawful age, being first duly sworn on his oath, states that he is the Petitioner (and Husband) named herein and that he has read the above and foregoing Agreement; he further states that the facts and matters contained therein are true and correct to the best of his knowledge, information and belief and he has executed this document voluntarily and of his free will.

_____
                       Petitioner

On this ____ day of _____, 20___ before me a Notary Public in and for said State personally appeared _____to me known to be the person described in and who executed the foregoing instrument, and acknowledged and stated under oath and/or affirmed that he executed the same as his free act and deed, and that the facts and matters contained therein are true and correct to the best of his knowledge, information and belief.

IN TESTIMONY WHEREOF, I have hereunto set my hand and affixed my official seal in the County and State aforesaid, the day and year first above written.

_____
                   Notary Public

My Commission expires: _____

STATE OF _____   )
) SS
COUNTY OF _____   )

_____, of lawful age, being first duly sworn on her oath, states that she is the Respondent (and Wife) named herein and that she has read the above and foregoing Agreement; she further states that the facts and matters contained therein are true and correct to the best of her knowledge, information and belief and she has executed this document voluntarily and of her free will.

_____
                      Respondent

On this ____ day of _____, 20___ before me a Notary Public in and for said State personally appeared _____to me known to be the person described in and who executed the same as her free act and deed, and that the facts and matters contained therein are true and correct to the best of her knowledge, information and belief.

IN TESTIMONY WHEREOF, I have hereunto set my hand and affixed my official seal in the County and State aforesaid, the day and year first above written.

_____
Notary Public

My Commission expires: _____

EXHIBIT "A"
Parenting Plan

EXHIBIT "B"
Division of Property

EXHIBIT "C"
Legal Description for Marital Residence

(Adapted from Settlement Agreement co-written with Kieran Coyne, an attorney in St. Louis, Missouri.)

JUDGMENT OF DISSOLUTION

When the entire case is over, whether because you reached a settlement or had a trial, the judge will enter a Judgment of Dissolution. A sample Judgment of Dissolution for a case involving a disabled or special needs child is included, to show you what one can look like. As with other documents, yours will vary based upon your local court requirements and the facts of your case.

SAMPLE JUDGMENT OF DISSOLUTION

IN THE FAMILY COURT OF SOMEWHERE COUNTY
STATE OF YOURSTATE

In Re the Marriage of:

PAUL JONES,   )
Petitioner,   )
) Case Number _____
v.   )
) Division _____
RITA JONES,   )
Respondent.   )

JUDGMENT OF DISSOLUTION

Now on this _____ day of _____, 20___ , this cause comes on for hearing; Petitioner, Paul Jones, appearing in person and with his attorney, (name). Respondent, Rita Jones, appearing in person and with her attorney, (name).

Whereupon, all matters contained in the Petition are submitted to the Court for trial. All parties announce ready for hearing. After hearing all the evidence, reviewing the Property Settlement Agreement and being fully advised in the premises, the Court finds that Petitioner has been a resident of the State of _____ for more than _____ days next preceding the commencement of this proceeding and that more than ___ days have elapsed since the filing of the Petition. The Court finds that the Respondent, Rita Jones, is not now pregnant. The Court finds that there remains no reasonable likelihood that the marriage can be preserved and that the marriage is irretrievably broken.

IT IS THEREFORE ORDERED, ADJUDGED AND DECREED by the Court that the parties hereto be and they are hereby granted the dissolution of their marriage and restored to all rights and privileges of single and unmarried persons.

The Court finds that the Property Settlement Agreement is presented to the Court and after being duly examined is found not to be unconscionable, and is to be made a part of the Judgment. The Court finds that said agreement disposes of all marital and non-marital property and debt.

The Court finds that there was one child born of the marriage, namely: Brian Peter Jones, born January 1, 2000.

THE COURT FINDS THAT SAID MINOR CHILD HAS A SPECIAL NEED, NAMELY AUTISM, WHICH SPECIAL NEED HAS BEEN COMPLETELY ADDRESSED IN THE SETTLEMENT AGREEMENT, PARENTING PLAN AND PROPOSED JUDGMENT. THESE DOCUMENTS HAVE BEEN APPROVED BY THE SPECIAL NEEDS COORDINATOR ASSIGNED TO THIS CASE.

The Court finds that it is in the best interests of the child for the parents to be awarded joint physical and joint legal custody of the child.

In determining the custody of the child, the Court has considered the wishes of the child's parents as to custody and the proposed Parenting Plan submitted by both parties; the needs of the child for a frequent, continuing and meaningful relationship with both parents and the ability and willingness of parents to actively perform their function as mother and father for the needs of the child; the interaction and interrelationship of the child with parents, siblings, and any other person who may significantly affect the child's best interests; which parent is more likely to allow the child frequent, continuing and meaningful contact with the other parent; the child's adjustment to the child's home, school, community; the mental and physical health of all individuals involved, including any history of abuse of any individuals involved; the intention of either parent to relocate the principal residence of the child; and the wishes of a child as to the child's custodian.

In the event either party relocates their principal residence, then you are advised pursuant to Section _____ of the Statutes of the State of YourState as follows: Absent exigent circumstances as determined by a Court with jurisdiction, you, as a party to this action, are ordered to notify, in writing by certified mail, return receipt requested, and at least 60 days prior to the proposed relocation, the other party of any proposed relocation of the principal residence of the child, including the following information:

1. The intended new residence, including the specific address and mailing address, if known, and if not known, the city;

2. The home telephone number of the new residence, if known;

3. The date of the intended move or proposed relocation;

4. A brief statement of the specific reasons for the proposed relocation of the child; and

5. A proposal for a revised schedule of custody or visitation with the child.

Your obligation to provide this information to each party continues as long as you or any other party by virtue of this order is entitled to custody of a child covered by this order. Your failure to obey this order of this court regarding the proposed relocation may result in further litigation to enforce such order including contempt of court. In addition, your failure to notify a party of a relocation of the child may be considered in a proceeding to modify custody or visitation with the child. Reasonable costs and attorney fees may be accessed against you if you fail to give the required notice.

The Court orders that each party pay their respective pro rata share of the 20__ personal property taxes based upon the assessed value of the vehicles awarded to each party. Each party shall pay their share prior to December 31, 20__.

The Court orders the Sheriff or other Law Enforcement Officer to enforce visitation or custody rights.

The Court orders Petitioner to pay to Respondent the sum of $_____ per month as and for Respondent's maintenance until further order of the Court. Said maintenance obligation shall be modifiable.

It is contemplated by and the intention and agreement of the parties that the amounts payable by Petitioner to Respondent under this Section shall be deductible on Petitioner's federal and (state) income tax returns and shall constitute income to Respondent for federal and (state) income tax purposes.

The Court orders Respondent to pay to counsel for Petitioner the sum of $_____ as and for a portion of Petitioner's attorney fees.

The Court orders Petitioner to pay all court costs incurred herein.

The Court finds that this Judgment has disposed of all marital and non-marital property and debts.

IT IS FURTHER ORDERED, ADJUDGED AND DECREED by the Court that the parties shall sign any and all documents necessary to effectuate the terms of this Judgment Entry.

IT IS SO ORDERED.

Dated this _____ **day of** _____, 20____.

_____
The Honorable _____
Case No. _____

APPROVED AS TO FORM:

_____
Attorney for Petitioner

_____
Attorney for Respondent

These pleadings and documents are intended to provide some insight and guidance into the ways your case can be different from a case that does not involve a disabled or special needs child. The pleadings and documents will be different in every case. Work closely with your lawyer to craft pleadings and documents that address all the issues important and relevant in your case.

Chapter 5

Child Custody and Visitation

Whether you settle the case or have to go to trial, one important issue that must be resolved by the parties or the judge is the issue of child custody and visitation. This issue must be determined on a case-by-case basis. It is supposed to be decided based upon what is in the best interest of the child. There are two types of custody—physical custody and legal custody. Physical custody refers to where the child lives. Legal custody deals with decision making and access to records. This chapter will be concerned primarily with physical custody and visitation issues. There will be discussion of legal custody later in this chapter.

In order to decide the issue of child custody in any divorce case properly, certain factors must be considered. The number of factors to be considered is quite lengthy but not all of the factors will be applicable to every case. Carefully read the factors and determine which ones apply to your case. Following the recitation of custody factors to consider is a discussion of factors which are of particular importance in the determination of custody and visitation in a divorce case involving a child with disability or special need.

CUSTODY FACTORS

Prior to the divorce being filed, which parent has been the primary caregiver for the child? In most cases one of the parents provided the majority of the caregiving time. Frequently in the family with a disabled child, one parent primarily focuses on being the breadwinner, while the other parent primarily focuses on the care of the child. Within this situation, both parents might be employed and both parents might provide care of the child, but they each have a particular focus on which they spend the majority of their time.

Whose schedule is most workable for taking care of the child after the divorce? If one of the parents is, for example, an airline pilot, her schedule will be less flexible than that of a parent who is a writer and can work flexible hours from home.

The next issue requires great candor and honesty. Which parent really wants to be most involved with the child? One parent's personality and temperament may be better suited to spending long hours caring for a sick child than that of the other parent. Sometimes one parent will give up her job to devote herself completely to the care of the child, only to find after several weeks or months that she cannot handle it. Then it is up to the other parent to become the primary caregiver, or they must find some other solution. These are heart-wrenching decisions. No one asks to be in this position. Even when you have done your very best, sometimes it is not enough. Not everyone is cut out to do this.

If both parents have been equally providing the care of the child, both parents have equally flexible and workable schedules, and both parents wish to be involved in the child's care on a daily basis, they should consider joint physical custody. This is not the usual situation in families with a disabled child or in families with a typical child. When it does happen, however, joint physical custody should be explored.

Another factor to be considered in evaluating physical custody of the child is whether either parent travels frequently, for business or pleasure. Travel is not necessarily a bad thing for any child. Travel can be an important part of a child's education and upbringing. Be aware however that you can run into accessibility issues when traveling with a child who has special needs. Medical care and prescriptions can be difficult to obtain when traveling. If your child has life-threatening allergies, extreme caution must be exercised and exquisite planning utilized when traveling with your child. Children who have difficulty with transitions may need special modifications when traveling. If your child has a seizure disorder, they may not be allowed to travel on commercial airlines.

Does either parent work long hours or have an unusual work schedule? If so, this could affect the parent's ability to transport the child to necessary therapy, treatments or activities.

Is either parent studying for a diploma or degree? If they are, what is the anticipated graduation or completion date? Can a custody and visitation schedule be fashioned that allows the student parent more time for studies while completing their schooling, then increases their parenting time during semester breaks and upon graduation?

Do both parents have very similar goals, interests, and values? If they do, they are more likely to achieve an amicable resolution of custody and other issues related to the divorce. They are also more likely to be good candidates for joint physical custody. On the other hand, if the parents are clearly an example of opposites attracting, they may well have great difficulty working together on the day-to-day care of the child.

Are you and your spouse able to work well together to resolve problems? Frankly, if you were, you probably would not be going through a divorce. However, just because two people are no longer going to be married does not mean they cannot be civilized and get along. I urge all divorcing parents, whether they have a disabled child or not, to consider themselves from that point forward as "business partners" in the business of raising their child. Treat each other with respect and courtesy. Discuss issues in an unemotional, non-accusatory manner. Do not incur large expenses or make important decisions on your own, any more than you would with a business partner. When the emotions are removed, the focus is put back on the child, and when the business partner model is used, many parents are able to work well together to parent their child. All parents need to make every reasonable effort to get along and work together cooperatively on issues involving the child. This is especially important when you have a disabled or special needs child. Sometimes parents are so busy fighting each other that the needs of the disabled child go unaddressed. This is shameful and inexcusable. Your child did not ask you two to marry each other, and your child did not ask you two to divorce each other. Your child is the one innocent party in this situation. Your child is also completely vulnerable in this situation. You have a higher duty to protect your child than the parent of the typical child. Your squabbles with your spouse are not as important as your child's well-being.

Surprisingly, after divorce, religion can be a bigger issue than it was during your marriage. One parent may have gone along with the wishes of the other parent while they were married, but may now feel free to exercise their own faith after the divorce. The family may have avoided the issue by not being observant of any faith during the marriage. After you and your spouse divorce and go your separate ways, one or both of you may wish to practice a faith. Do you and your spouse agree on the religion in which the child will be raised? An entire chapter could be written on the unique aspects of faith in the life of a child with a disability or special need. It is an important issue.

Do you and your spouse agree on the education plan for the child? Usually one or both parents move after the divorce, unless the move or moves already took place during or prior to the divorce. The location of the custodial parent's residence can have a huge impact on where the child is eligible to attend school. It can also affect the child's eligibility for certain therapy and treatment programs. These factors should be discussed. Think ahead to the next level of school your child will be in, whether that is middle school or high school. If your child is in homebound education, how will the addresses of your residences affect eligibility?

Do you and your spouse agree on medical care for the child? If this has been an ongoing battle throughout the marriage, expect it to get worse, not better, following the divorce. Frequently, one parent wants to try treatments or therapies with which the other parent might not agree. Sometimes one parent is in denial about the child's condition. For that parent to agree to treatment for the condition, the parent would have to face the reality of the child's condition and admit the child's disability. One form of denial is for a parent to minimize the severity of the child's condition or be insistent that the child will "grow out of it."

Do you and your spouse agree on extracurricular activities for the child? Again, if this has been an ongoing battle throughout the marriage, it is likely to get worse after the divorce. One parent might want to encourage the child in mainstream activities for the child to have as much normalcy as possible and for socialization. The other parent might want to protect the child from possible cruelty of other children, or from the child being embarrassed by her disability. If you look deep within, you may even find that one parent is embarrassed by their child and wants to minimize awkward and embarrassing situations.

Is either parent involved with or dating someone? If so, how is that likely to impact on their involvement and relationship with the child? Will it result in the parent moving to another location? Does your child have asthma? Does the "significant other" smoke cigarettes? Is your child allergic to pets? Does the significant other have pets? While these and many other factors need to be considered, many times it is a good thing when significant others come along. A person who is happy and in a good relationship is more likely to be cooperative. Starting a new relationship can give a person something else on which to focus their attention, rather than continuing to fight with their former spouse. Is important, however, to set boundaries for new significant others. If they try to take over, or they stir up fights, they can become a huge problem.

How will grandparents be involved in the child's life after the divorce? Grandparent involvement may increase or decrease after the divorce. If grandparents provided a significant portion of the childcare, transportation or sick day coverage during the marriage, it is an important factor. You need to try to determine what their involvement will be following the divorce. Ideally, you will all set your hurt feelings and differences aside and work together as a team for the best interests of the child.

This factor is huge: Are both you and your spouse good, competent, responsible parents? Of course, nearly all parents would immediately insist that they are. Unfortunately, sometimes people see themselves as they want to be, not as they actually are. Human beings can be selfish, spoiled, petty, immature, reckless, irresponsible brats. If you are able to step back for a moment, you will admit this is not a good situation for a child. None of us want to think of ourselves as bad parents. Some people, however, simply are.

Another important factor is what the child wants. Who does the child want to live with after the divorce? The child should have the level of input that is appropriate to the child's age and emotional development.

VISITATION FACTORS

When you are formulating a plan of visitation, all of the factors discussed within the custody factors section need to be revisited from the perspective of visitation, not custody. In addition to reviewing all of those factors, additional steps are required in properly formulating a visitation plan.

How far will the noncustodial parent live from the custodial parent's home? How far will the noncustodial parent live from the child's school? How far will the noncustodial parent live from their place of work? This will affect whether one midweek overnight visitation is feasible. A work commute might make sense when the noncustodial parent is driving directly from his home to his job in the morning. However, if he has the child for overnight visitation and the child's school is in the opposite direction from the parent's job, driving the child to school in the morning after an overnight visit might not be feasible. If the noncustodial parent has to be at work at 5 am, for example, and the child's school does not start until 8 am, this would cause a problem. In this situation, it may be better for the noncustodial parent to exercise evening visitation but not overnight visitation during the week on school nights.

Afterschool activities and daycare rules must be taken into account. If the child must be picked up from daycare or afterschool care no later than 6 pm and the parent does not get off work until 6:30 pm, they will have to make other arrangements. If the child's afterschool activities do not provide transportation, this can affect the logistics of the visitation schedule as well.

Is the child in religion school or other religious observance? If so, determine what the scheduling requirements are and factor them into the visitation schedule.

When you are determining the custody and visitation schedule, try to allow sufficient time for the child to spend time with their friends, grandparents, and other relatives. Divorce is disruptive enough for a child.

To no longer be able to play with their cousins, hang out with their friends, or bake cookies with Grandma is simply wrong.

If the family visits out-of-town relatives, does the holiday schedule accommodate travel time for those out-of-town visits? This can usually be resolved by tailoring the holiday schedule appropriately.

Is the child active in sports leagues, music lessons, dance classes, or other ongoing activities? To the extent possible, the child should not have to sacrifice their activities because their parents divorced. Good communication and cooperation between the parents usually manages these issues nicely.

Try to ensure that the summer visitation schedule allows each parent sufficient blocks of time for travel. Also try to ensure that the summer visitation schedule does not prevent the child from participating in their summer camps, sports leagues, and tournaments.

When formulating the custody and visitation schedule, be careful that the child is not being shuffled around too much. There are many ways to work a schedule in order to minimize the number of times the child goes back and forth between parents while not reducing the noncustodial parent's time with the child. Make sure the child is not living out of a suitcase. The child needs to have a clear sense of where home is.

At both households, the child needs to know she is not an afterthought. Does the child have a bed to sleep on? Will she have to sleep on the sofa or a pallet on the floor, or share a bed with others? Will she have any space to herself and any place for privacy besides the bathroom?

The child needs to feel as though she still has two parents, not just one parent and a visitor. This is important for the parent and the child.

UNIQUE CUSTODY AND VISITATION FACTORS
FOR A CHILD WITH SPECIAL NEEDS

In addition to evaluating carefully all of the custody and visitation factors discussed above, when formulating the plan for custody and visitation with a child who has a disability or special needs, there are additional factors which should be considered. While it can be more difficult to formulate a workable plan that meets the needs of the parents and the disabled child, it is possible, with the correct information.

Primary caregiver parent

Which parent has been the primary caregiver since the special need or disability was diagnosed? This issue does not just go to which parent has spent the most time with the child. This issue focuses also on the disability or special need. Has one parent taken on the challenge of managing the child's special needs issues? Has the other parent left the specialized disability issues primarily in the hands of the primary caregiver parent? People tend to fall into roles in a marriage. One spouse might be the one who arranges travel plans. The other spouse might be the one who does meal planning and preparation. One spouse might handle issues involving the vehicles, while the other handles home improvements and repairs. It is similar with the care and management of a child with a disability. Frequently one parent will learn as much as they can about the child's particular special need, and shoulder the bulk of the responsibility for that care.

Has one parent not truly bonded with the child? Sadly, sometimes a parent does not bond with their disabled child. It may be a self-defense mechanism, not wanting to get too close to the child in case the child does not survive. It may be that the parent does not relate to the child because of the child's differences. Some parents see their children primarily as trophies. To this type of parent, a disabled child might not measure up to the parent's expectations. If one parent has bonded with the child and the other has not, this should be a factor which is considered in the development of custody and visitation plans.

Has each parent been supportive and cooperative of the child's special needs and treatment? Some parents will without hesitation devote their lives to doing whatever they can for their disabled child. Other parents will turn their backs, minimize the situation, or even treat the child with cruelty, blaming the child for the stress and expenses.

Evaluate how involved each parent is in the child's daily care. This includes home therapy and modifications, administration of medication, as well as transportation of the child to doctors, therapists and treatments. Which parent handles administrative aspects of the child's special needs, such as making appointments, handling insurance issues, researching options available for the child, and determining a course of treatment or an action plan?

How has each parent's life changed since the child was diagnosed? This can be particularly telling when you're dealing with a child with serious medical issues. If one parent has gone on with life as usual, it is highly unlikely they are very involved in the care of the child. Raising a child takes a great deal of work even when the child does not have serious health issues. When the child does have serious health issues, something else has to give in order for the child to receive the care they need and deserve. If both parents truly are involved in the child's care, then both parents have sacrificed something from their schedules and their lives in order to make the time to care properly for the child. If there is no significant change in a parent's life, then they are not significantly involved in the care of the child.

Parent training

Has the noncustodial parent completed appropriate training to be qualified to take care of the child's medical needs? Does the noncustodial parent have a backup plan in case there is an emergency while the child is in his or her custody? How will the child get to emergency medical care from the noncustodial parent's house?

Has the noncustodial parent educated himself or herself on the child's disability? Has the parent learned as much as possible about the child's treatments, therapies, and medications? Is the parent involved in the local chapter of the organization which serves the particular disability? Does the parent even understand the jargon used by the educators and service care providers when discussing this particular disability? How involved has the parent been in school meetings, teacher conferences, and the formulation of Individualized Education Plans (IEP) for the child?

Logistical considerations

All of the logistical considerations previously discussed are highly relevant with a child with a disability. The child still needs to be able to get to her school, therapy, treatments, and activities consistently and on time. She needs to have her equipment and supplies with her. If possible, she should not have her commute times increased significantly.

Parental denial

How has each parent responded to the child's special needs? Some parents live in denial of their child's disability. They don't want their child to be disabled, so they stick their heads in the sand and ignore it. They will fight with the doctors, and about medications, treatments, and therapies. Still others are simply too irresponsible to administer the child's medications reliably or to have a critically ill child's life in their hands for extended periods of time. Some parents are passive aggressive, and will agree to do things they don't want to, but will then not follow through.

Lack of cooperation / medical or educational neglect

When determining the details of the visitation schedule, you should consider the likelihood that the noncustodial parent will properly follow through on the child's medication, dietary restrictions, treatments, and therapies during that parent's period of visitation. How has this parent done on these things before and during the divorce? Has the child missed medication or missed therapy or treatments when with this parent?

You should also consider the likelihood of the custodial parent properly handling the child's daily care when the child is with them. Although you are not physically present during those visits, there are ways to tell what happens at the other parent's house. Does the child come home dirty, smelly, hungry, or tired from the parent? Do the child's clothes come home dirty or not at all? Does the child's homework get done with that parent?

Another factor is the likelihood of the noncustodial parent following the consistent schedule and routine of the child when at the other parent's home. Special needs children usually require more consistency and predictability than typical children. If one parent refuses to maintain the routine the child is used to, it will be disruptive for the child. Both households need to maintain consistent schedules for mealtimes, bathtime, bedtime, waking up time, and other routine daily matters.

Unfortunately, some parents commit medical neglect or educational neglect through their irresponsible actions, or through their passive-aggressive behavior. If your case reaches that level, you need to determine the appropriate action, whether that is notifying the Guardian-ad-Litem, the school administration or a child protective agency. You would, of course, have already tried diligently to make sure the other parent knew the proper care of the child and how to implement it.

Child's schedule

What is the usual daily schedule of each parent? Special needs children have three times as many sick days and school absences as typical children. Which parent will be available for care of the child on all these days? Which parent's work schedule will be most accommodating?

If the child is in therapy or treatment for which the parents must provide transportation, this must be factored into the schedule. Frequently therapy and treatment times are only available between 9 am and 5 pm.

Before signing off on a custody and visitation plan, carefully and thoroughly walk through how that custody and visitation plan will impact the child's schedule, comfort, treatments, therapies, schooling, and medication administration. Rarely will a "cookie-cutter" custody and visitation schedule work with the logistics of these factors. Frequently, however, a somewhat standard custody and visitation schedule can be tailored to meet the best interests of the child, when the right questions are asked.

While you do not want to draw them into your personal matters, sometimes the child's teachers, therapists, and medical professionals can be a great resource for suggestions as to custody arrangements that would be in the child's best interests. They see many special needs children whose families go through divorce. They have seen arrangements that work well and arrangements that fail miserably.

I am repeating the issue of considering what the child wants. This must be done carefully and appropriately. You should never pull your child into the divorce. That is highly inappropriate and harmful to the child. You should, however, consider the child's wishes. Your child has already faced and endured more than many people will during an entire lifetime. Your child deserves to be treated with respect and dignity.

Environmental modifications

Now think about where the visitation will occur. Is the noncustodial parent in a temporary housing situation, sleeping in the basement at a friend's house? Is the parent staying in a hotel until they find an apartment or buy a house in the city to which they have moved? Whatever the situation, is it an appropriate setting for the child's medical condition? Will the child be comfortable and safe there? Will the environment be appropriate for the child? It may be necessary to draft one custody and visitation plan that will be in effect while the parent is in the temporary housing, with a second custody and visitation plan to be in effect when the parent obtains appropriate permanent housing.

Other factors to consider about where the visitation will occur include who else lives or stays over at that household. If your child is nonverbal, he is a natural target for abusers and child molesters because he cannot report what happens to him. If your child has asthma or other breathing or lung problems, carefully evaluate the household to determine if there are smokers, pets to which the child might be allergic, or other factors which could trigger an emergency respiratory situation. If the child has life-threatening allergies, for example to peanuts, all persons within the household must be educated on the seriousness of this condition and the behaviors which must be avoided at all costs.

Further logistical factors include whether your child's wheelchair will fit into and throughout the house. Is there a ramp so your child can get inside the house without the indignity of having to be carried? If a child is not ambulatory, how will transfers to and from her chair be handled? Is all the necessary equipment properly installed?

Has any necessary therapy equipment been properly installed in the noncustodial parent's home? Has an extra set of medication, inhalers, nebulizer, and other necessary medical treatment equipment been obtained and placed within the noncustodial parent's home? Has the noncustodial parent completed sufficient training to be proficient on his or her own with this equipment, especially in case of emergency?

If other environmental modifications are necessary, such as locks on the stoves, alarms on the doors, locks on the toilet seats, padding on sharp corners and fireplaces and tall or heavy furniture being bolted to the wall studs, have all of these modifications been completed? Has everyone within the noncustodial parent's household been thoroughly instructed concerning all the applicable safety factors with this child?

What does physical custody mean?

Physical custody means where the child lives. The parents might share a joint physical custody. If they do not share joint physical custody, then one parent is usually designated as having primary or sole physical custody. In some states, different terminology is used. You should check with your divorce lawyer on the appropriate language to be used in your case. When a child is physically with the custodial parent, it is usually not referred to as visitation. Visitation usually refers to the time a child spends with the noncustodial parent.

What does legal custody mean?

Legal custody refers to decision-making authority and access to records. When parents share joint legal custody, it means both parents have to discuss and try to reach agreement concerning the major decisions concerning the child's life, such as medical care, education, and religion. Other subjects sometimes included in the area of legal custody include use of birth control by the child, sex education, driving privileges, and college issues. Generally the parent with whom the child is staying at any given moment has the authority to make the smaller, day-to-day decisions concerning the child, such as what they will have for dinner. Regardless of the type of legal custody the parents have, if a child has a medical emergency, the parent who has the child at that moment is to seek immediate appropriate medical care and notify the other parent as soon as possible. Cell phones have made this much less of an issue than it used to be.

You need to discuss all of these custody issues thoroughly with your lawyer. These issues are highly relevant at all stages of the divorce—at the time the case is filed with the court, when the Answer and Counter Petition are filed, when discovery is being done, and when the Parenting Plan is written. These issues are vital during settlement or trial, and when writing the final documents and pleadings. You must be prepared on these issues to advocate properly for your child's disability or special need.

Chapter 6

Child Support

Child support needs to be very different from the standard calculations when you have a disabled or special needs child. Many courts use standardized child support calculation forms or tables. There are very good reasons for the use of these standardized calculation tools. They make it quicker and more efficient to calculate child support. They result in much more uniform results from one judge to another within the jurisdiction that uses that calculation tool. They also provide some predictability for people going through divorce, to know what to expect in their result. While these child support calculation tools can be quite helpful in the standard case, they rarely achieve a fair or appropriate result in cases involving children with disability or special needs.

There are many costs of raising a disabled child that exceed the costs of raising a typical child, and that are not covered by health insurance. Health insurance is highly unstable, as existing coverage can disappear with a job change, and insurance companies may cancel coverage or amend their policies to exclude certain treatments. Healthcare legislation is unreliable at the current time, with recent passage of initial legislation certain to be followed by numerous amendments for many years to come.

Federal and state funding programs are in a constant state of flux, with no end in sight. Funding programs can terminate with a scheduled end date or by the exhaustion of funds.

There are frequently waiting lists of months and even years for children to get the therapy and treatment they need. If your child loses her treatment because the funding (health insurance or government funding) is terminated, she might have to wait months or years to resume her treatment even after a new source of funding is located.

There are direct costs and indirect costs of raising a child with a disability or special need. Many health insurance companies specifically exclude coverage for any type of treatment for certain diagnoses. The direct costs are grossly under-funded by health insurance and government programs. The indirect costs are paid almost completely out-of-pocket by the families.

Direct medical costs can include the expenses for doctors, hospitals, out-patient treatment, therapists, medications, supplements, specialized equipment, home environment medications, co-pays, deductibles, and all other medical costs. For these direct costs to be properly addressed in the divorce, make sure you maintain receipts and billing statements and all other documentation available. Some of these costs are one-time costs, such as certain home modifications. Others are on an ongoing basis, such as a specialized nutritional regimen for a child with a metabolic or digestive disorder. Still other costs occur on a periodic basis. These can include orthopedic devices which must be replaced as the child grows, leg braces, wheelchairs, lift equipment, and transportation devices. As a child progresses through therapy, he will need different equipment for the next stage of therapy. As a terminally ill child's condition worsens, his equipment, treatment, and palliative care needs will be modified.

Indirect costs associated with raising a child with a disability or special need can be massive. These are seldom covered by health insurance or government programs. On average, indirect costs will equal the direct medical costs. It is essential to itemize as many of these costs as you can and provide the data with backup to your lawyer. Keep receipts, invoices, purchase orders, brochures, and all other information you can obtain. It can be very helpful to keep track of these items using a line item approach. The direct and indirect costs will vary in each case, however, the following line item list should provide you some guidance and get you started in creating a list appropriate for your case. This list is not exhaustive, as there can be many other costs in any given case.

Additional costs of raising a child with special needs

- Increased health insurance premiums.
- Co-pays and deductibles, which are often at a higher rate due to more specialists and some out-of-network providers.
- Medications.
- Treatments.
- Therapies.
- Equipment.
- Supplements.
- Dietary costs and specific nutritional regimens.

- Sensory therapy items, special clothing due to sensory issues, and other sensory items.

- Respite care.

- Professionals.

- Modifications to the home environment.

- Modifications to transportation, handicap van, etc.

- Seminars and conferences.

- Travel to out-of-local-area for medical care and treatment.

- Lodging and meals at nonlocal hospitals and other sources of medical care and treatment.

- Meals when your child is hospitalized locally.

- Childcare for your other children when you need to be with your disabled or special needs child within or outside of the home, doing therapy, taking the child for treatments, staying with the child at the hospital, etc.

- Extra laundry, if the child has vomiting or diarrhea, is incontinent, or is bleeding on clothing, sheets, blankets, and towels.

- Other costs caused by the constantly changing needs of the child.

It is unlikely that your lawyer has lived through the experience of raising a child with your child's disability. As such, no matter how well intentioned he is, he will be completely unaware of many of the costs associated with raising your child. Educate your lawyer on these costs, and provide as much detail and proof as you can, so your lawyer can advocate for you. He cannot argue to the judge that you need a higher child support amount if he does not know why you and your child need the higher amount.

CURRENT EXPENSES

As you create your own line item list and collect your receipts and other proof of costs, make sure your lawyer understands that these costs are in a constant state of change. To the extent possible, there should be provision for informal modification of child support amounts to track the actual costs when they change.

THERAPY, EQUIPMENT, AND MEDICATIONS

There are many types of therapy. A partial list includes physical therapy, occupational therapy, language therapy, communication therapy, sensory integration therapy, music therapy, art therapy, therapeutic horsemanship, behavior therapy, group or individual therapy, and socialization therapy. There are many others.

Equipment needs must be addressed in a unique manner, because they can have many unpredictable changes. The equipment can be outgrown physically as a child grows. Some equipment may be workable for the child for a year or even two. The child may then have one or more growth spurts and outgrow his orthopedic equipment, leg braces, and wheelchair two or three times within one year. A fixed child support amount will not properly address this situation.

Periodically, a new type of therapy may become available in your area, which requires special equipment. As your child progresses, she may move on to a different level or type of therapy and require different equipment. If her condition worsens, she may need an in-home hospital bed instead of a wheelchair, a wheelchair instead of leg braces, or other modifications.

Medication costs can vary with little or no warning. Sometimes medication that has been covered by your insurance will no longer be covered. A change in your child's condition or in his age may require a change in medication. In some situations, diabetes that had been controlled by diet and pills might require insulin injections for proper control. Pharmaceutical companies are constantly developing new drugs and medications. Some medications work one way before your child hits puberty and in a different manner after your child is at puberty. A child can take certain medications for months or even years without any side effects, and then, without warning, have an adverse reaction to that medication and have to be switched to a different medication.

Another medication cost issue is the fact that when the parents set up two households, medication should be maintained in both households if appropriate. Notify your doctors and pharmacists of the situation and request that prescriptions be filled into two bottles or containers.

SUPPLEMENTS, DIETARY COSTS, AND SENSORY ITEMS

Often children with disabilities or special needs have digestive disorders, metabolic disorders, compromised immune systems, difficulty sleeping, and other issues. It is often prudent, with medical advice, to give these children supplements that are different than or superior to the usual grocery store brands many children take. Insurance seldom covers these supplements, and many are quite expensive.

Many children with disabilities or special needs have to be on special diets. If a child with phyloketonuria (PKU) has the wrong type of food, it can cause serious health problems and permanent damage. Children with diabetes, celiac disease and many other disorders must be on very rigid diets. These are medically necessary, and great harm can result if they are not followed strictly. They are also not a lot of fun. Imagine being in elementary school and attending a friend's birthday party. If you cannot eat things that contain wheat, gluten, casein, or sugar you cannot eat the birthday cake. If you cannot eat things that contain sugar or milk or many other ingredients you cannot eat the ice cream. Soda and snacks are usually off-limits as well. While all the other kids are stuffing their faces with cookies, cake, ice cream, soda, candy, and snacks, the child with strict dietary restrictions may be relegated to having a juice box and some carrot sticks or specially prepared items. Another aspect of dietary restrictions is the great concern that the child receives sufficient nutrients through the foods they can consume. Often these other foods are not available at the regular grocery store and must be purchased at specialty stores or online. They are frequently more expensive than foods found in the regular grocery store.

Children with disabilities or special needs often have sensory issues in addition to or as a component of their disability. For children with sensory issues, certain textures, tastes, sounds, flashing lights, moving objects, and other things can cause them to be in great pain, miserable, nauscous, and even to have seizures. Their brains interpret sensory input in a different way than that of a typical child. They may be extremely oversensitive to certain stimuli and extremely undersensitive to other stimuli. Some of the sensory issues can be relieved by certain sensory equipment, special clothing, and shoes and items that you need to take when you're out of the house, to use when you find yourself in a situation that triggers the sensory reaction or problem.

RESPITE CARE

When you are the parent of a child with a disability or special need, the child's needs continue 24 hours a day, seven days a week, 365 days per year. You don't get to "clock out" and go off duty. Often parents of a child with a disability will "tag team" and take turns shouldering the responsibility. It can be extremely draining, emotionally and physically, to have the responsibility of a child with serious medical needs on your shoulders. It has been compared to working as a nurse in the ICU, triple shifts every day, 24 hours a day, seven days a week. Clearly, no one could keep up that grueling schedule. They would collapse. Yet many parents of disabled or special needs children go for months and even years without ever being off duty. The situation becomes even more difficult when the parents of a disabled child separate, as then there is only one adult in the house to provide this 24-hour-a-day care.

All parents need to take care of and supervise their children. The level of care is much higher when your child has cancer, respiratory issues, a heart condition, or other serious medical issues. And if you have other children, how can you take care of all of your children, day in and day out, without ever being off duty or getting a break? If your child is undergoing chemotherapy, for example, you should not drag her all over town to run errands such as grocery shopping, exposing her compromised immune system to cold and flu germs. Neither can you just leave her at home alone to go do the necessary errands.

Respite care means having trained caregivers provide the appropriate level of professional care necessary so you can do other things that are necessary. When you have a child with a serious medical issue, you cannot just hire the teenage babysitter down the street to watch your child if you have to take one of the other children to an activity. You need a trained caregiver who may need to know how to resuscitate a child, how to use the medical equipment, how to properly transfer your child from bed to wheelchair, from wheelchair to toilet, or how to deal with an autism meltdown. A caregiver with this level of training will cost more than the usual teenage neighborhood babysitter. When you're calculating your child costs for your divorce, you should estimate the respite care for ordinary days as well as for sick days. Then you need to get written verification of the costs from the respite care provider.

PROFESSIONALS

The proper care of a child with a disability or special needs may require the involvement of many professionals. These professionals can include specialty physicians, physical therapists, psychotherapists, occupational therapists, behavioral specialists, social skills therapists, medical assessors, support group facilitators, tutors, parent training teachers, and special education lawyers, among many others. These costs should be itemized for your lawyer, with supporting backup provided. The courts will not automatically know which professionals are treating your child or providing support services. They are unlikely even to know which types of professionals are necessary for your child's situation. Special needs and divorce is a new field of law. You will have to educate the lawyers and judges involved in your case. They want to help, but they do not know how to help unless you tell them your family's unique circumstances.

HOME MODIFICATIONS

Modifications to the home environment are frequently necessary for children with disabilities and special needs in order to provide for the child's safety and well-being. Carpet may need to be removed and hard flooring installed for the child's wheelchair or other orthopedic devices. You may have to have light switches lowered, and lower sinks, countertops, and door handles for the wheelchair-bound child to reach. Special showering and bathing fixtures may be necessary for a child with mobility issues. You may have to install lift equipment and therapy equipment. Hallways may have to be widened and ramps built. As the child grows into a larger wheelchair, some doorways and hallways may no longer be large enough, and they may have to be widened to accommodate the wider wheelchair.

A child with balance issues may need semi-permanent cushioning blocks to be installed on the corners of fireplaces and walls in case she falls or crashes into them. You may need to bolt bookcases and heavy furniture to the walls to prevent a child from accidentally pulling this furniture down on herself.

Some children with disabilities have no sense of danger, and will require locks to be put on toilets to prevent drowning, and on the stove doors and on stovetop controls to prevent burns. If your child is a "runner," meaning she leaves the house without warning and wanders off, you may have to put alarms on all your doors to alert the family, especially if the child wanders off in the middle of the night or during a blizzard.

Include in the child support calculations the cost of all necessary home environment modifications to be made in both households, and include costs for these renovations if either parent is contemplating moving during or after the divorce.

FUTURE CHANGES IN THE CHILD'S
CONDITION OR NEEDS

If there are known costs anticipated for the child, such as an upcoming surgery, an out-of-town treatment or consultation or other known future cost, include it in the child support calculations. While it may not be possible to calculate the exact costs for these future items, you should work with your lawyer to try to devise a mechanism by which these costs will be distributed between parents and paid in a timely manner.

Try to build in a mechanism by which the child support can be informally modified in the future when there are changes in the child's condition. Your money is better spent on paying for things your child needs, than on years and years of legal fees, constantly going back to court in battling over things throughout your child's lifetime. Sometimes it is necessary to go back to court to deal with unresolved new issues, but good planning at the time of the divorce can help you avoid some of the trips back to court.

It is absolutely vital that sufficient resources are allocated for the child's care through the divorce courts. Care of a disabled child is stressful and daunting enough, even when there are sufficient resources. The care of a disabled child is more expensive than the cost of raising a typical child. Meyers, Lukemeyer, and Smeeding (1996) found that nearly two-thirds of families with special needs children have incomes at or below the poverty line. Meyers *et al.* also found evidence that families with special needs children have more hunger, more evictions, more utility shutoffs, and more homelessness.

In most cases, following the divorce one of the parents will become the primary caregiver for the disabled child. That primary caregiver parent will have less opportunity to earn income to pay for his or her own living expenses as well as for those of the disabled child and any other children in the household. The increased burden of daily care of a special needs child as well as the unpredictable nature of having to deal with unexpected medical, emotional and other crises in the child's life present barriers to employment and to advances in career of the parent (Meyers *et al.* 1996). Meyers *et al.* found that primary caregiver parents spend a median of four hours and 42 minutes per day, seven days a week, 365 days a year in caring for severely disabled children, with some primary caregivers spending up to 20 hours per day caring for their disabled children. The courts must do a better job of providing sufficient support for these children.

Itemize costs on an ongoing monthly basis as well as on a periodic and future basis. Start with the list below, and add to it everything else that is relevant in your case. This list is merely a starting point. Every case will be different. Then make three copies of your list. Title one list "ongoing monthly costs." Label the second list "periodic costs," and the third list "future costs." Keep these lists handy and add to them as appropriate.

Special needs costs

- Doctors.
- Therapy.
- Medical treatment.
- Other medical expenses.
- Supplies.
- Equipment.
- Transportation.
- Training.
- Conferences.
- Caregiver.
- Professionals.
- Companion.
- Prescription medication.
- Nonprescription medication.
- Supplements.
- Dietary regimen.
- Daily and personal care items.
- Household environmental modifications.
- Respite care.
- Activities.
- Sensory items.
- Meals and lodging when traveling to treatment.
- Other special needs items.

Items that have a predictable monthly amount can be added into monthly child support. This can be accomplished by itemizing and adding them as child-rearing costs on the child support calculation chart or other calculation means used by the court. Many child support calculation charts provide a line for extraordinary medical expenses or other extraordinary costs of that child. Frequently, however, people do not know what to enter on this line. This is where your lists will be extremely helpful. Again, the lists given in this chapter are mere guidelines. There is a multitude of possible costs in any given case. Do not forget to add the indirect costs into your lists.

Items that do not have a predictable monthly amount need to be handled by some means. Work with your lawyer to try to achieve the best means in your jurisdiction to handle the payment of these costs. Also work with your lawyer to try to find a way to make changes informally as your child's needs change.

There may be additional costs caused by the divorce itself. Divorce is stressful for everyone concerned, even those without a disability. Sometimes, when their family is going through divorce, a special needs child may regress and lose previously achieved skills. They may need to have medication increased temporarily. The child may need more therapy or to go back to a previous stage of therapy, or need to undergo counseling. All of these things have associated costs, which need to be to dealt with in the divorce.

You need to be fully prepared on all the issues relevant to the amount of child support your child needs. Collect your information and proof of costs. Work closely with your lawyer, and make sure you include every direct and indirect cost. The information in this chapter is only the starting point. Every case will have different costs. Add to this all the other costs relevant to your case. With this information, you can properly advocate for the child support your child deserves to take care of his or her disability or special need.

Chapter 7

Alimony (maintenance or spousal support)

During the marriage, often one parent will quit their job or go from full-time to part-time employment in order to care properly for the needs of the disabled child. The family may be able to make it financially during the marriage because of the income earned by the other parent. When divorce is imminent, however, the primary caregiver parent will not be able to survive financially being unemployed or underemployed. During and after the divorce, this parent will need financial assistance from the other parent in order to survive. This financial assistance is known as maintenance, also as alimony or spousal support.

PRIMARY CAREGIVER'S JOB FUTURE

Often the job loss or going from full-time to part-time employment is not voluntary on the part of the primary caregiver parent. There are huge barriers to employment for parents caring for a child with a serious medical issue. Newacheck *et al.* (1998) found that children with special needs have on the average three times as many sick days as typical children. The parent who takes time off work to take care of the sick child on those days will soon find herself without a job. It is difficult if not impossible for the primary caregiver to maintain steady full-time employment when caring for a child with serious disabilities or special needs.

The primary caregiver parent is unable to devote the time and attention to her career that she otherwise would, if she were not caring for a child with a serious disability. In order to manage the care of a child with a serious disability properly, the primary caregiver parent has to manage doctor and therapy appointments, often do therapy with the child, do research to find additional resources and treatment options, deal with insurance companies, battle school systems, find funding, obtain funding and maintain funding for the child's expenses, as well as doing all of the actual care of the child.

Frequently schools, therapists, and others who work with a disabled child require that only one person is designated as the primary contact person, and that that person must be readily accessible at all times whenever the child is not physically with that parent. Being on call at all times for any crisis with your disabled child, having to leave work frequently and without warning to pick up your child from school or daycare and deal with frequent crises, being physically and emotionally exhausted, being distracted and unable to maintain complete focus on the job at hand all work together to create an employee who, from the perspective of the employer, is unreliable, unpredictable, and frequently absent. This does not bode well for job security, much less career advancement.

Even when a child with a disability or special need is not currently acutely ill, the child may require many more hours per day of caregiving by the parent. As discussed by Msall *et al.* (2003) many of these children have major limitations in the areas of mobility, self-care, communication, and/ or learning. Meeting the needs of and providing the proper care for these children takes much more work and time.

Giving up a career and retirement contributions to care for a disabled or special needs child can have a huge impact on the primary caregiver parent's immediate and lifelong financial picture. Maintenance should consider the impact, short term and long term, that caring for the person with special needs has on the career of the caregiver.

Managing the care of a disabled or special needs child can take as much time as a full-time job. Taking the child to doctor appointments, treatments, and therapy, scheduling appointments for the child, dealing with concerns of therapists and teachers and responding to crisis after crisis, makes it difficult if not impossible to keep a full-time job. The primary caregiver spouse is often exhausted, sleep deprived, and stressed out.

The primary caregiver spouse may be unemployed or underemployed. She may have unstable employment because of caring for the special needs of the child. It can be difficult to obtain appropriate childcare for a special needs child and it may cost more than the primary caregiver spouse earns. A case that might otherwise not be a maintenance case may become one because of the care necessary for the child. The primary caregiver parent often gives up her current career, her future career potential, her current and future financial opportunity, as well as her current and future contributions to retirement accounts. If these special needs cases are not treated differently from standard cases, the primary caregiver parent will be penalized financially and may be destitute in old age.

PRIMARY CAREGIVER'S
FUTURE RETIREMENT SAVINGS

As already stated, when the primary caregiver parent goes from full-time to part-time employment or becomes unemployed, she is usually no longer eligible to participate in employer retirement programs. Looking down the road, you have an exhausted parent who has sacrificed everything for her disabled or special needs child. This parent has little or no income. She has an adult disabled child still living with her and dependent on her every day. She might not be receiving child support from the child's other parent.

It is a grim reality—the vast majority of single parents with a disabled or special needs child in the household are in abject poverty within two years of the divorce. The courts don't know this. Make sure you educate them, so they know the actual result of their decisions. Take care of your family. Both parents have to work together after the divorce to prevent the child and primary caregiver parent from falling into poverty.

HOW THE NONCUSTODIAL PARENT CAN HELP

There are things the non-primary caregiver parent can do to help keep the primary caregiver parent and the disabled child from being in poverty after the divorce. The non-primary caregiver spouse can contribute financially, and all those who have the financial ability to do so should. He can also help in other ways. If he does shift work, he can try to coordinate his shift with yours, so he can provide free childcare while you are at work. This will enable you to work after the divorce, be eligible for health insurance and participation in employer retirement accounts. This childcare is vital. Appropriate childcare for a disabled child is usually more expensive than for a typical child. Many daycare centers will not take a disabled child. An important part of his providing this free childcare is that he handles all the sick days, school absences, school days off, therapy appointments and other things your child needs during his shifts, just as you are providing during your shifts. Realize that this could still leave you with twice as many hours of responsibility for your child as the other parent, as you will be caring for him when neither parent is working.

You need to advocate properly for the maintenance and other help that are necessary in order for you to provide a home for your child after divorce, without being in a pit of poverty. Your child's best interests demand that you have sufficient financial resources to heat and cool your home properly, live in a safe neighborhood, be able to buy nutritious food, and keep your child properly clothed and cared for. You cannot do this if you are in poverty. Use this information to advocate for sufficient financial resources to provide the home your child needs and deserves.

Chapter 8

Property Distribution and Retirement Accounts

In the process of divorce, the court needs to divide the property of the parties. This can include real estate, timeshares, vehicles, household goods, bank accounts, investments, debts, retirement accounts, personal goods, and any other property. It can be helpful to write up a list of everything you and your spouse own, together or separately. When you have listed all the property, then estimate and write up the current and future impact of your disabled or special needs child on the career of the primary caregiver parent and on his or her ability to contribute to their income, bank accounts, investments, and retirement accounts. This should be considered when awarding property to either parent.

HOW DO WE SPLIT UP THE HOUSE AND OTHER PROPERTY?

The primary caregiver parent often has limited opportunity to contribute to his or her income, bank accounts, investments, and retirement accounts. She will have less ability to replace household items and vehicles when they wear out or break down. Taking care of the disabled child will make demands on her time that can prevent her from earning a sufficient income and from advancing in her career. The non-caregiver parent has much greater opportunity to focus on his career, earn a sufficient income, advance his career, and contribute to his bank accounts, investments, and retirement account. He will have greater opportunity to replace household items and vehicles when they wear out or break down. Over time, the items awarded to the primary caregiver parent in the divorce will no longer be usable or functional, and she will have less opportunity to replace or repair them.

The primary caregiver parent will need to maintain a household that is appropriate for a disabled or special needs child. This may involve requirements that would not be necessary for a typical child, such as wider hallways and doorways to accommodate a wheelchair, lower light switches and countertops, and lift equipment to lift the growing child from bed to wheelchair, and from chair to bath or shower. It can also involve ramps to enter the house, electric chairs to get the child up and down stairs, physical therapy equipment, an alarm system for a child who wanders off in the night, and many more environmental household modifications. These modifications can be expensive, and they do not last forever. They break down and often require specialized repair personnel. As the child grows or as his condition changes, more modifications may be necessary. The primary caregiver parent will have less financial ability to pay for these modifications, or for their repair or replacement, than the other parent.

Disabled or special needs children are sick far more often than typical children. When the child is sick, usually the primary caregiver parent is the one who stays home from work to take care of the child. As disabled or special needs children have on average three times as many sick days as typical children, the primary caregiver parent frequently finds herself without a job, due to excessive absences from staying home with her sick child. Even when these children are not acutely sick, their day-to-day care can take several hours a day, even up to 20 hours a day. They often have major limitations in mobility, self-care, communication, and/or learning. They cannot be left unattended. The combination of frequent sick days and the extra hours of care often make it impossible for the primary caregiver parent to be gainfully employed at a sufficient wage to pay her living expenses, much less bear the increased expenses of a disabled or special needs child.

Many people have careers that do not adapt to the demands of caring for a disabled or special needs child. If you are a surgical nurse, you cannot leave in the middle of a surgery because the school has called and your child has had a crisis. If you are a flight attendant, you cannot do your job of being on flights all over the country if you have to be available to pick up your child at a moment's notice. Very few jobs can accommodate a worker who frequently has to leave work, and at a moment's notice.

Specialized childcare that is appropriate for a disabled or special needs child usually needs to be one-on-one, and can cost more than the primary caregiver parent earns. You cannot hire the teenaged kid down the street to take care of a disabled or special needs child. You need trained experienced professionals who are able to handle whatever crisis may arise. The caregiver may need to resuscitate your child, deal with seizures, handle your child's equipment, transfer your child from bed to wheelchair, and do many other things that require training and experience.

The primary caregiver parent is usually physically and emotionally exhausted. Having a critically ill child takes its toll. Despair, sadness, and depression are common when contemplating your child's condition.

If you have other children, meeting their needs on top of the needs of your disabled or special needs child can further tax your time and energy. You will need to arrange appropriate childcare for your disabled child while you do the cooking, cleaning, laundry, grocery shopping, errands, and all the other things necessary to maintain a home.

Often you also do therapy with your child at home. And you are managing your child's care, which involves taking your child to his appointments for doctors, treatments, therapy, assessments, fittings, blood tests, surgeries, and rehabilitation. You are also handling the scheduling of all of these appointments, battling the insurance company when they refuse to pay medical bills, dealing with the school district, and searching for new treatment options and medications for your child. Since your child has many school absences, you are also tutoring him at home, and if he has a learning disability, cognitive impairment, or communication disorder, this can take several hours every day. All of this is on top of taking care of your disabled or special needs child's bathing, dressing, grooming, self-care, mobility, and other issues.

Clearly, the primary caregiver spouse will quickly dissipate her assets without help from the other parent. This is especially true if the property distribution at the time of the divorce is the standard 50/50 arrangement, where husband and wife split up the assets relatively equally.

The primary caregiver parent has much greater needs than the other parent, and it is because of the disabled child of the marriage. These costs should be viewed as a marital debt or expense, and should be shared by both parents for as long as they continue.

The primary caregiver spouse usually needs a greater portion of the assets of the marriage, to offset her decreased income and career potential, her decreased ability to contribute to her retirement account, and her shouldering more than 50 percent of the care of the disabled or special needs child. Taking these factors into consideration, both fairness and the best interests of the disabled or special needs child may require that the primary caregiver parent gets more than 50 percent of the marital assets. She may need to receive a larger proportion of the bank accounts or investment accounts to have a fund from which to meet these needs.

Sometimes it is appropriate to remove the dollar value of the house from the total property calculations, awarding it to the primary caregiver parent because of the special needs of the child. These things must be determined on a case-by-case basis.

The primary caregiver parent is less likely to remarry than the other parent. She has less opportunity to pursue a social life after the divorce, and many potential new spouses do not want the responsibility and restrictions of a household with a disabled child. As such, the primary caregiver parent has less likelihood of another source of income or financial stability.

WHAT SHOULD WE DO ABOUT THE DEBTS?

Usually the debts become the responsibility of the party who receives the asset for which there is debt. For example, if a person receives a car, he usually will have the responsibility to pay the loan on that car. If, however, the primary caregiver parent receives an asset for which there is a large amount of debt, such as the house, she may need contribution from the other parent in order to pay the mortgage on the house. This can be justified when there is a large difference in the incomes of the husband and wife.

The non-caregiver parent may be in a much better position than the primary caregiver parent to pay more of the debts. This can apply to any of the debts, including mortgage, car loans, credit card debts, and other debts. If the debt apportionment causes the primary caregiver parent to be financially precarious or destitute, that is not in the best interests of the disabled or special needs child.

If the ability of the primary caregiver parent to pay debts is decreased by the time and work she spends taking care of the disabled or special needs child, the debt apportionment should be modified to reflect this. Debts should, in general, be apportioned based upon ability to pay.

HOW DO WE HANDLE
THE RETIREMENT ACCOUNTS?

Depending on the laws of your state, the portion of retirement accounts accumulated during the marriage is generally considered marital property. As such, they are often divided 50/50, or equally, between the husband and wife when they divorce. This general approach needs to be re-examined when your case involves a disabled or special needs child.

If the primary caregiver parent devotes sufficient time to the care of the disabled child such that she is unable to maintain full-time employment, she will probably not be eligible to participate in her employer's retirement program. She will suffer over the long term, as compared to the other parent, who is able to maintain full-time employment, contribute to his retirement programs and continue to build his retirement account after the divorce. This may well result in her being financially destitute in her old age, and taking care of the disabled child, who is then an adult but still disabled and in need of daily care and supervision.

She may be doing this without any financial contribution from the other parent. In some states, child support ends at age 18, even with a disabled child. The primary caregiver parent and disabled adult child then have to try to survive on social security and other subsistence programs. The other parent may, at that time, be enjoying a comfortable retirement and financial security, due to having been able to work full time after the divorce and continue to contribute to his retirement account.

Clearly this situation is not fair. Even more important, it is not in the best interests of the disabled or special needs child. Living in poverty is not in any child's best interests, especially when the divorce courts can help prevent it. It is particularly wrong when dealing with a disabled or special needs child.

There are ways to prevent this bleak future. The courts should consider the role of the primary caregiver parent as a job equal to that of the other parent. They should develop a formula for assigning future retirement contributions of the other parent to the retirement account of the primary caregiver parent. Sometimes this can be accomplished by awarding more than 50 percent of the current retirement accounts to the primary caregiver parent, knowing that she will not be able to contribute to it in the future.

Caring for the special needs of the child is a job, it is a joint venture which involves both parents. They did make or adopt this child together. It is logical that future contributions to retirement accounts should be distributed to the joint venturers. This is an economic partnership, a shared enterprise. The courts and lawyers will need to devise means to do this within each case, depending on the type of retirement accounts and rules governing those accounts—but it can be done, and it should be done.

Divorces involving disabled or special needs children may need to result in an award of maintenance, in an unequal distribution of property and debts, and in creative distribution of current and future retirement accounts. The primary caregiver parent will have less financial opportunity after the divorce, and will have greater time and financial burdens. The courts need to deviate from the usual approach to maintenance, property, debt, and retirement account distribution in order to meet the needs of the primary caregiver parent and disabled or special needs child properly.

Chapter 9

How You Can Help Your Lawyer Get the Best Result

It is imperative that you work well with your lawyer if you are going to achieve the best results you can in your divorce and properly advocate for your disabled or special needs child. If you used the information in Chapter 2 on how to hire a good divorce lawyer for your case, you will be miles ahead of someone who chooses their lawyer out of the phone book. Let's assume you hired the best lawyer you could get in your area, for this type of case. Still, your lawyer might not have ever handled a divorce case involving a disabled or special needs child before, so you will need to diplomatically give your lawyer the information she needs to get the best possible results.

Reasonable expectations

This is a new field of law. Traditionally, the interests of disabled or special needs children have not received much attention from the divorce courts. Our court system is based on tradition, and you are asking the courts to go against their tradition. Big changes in our legal system take many years. As such, you need to realize that you will probably not get everything you need, especially at the divorce. It is sometimes possible to get additional help from the courts later on, after the divorce, but even then, do not expect to get everything you need.

In divorce cases that do not involve disabled or special needs children, people often do not get everything they need. There is just not enough money to go around. In your case, there are probably greater needs than in a typical divorce case. In addition, since one parent often has reduced income due to caring for the child, there is less income to go around in these cases.

This does not mean you should give up. You must educate your lawyer and judge. The change begins with you. You are fighting for your family and for all the families who come behind you.

You also have to advocate for your child's special needs because by doing so, you should get better results than if you did not try at all. Although you may not get everything you need, by being informed and prepared on your child's issues you should get better results than you otherwise would.

BE COOPERATIVE, NOT CONFRONTATIONAL

You may be in the habit of having to battle to advocate for your child. You battle insurance companies when they refuse to pay legitimate medical claims. You battle school districts to get an appropriate education for your child. You may even have to battle people in your own family who say stupid things about your child's disability. And you are going through divorce, which can be one ugly battle.

Do not fall into the trap of constantly battling with your spouse or your lawyer during the divorce. Constant confrontation will harm your child. It will also cause you to lose credibility with the court. It can cause you to get a bad result in your case, which will harm you and your child.

Do not be a doormat, but do not be stuck in battle mode. Pick your battles wisely. Navigating a family with a disabled or special needs child through divorce court takes a great deal more ability on the part of your lawyer than a typical case.

If you are causing problems in the case, you are taking your lawyer's time and attention away from working on your case. If you drown your lawyer with emails and telephone calls, your legal fees bills will skyrocket. You will run out of money and not be able to pay the lawyer for the most important part of your case—advocating for your child's needs.

COLLECT MEDICAL AND EDUCATIONAL DOCUMENTS

Throughout this book, we have discussed many documents that can be important in divorce cases involving disabled or special needs children. These can be medical records, pharmacy records, school records, treatment records, hospital records, therapy records and many other types of records, depending on your case. Work with your lawyer to get these documents.

It can be expensive to get copies of records. Many places charge by the page for copying records. Before you start, talk with your lawyer to find out how you should get these records, so they will be admissible in court. Otherwise, you may have to pay twice for the records, in order to have admissible records.

You and your spouse may have to sign several records releases. Sign these promptly, as it can take many weeks to get records. It does no good to have paid for records that arrive a week after your court date.

Help educate your lawyer on your child's special needs

Go back to the day you found out your child had a disability or special need. Now think of how much you have learned since then. Most likely, your lawyer and the judge will be back at day one on the learning curve of your child's particular disability or special need.

Make it easy on your lawyer and on yourself. Get a couple of good, concise articles or book excerpts that explain your child's condition. Do not drown your lawyer in materials—he will not read them. You can't afford to pay him to read entire books on your child's condition. He does not need to know as much on the subject as your child's doctors or therapists. He needs to be able to argue your case to the judge and to negotiate with the other side. He needs to be able to draft appropriate pleadings and other documents that properly raise your child's issues.

In addition to getting a couple of good concise articles or book excerpts, type a narrative for your lawyer on your child's medical history, the diagnosis of disability and what has happened since the diagnosis. Write a summary of "a day in the life" of your child and yourself. Again, do not drown your lawyer in exhaustive material. If you go overboard, you will risk your lawyer not having the time to do more than just skim what you give him.

Get evaluations and reports

If your child still needs evaluations on certain aspects of her disability or special need, talk with your lawyer and get the appropriate evaluations done. Of course talk with your spouse about this before scheduling evaluations. You would not appreciate your spouse taking your child for evaluations behind your back, so don't do it to him or her.

Do not use the child as a pawn. Do not subject the child to unnecessary invasive testing just to try to get more money. Always put your child's interests first.

That being said, do not put off necessary evaluations or testing until after the divorce. Your child's disability or special need is vitally important. It needs to be addressed by the divorce court. If you do not deal with this issue during the divorce, you will probably have to come back to court after the evaluations and testing are done, in order to get what your child needs. In some states, you are not allowed to come back to court for a certain amount of time after the divorce. This can be two or three years. Some judges will say that if you knew about the disability at the time of the divorce, you should have brought it up then, and they will not allow you to raise the issue later.

Talk with your lawyer about the reports that already exist. You might not need to have further evaluations or testing done. You might just need to get the records that are already out there. Make sure proper procedure is used to get these reports and records, so they will be admissible at court.

GUARDIAN-AD-LITEM

It can be very helpful to have a Guardian-ad-Litem (GAL) appointed to handle your child's disability or special needs. This person is usually a lawyer. She will evaluated the situation and make a recommendation to the judge as to what should be done for your child. She will represent your child—not you and not your spouse. Her job is to act in your child's best interests.

Standard court forms do not always work well for the appointment of a GAL to deal with the disability or special needs issues of a child. A GAL is usually appointed because of credible claims of child abuse or neglect, or in cases involving highly contentious custody battles.

I have included sample documents your lawyer can modify to use in your case. These samples are for guidance only and are merely a starting point. They will need to be modified to comply with the laws and procedure of your state and local court. Your lawyer needs to draft the actual motion and order.

SAMPLE MOTION FOR APPOINTMENT OF GUARDIAN-AD-LITEM

IN THE FAMILY COURT OF SOMEWHERE COUNTY
STATE OF YOURSTATE

In Re the Marriage of:

PAUL JONES, Petitioner,	))) Case Number _____
v.	)) Division _____
RITA JONES, Respondent.	))

MOTION FOR APPOINTMENT OF GUARDIAN-AD-LITEM

Comes now the Petitioner, Paul Jones, by and through his attorney, _____, and respectfully requests the Court appoint a Guardian-ad-Litem for the minor child(ren): _____ for the following reasons:

_____ credible allegations of child neglect

_____ credible allegations of child abuse

_____ special needs of the child(ren), specifically: _____

      I AM/AM NOT AWARE OF ANY SPECIAL NEEDS OF THE CHILD(REN), SPECIFICALLY: _____

_____ other

This Motion for Appointment of Guardian-ad-Litem is supported by a sworn affidavit, a true and correct copy of which is attached hereto and marked as Exhibit 1.

Respectfully submitted,

_____

Attorney for Respondent

CERTIFICATE OF SERVICE

I hereby certify that a true and correct copy of the foregoing was deposited in the U.S. Mail, postage prepaid to:

Opposing Counsel's Name, Street Address, City, State ZIP

this _____ day of _____, 20___.

_____

Attorney for Respondent

SAMPLE ORDER APPOINTING GUARDIAN-AD-LITEM

IN THE FAMILY COURT OF SOMEWHERE COUNTY
STATE OF YOURSTATE

In Re the Marriage of:

PAUL JONES,	)
Petitioner,	)
	) Case Number _____
v.	)
	) Division _____
RITA JONES,	)
Respondent.	)

ORDER APPOINTING GUARDIAN-AD-LITEM

IT IS HEREBY ORDERED that _____ shall be appointed as Guardian-ad-Litem for the minor child(ren): _____ for the following reasons:

_____ credible allegations of child neglect
_____ credible allegations of child abuse
_____ special needs of the child(ren), specifically: _____

    THE PARTIES STATE THAT THEY ARE/ARE NOT AWARE OF ANY SPECIAL NEEDS OF THE CHILD(REN), SPECIFICALLY:

_____

_____ other

SO ORDERED:

_____

The Honorable _____

EXPERT WITNESSES

You might need to hire expert witnesses for your case. Expert witnesses can be appropriate to provide evidence to the court on matters that are not common knowledge. They can be appropriate when someone with specialized training, knowledge, and/or experience is necessary to present information to the court.

There are several issues in which an expert witness can be helpful in a divorce case involving a disabled or special needs child. Your child's disability, the level of care necessary for your child, the costs of your child's disability, and your child's likely future are all subjects for which an expert might be needed. The economic impact on you and the family can also be explained to the court by an expert witness.

Discuss the issue of expert witnesses with your lawyer. Realize that expert witnesses can be very expensive. Some experts may have to travel to your town to testify for you. In that situation, you may have to pay travel costs, records review costs, preparation costs, and appearance fee. This needs to be carefully planned with your lawyer.

TRANSLATE THE JARGON FOR YOUR LAWYER

Every area of medicine has its own jargon—words and phrases that are not understood by the general population. You probably did not know these words before your child was diagnosed. Make a list of helpful words and definitions for your lawyer to use when she reads medical records, Individualized Education Plans, therapy notes, and other material in your case. Make sure she will be able to understand the terminology that will be used at court hearings and in depositions. You don't want her to be in court and have to guess at what someone means.

Working with your lawyer as a professional team will result in the best possible results for your case. When that happens, you are advocating for your child at the highest level. You need to have reasonable expectations and to be cooperative, not confrontational. You need to choose your battles carefully. Gather the medical and educational documents your lawyer will need. Educate your lawyer on your child's disability. Don't put off getting necessary evaluations done until after the divorce. Consider having a GAL appointed to help advocate for your child. Talk with your lawyer about hiring expert witnesses to provide testimony and/or reports for the court. And translate the jargon so your lawyer can understand all this stuff! Following these steps will help your divorce be less stressful, and can result in getting a better result for your child's disability or special need.

Chapter 10

Tying up Loose Ends

You need to make sure the issue of special needs is addressed in the pleadings and documents at all points during the divorce. (Making sure that the issues are included in every phase of the litigation process will help prevent special needs issues from slipping through the cracks. Frequently a special needs issue is raised early in the case, but is not considered later, when the case is ending.) Samples have been provided throughout the text of several of these documents. At the end of your case another document may be necessary—an Affidavit for Judgment. This document should contain a statement of whether there are any known special needs. A sample has been provided as a starting point for your lawyer. Your lawyer will need to modify this sample to comply with your state and local laws and rules. It will also need to be modified to contain the facts of your particular case.

SAMPLE SPECIAL NEEDS AFFIDAVIT FOR JUDGMENT

IN THE FAMILY COURT OF SOMEWHERE COUNTY
STATE OF YOURSTATE

In Re the Marriage of:

PAUL JONES, Petitioner,	))) Case Number _____
v.	)) Division _____
RITA JONES, Respondent.	))

AFFIDAVIT OF PETITIONER REQUESTING
DISSOLUTION OF MARRIAGE—SPECIAL NEEDS CASE

Petitioner, upon his oath submits the following affidavit pursuant to local rules, to form a basis for the court's entering a judgment in this case upon affidavit and without the necessity of a formal hearing.

1. The Petition in this case was filed on _____, 20____.

2. Respondent was served with summons in this case on _____ (date) and filed a responsive pleading on _____ (date).

3. Respondent is and has been a resident of the State of YourState for more than _____ days/months immediately preceding the filing of the Petition in this case.

4. Both parties are over eighteen years of age.

5. At the time of filing, Petitioner resided at _____ (street address, city, county, state, zip code).

6. At the time of filing, Respondent resided at _____ (street address, city, county, state, zip code).

7. Petitioner's social security number is xxx-xx-xxxx. (if applicable)

8. Respondent's social security number is xxx-xx-xxxx. (if applicable)

9. Petitioner is represented by _____ (attorney name and address).

10. Respondent is represented by _____ (attorney name and address).

11. Petitioner is employed as a _____ (occupation) at _____ (employer name) located at _____ (employer address).

12. Respondent is employed as a _____ (occupation) at _____ (employer name) located at _____ (employer address).

13. Petitioner and Respondent were married on _____(date) at _____ (city, county, state). The marriage was recorded in the County of _____, State of _____.

14. Petitioner and Respondent separated on or about _____, 20___.

15. Petitioner believes that there is no reasonable likelihood that the marriage of Petitioner and Respondent can be preserved and, therefore, believes that the marriage is irretrievably broken.

16. Petitioner is not on active duty with the Armed Forces of the United States of America or its allies.

17. Respondent is not on active duty with the Armed Forces of the United States of America or its allies.

18. Petitioner is not pregnant.

19. The parties have entered into a written agreement for the division of their property which includes all assets and debts and identifies and divides the marital property and debts and sets apart to each party his or her non-marital property. This agreement is attached to this affidavit and incorporated herein by reference.

20. Petitioner and Respondent have agreed that spousal maintenance is payable by Respondent to Petitioner in the amount of $ _____ per month as and for Petitioner's maintenance until further order of the Court. Said maintenance obligation shall be modifiable. The parties ask that the court incorporate this agreed upon spousal maintenance in the Judgment of Dissolution.

21. Petitioner is unaware of any genuine issue as to any material fact in this proceeding.

22. There is one minor, unemancipated child of the marriage, namely: _____ DOB: _____

23. SAID CHILD HAS SPECIAL NEEDS, NAMELY AUTISM, WHICH SPECIAL NEEDS HAVE BEEN COMPLETELY ADDRESSED IN THE SETTLEMENT AGREEMENT, PARENTING PLAN AND PROPOSED JUDGMENT. THESE DOCUMENTS HAVE BEEN APPROVED BY THE SPECIAL NEEDS COORDINATOR ASSIGNED TO THIS CASE.

24. The child has lived with Petitioner and Respondent at _____ (street address, city, county, state) for six months immediately preceding the filing of this Petition.

25. That Petitioner has not participated in any capacity in any other litigation concerning the custody of the child in this or any other state. Petitioner has no information of any custody proceeding concerning the child pending in a court of this or any other state; and knows of no person not a party to these proceedings who has physical custody of the child or claims to have custody or visitation rights with respect to the child.

26. Petitioner and Respondent have entered into a custody agreement, which is attached and incorporated herein by reference. Petitioner and Respondent request that the Court incorporate the terms of the custody agreement in the Judgment of Dissolution.

27. Attached hereto is a special needs child support worksheet which has been agreed to by both parties. Petitioner attests to the truth of the contents of the child support worksheet.

28. The parties agree that the amount of support calculated by the special needs child support worksheet is not rebutted as being unjust or inappropriate and agree that Respondent shall pay $____ per month child support.

29. Costs paid by Petitioner.

30. Petitioner shall pay maintenance to Respondent in the amount of $_____ per month. This maintenance is modifiable.

_____

Petitioner

STATE OF _____   )

)

COUNTY OF _____   )

_____ personally appeared before me on _____, who upon being duly sworn stated that the foregoing statements were true and accurate to their best knowledge and belief.

_____

Notary Public

CERTIFICATE OF MAILING

I hereby certify that a copy of the foregoing was mailed on the ___ day of _____, 20__ by U.S. Mail, postage prepaid to: _____
(opposing counsel's name, street address, city, state and zip code)

The Judgment should also address the issue of special needs, with a statement of whether there are any known special needs, and that those needs have been fully met in the final documents. A sample Judgment has been provided in Chapter 4, with the sample Parenting Plan and Settlement Agreement.

SHARE INFORMATION

In order to save yourselves money on legal fees, you should be as cooperative as possible in tying up the loose ends at the end of your divorce case. Your money will be better spent on your child and your future than on unnecessary legal fees. Work together, share names of financial institutions, addresses, contact information, and other practical information to facilitate getting things done at the end. If you are not cooperative with your spouse, do not expect her to be cooperative with you.

SIGN RELEASES AND AUTHORIZATIONS

It will probably be necessary for both of you to sign releases and authorizations when wrapping things up at the end of the divorce. Briefly check with your lawyer before you sign things, then be prompt and cooperative. You do not want to spend the rest of your life stuck in this phase. Cooperate and move on with your life. You may need to make a phone call or two to give people permission to speak with your spouse or to give copies to him or her.

PAPERS TO SIGN

After the case is settled or resolved by trial, there are often many documents to be signed. You need to make sure these documents are completed correctly and filed in the proper location. People have been known to get signed car titles and other documents after the divorce, but not properly file them. Then years later, when they try to sell the car or boat or house, they cannot find the signed documents. File the signed documents right away and avoid this problem. Cooperate with your spouse if you want him or her to cooperate with you. Do not waste legal fees fighting over silly petty things.

CAR TITLES, MORTGAGES, AND QUITCLAIM DEEDS

You lawyer can advise you on the proper procedure in your state for handling car titles, mortgages, and deeds. In some states you can simply sign the back of the title for whatever vehicles your spouse receives in the divorce. In other states, gift affidavits or other documents are required.

If real property, such as the house, is awarded to you or your spouse, documents will probably have to be signed. When one person receives the house, the other person usually signs a document called a quitclaim deed, which transfers all the interest of that person to the other person. When one person is just living in the house until it is sold, a quitclaim deed might not be necessary.

There are two important documents relating to the house—the mortgage and the deed. The mortgage is the contract between the lender and you and your spouse. The deed is the document that shows ownership. If your spouse receives the house and is required to pay the mortgage, they may need to refinance to get your name off the debt. If you sign a quitclaim deed but your spouse does not get your name off the mortgage, you are still liable on the debt—but you have no ownership of the house. Discuss this with your lawyer to make sure you are protected.

BANK AND FINANCIAL ACCOUNTS

After the divorce you will probably close some accounts and take names off other accounts, depending on what was agreed to or ordered by the judge. Consider closing all your old accounts and opening new accounts in a financial institution in which neither you nor your spouse have ever had accounts. People working at financial institutions have been talked into giving former spouses copies of statements on accounts that no longer belong to them. They have even been able to clean out accounts after the divorce. The best way to avoid this is to open new accounts in new banks and financial institutions. This applies to brokerage accounts, bank accounts, and all other financial accounts.

EMPLOYERS AND INSURANCE

Your employer will need to know about the divorce for several reasons. Your tax status will have changed, so you will need to fill out new tax forms for your employer. Your employer might provide life insurance as part of your benefits package. If so, make sure you change the beneficiary if your former spouse is listed as your beneficiary. Your employer will need to know about the divorce for health insurance reasons, which may affect not only you, but also your former spouse and the children. Your employer will also need to know what to do about your pension and retirement accounts.

Think about other types of insurance you may have as well—term life, whole life, variable life and other types of insurance. Evaluate who the beneficiaries are, and whether you want to make a change on this. Do not violate any terms agreed to or ordered in the divorce. If the Settlement Agreement or Judgment requires you to carry life insurance with the children as beneficiaries, for example, you have to do so.

RETIREMENT ACCOUNTS

Distributing retirement accounts after the divorce can be a lengthy and expensive process. Some types can be distributed by a letter of instruction. Other types have to be distributed by a Qualified Domestic Relations Order (QDRO). You will need to work with your lawyer to make sure this aspect is done properly. Be aware that distributing retirement accounts can take longer than the divorce did. Be patient and cooperate. It is the best way to get through this phase.

SCHOOLS, DAYCARE, THERAPISTS, AND DOCTORS

You need to let your child's school, childcare provider, doctors, therapists, and other healthcare providers know about the custody provisions of your decree. Tell people this information face-to-face, and give them written information if appropriate. Keep in mind that there will be highly personal and private information contained in your court documents, and you don't want to be the subject of gossip. Provide what people need in order to do their jobs properly. Don't give people copies of documents for the purpose of embarrassing your former spouse. You may need to update contact information for yourself and your spouse with the school, childcare provider, doctors, therapists, and other healthcare providers. If you handled the contacts with the school and others before the divorce, sign the necessary forms so your former spouse can get the information they are allowed to get under the decree.

The childcare provider will need to know who will be responsible for payment. The healthcare providers will need to know who is supposed to pay the co-pay, deductible, and uncovered medical expenses.

Chapter 11

Life after Divorce

It is done. You made it through your divorce. You advocated for your child, and you got the best result possible under the circumstances. There were difficult times along the way, but things went more smoothly than you had initially feared.

You grew and became stronger than you would have ever believed possible. You did your part to help change the divorce courts to be more receptive to the needs of families with disabled or special needs children. Now what?

YOUR NEW REALITY

Your new reality is that you are the newly divorced parent of a child with a disability or special need. You are facing an uncertain future. If you are the primary caregiver parent, your daily life can be daunting. You will need to find ways to delegate. Not all tasks have to be done by you. If you have other children, recruit them to help with the routine chores. Just a few decades ago many children in this country used to do two or three hours of farm chores before going to school. It will not do your children any good for you to work yourself to complete exhaustion and physical breakdown.

There are other practical things you can do to ease some of your daily burden. Using paper plates and cups can greatly reduce the amount of dishes to wash. Buy lots of socks and underwear for everyone in your household. You no longer have backup help, and when one of the children is sick, laundry may have to wait.

Develop a higher tolerance for clutter and imperfection. You are not Martha Stewart. She has a team of assistants, and is not a single parent raising a special needs child. Don't be so hard on yourself.

It is critical that you get good sleep. While you might not get eight hours sleep a night, or even six hours sleep a night, the sleep that you do get has to be restful. Five hours of restful sleep can be better than

157

seven hours of tossing and turning. When you get all the children to sleep, light a candle or two. Brew some herbal calming tea. Practice relaxation techniques, like meditation. Doing tai chi can help your body relax for sleep. Take care of yourself so you can take care of your child.

TWO HOUSEHOLDS AND VISITATION

After the divorce, if not before, there will be two households. The children will forget things at your house that they need when they are with your spouse. They will leave things over there that they need for school tomorrow. They will forget to tell you about the project that is due tomorrow. Plan on these things happening and they will be less stressful when they happen. There will be more transportation and things will be more complicated.

Realize that about half of all marriages end in divorce. There are millions of people who are dealing with visitation issues. Approach it with a good attitude. If you are determined to be angry and resentful, I guarantee you will be miserable. Don't be a doormat, but let many things roll off your shoulders.

There will be changes to the visitation schedule. Be as cooperative as possible when your former spouse requests a change to the schedule. If you refuse to accommodate the changes your spouse wants, do not expect cooperation when you request a change in the schedule. And you will need to ask for changes to the schedule.

There is no rule that people have to hate each other just because they are divorced. You are simply no longer married. That is all. Many people find they get along much better after divorce than they did during the marriage. Make that your goal and your life will be much better.

LESS MONEY, MORE EXPENSES

Do not expect to be able to spend money as you did during the marriage. There is now less money and there are more expenses. You now have two households. Many expenses will thus be twice as expensive as before. Two mortgages or rent payments, two electric bills, two gas bills, two water bills, and so on.

For some money issues there are no easy answers. You can only cut back so much. Coupon clipping, shopping sales, and strict budgeting will help, but you may need to make more drastic changes. You will need to take a hard, cold look at your financial picture and plan accordingly. This is no time to be in denial.

FUTURE RELATIONSHIPS

Problems can arise when either you or your former spouse start a new relationship. If you start a new relationship, your former spouse might get jealous even though you are divorced, and may retaliate by causing visitation problems or paying maintenance or child support late. The new person in your life might not get along well with your children. Your children might not want to give the new person a chance. They may feel confused and feel put in the middle. They may be scared that you will care about the other person and not love them anymore, or that you will move away with the other person.

If your former spouse starts a new relationship, their new person might be jealous of the time and money your former spouse spends on the children. The new person may be especially jealous of the extra time and attention your disabled or special needs child requires. They might try to interfere with visitation and cause confrontations, to establish their position with your former spouse.

You and your former spouse need to work together to disempower new people from interfering and causing problems. You must communicate well and frequently, so the new people cannot turn you against each other. And you both need to set boundaries with new people in your lives.

It may be necessary for new people in your lives to read books and get training in order to care properly for your disabled or special needs child, if they are going to be seriously involved in your or your former spouse's life. The new person can actually be a great asset in this regard, depending on the person and how things are handled. Guard against the new person coming in and taking over. They haven't lived through what you and your spouse have with your disabled or special needs child, so it is easy for them to waltz in and criticize how you are doing things. Although it is highly tempting, do not let this turn into a brawl. Speak to your former spouse separately and stop this behavior early. Again, set boundaries. And do the same thing with people with whom you get involved.

PROTECTING YOUR CHILD

Make sure your child knows the divorce was not her fault. Let her know every day that she is loved and important to you. She probably knows she creates a lot of work and expense for you. Don't ever let your child assume that your life would be better without her. Your child has enough to deal with handling her disability. She does not also need the weight of the world on her shoulders.

Your child needs to love both of his parents. Don't ever bad mouth your former spouse within the child's hearing, and don't allow others to do so either. Keep any difficulties between you and your former spouse—do not air them in front of the child. You might need to keep your mouth shut about certain things your former spouse did in order for your child to be able to love him or her. This is about your child's happiness, not about scoring points against your former spouse. Your child will love you because you take care of him and love him. He does not need to hate his other parent in order to love you.

Chapter 12

What to Do When Things Change in the Future

Life with a disabled or special needs child can be highly unpredictable. If things change significantly and the changes are expected to last for a while, talk with your lawyer about whether the decree needs to be modified for the needs of the child.

WHEN CAN THE COURT HELP ME IN THE FUTURE?

There are many things that can change. Your child's condition can improve or worsen. A special need may arise that did not exist or was not diagnosed at the time of the divorce. Your child might get well. A new treatment, surgery, or medication may be developed that improves your child's outcome. Or your child might have been in remision at the time of the divorce, and then the cancer might come back a year or two down the road.

Your child's financial needs may increase or decrease. Your financial condition or that of your former spouse may change. The parent receiving maintenance might get married, and lose maintenance. The parent receiving maintenance might receive a large inheritance and no longer need maintenance.

WHAT SHOULD I DO THEN?

When there are significant lasting changes, talk with your lawyer to find out whether your case merits a modification. Modification can be done formally or informally. Your lawyer will be able to advise you on your local rules and laws governing modification. Sometimes modifications can be done by agreement of both parents. When they cannot be done by consent, they usually have to go through the courts.

When the modification goes through the courts, it is usually done by filing a Motion to Modify. A sample is included, to give you a starting point. Your lawyer will need to adapt this to the facts of your case and your local laws and rules.

SAMPLE MOTION TO MODIFY

IN THE FAMILY COURT OF SOMEWHERE COUNTY
STATE OF YOURSTATE

In Re the Marriage of:

PAUL JONES, Petitioner,	))) Case Number _____
v.	)) Division _____
RITA JONES, Respondent.	))

MOTION TO MODIFY—SPECIAL NEEDS

Comes now the Petitioner, Paul Jones, by and through his counsel,_____, and for his cause of action, alleges and states:

1. On _____ this Court entered a Decree of Dissolution in this matter.

    There was one child born of the marriage, namely:

    _____ born _____.

THE COURT FOUND THAT SAID MINOR CHILD HAS SPECIAL NEEDS, NAMELY AUTISM, AND FOUND THAT THE SPECIAL NEEDS HAD BEEN COMPLETELY ADDRESSED IN THE SETTLEMENT AGREEMENT, PARENTING PLAN AND PROPOSED JUDGMENT. THESE DOCUMENTS WERE APPROVED BY THE SPECIAL NEEDS COORDINATOR ASSIGNED TO THIS CASE.

2. The Decree of Dissolution further awarded Petitioner and Respondent the joint physical and legal custody of the minor child.

3. The Decree of Dissolution awarded Respondent as support for said child the sum of $_____ per month.

4. The Decree of Dissolution further ordered Petitioner to pay maintenance to Respondent.

5. The Decree of Dissolution has not been modified.

6. Since the date of the original Decree of Dissolution was entered, there have been changed circumstances so substantial and continuing as to make the terms of said Decree of Dissolution unreasonable in regard to the children. As a result of such changed circumstances, a modification of the Decree of Dissolution is necessary to serve the best interests of the parties.

7. The changed circumstances include but are not limited to the following:
   _____.

8. Petitioner requests the court award sole physical and legal custody of the minor child to him due to the change of circumstances listed above.

9. Petitioner requests the visitation schedule originally ordered be modified as follows:
   _____.

10. Petitioner is unable to provide the ordered child support originally ordered due to the change of circumstances listed above.

11. Petitioner is unable to provide maintenance to Respondent.

12. Petitioner is presently employed by _____.

13. Respondent is presently employed by _____.

14. As a result of the above, all of which involve a substantial and continuing change of conditions and circumstances, the Petitioner prays that a new Order be entered by this Court.

WHEREFORE, Petitioner prays that the Court enter an Order modifying the Decree of Dissolution to award visitation as stated above to serve the best interests of the minor child; to decrease the child support paid by Petitioner, retroactive to the date of the service of this Motion, to a sum which is reasonable in light of the above-described changes in conditions and circumstances; awarding custody of the minor child to Petitioner; to decrease the award of maintenance paid by Petitioner; and further Ordering that in all other respects, the Court's Order entered _____, 20___, shall remain in full force and effect; and for such further Orders as to this Court shall seem just and proper.

_____
Attorney for Petitioner

STATE OF _____   )
) SS
COUNTY OF _____   )

Comes now Paul Jones, Petitioner, being first duly sworn according to law, and states that he has read the foregoing Motion to Modify and states that the facts contained therein are true and correct according to his best knowledge, information and belief.

_____

Subscribed and sworn to before me this _____ day of _____, 20___.

_____
Notary Public

My commission expires: _____.

With this information, you and your lawyer can work together to decide if a modification is appropriate. If a modification is appropriate, determine if it will be by consent or contested. A consent modification can often be done informally. If you need to handle the modification formally, your lawyer may have to file papers and seek relief from the court in order to serve the best interests of your disabled or special needs child.

Checklists

These checklists are for your guidance only, and are not intended to be exhaustive. Each case is different. Your case may required additional factors.

  A. Disability or special needs information

  B. Should you have your child's disability or special need evaluated?

  C. Information you will need for your first meeting with your lawyer

  D. Financial information to collect for your lawyer

  E. Special needs issues for Answer and Counter Petition

  F. Discovery summary list

  G. Costs of disability and special needs

A. DISABILITY OR SPECIAL NEEDS INFORMATION

- All disabilities or special needs of all of the children. These can include any physical, mental or emotional disability, learning disability, behavior or mood disorder, or any other issue that might require special consideration in the divorce, for purposes of medication, medical treatment, therapy, custody, visitation, or child support.

- Whether any of the children receive special assistance at school.

- Whether any of the children have an Individualized Education Plan (IEP) or 504 Plan at school.

- Whether any of the children are on medication or receiving medical treatment.

- Whether any of the children are in counseling, physical therapy, behavior therapy, or psychological counseling.

- The official diagnosis of every disability or special need.

- The name of the person who made the diagnosis.

- When the diagnosis was made.

- When the first symptoms appeared.

- What testing or screening was done to evaluate or diagnose the child's condition (include testing that was done that ruled out other conditions).

- The reason the child was seen by the person who made the diagnosis. (What made people think the child needed to be evaluated?)

- Names of all other professionals who confirmed or agree with the diagnosis.

- The child's current condition.
- The child's prognosis (expected outcome).
- Whether the condition is curable, treatable, or terminal.
- Whether the child is expected ever to be able to get a high school diploma, get a college degree, live on her own, hold a regular job, live completely independently, marry, have children.
- The child's life expectancy.
- How the disability affects the child's life now and how it is expected to in the future.
- How the disability affects siblings' lives now and how it is expected to in the future.
- How the disability affects the parents' lives now and how it is expected to in the future.
- Identify who the primary caregiver is.
- How the disability has impacted the careers of the parents.
- How the disability will impact the parents' career advancement and retirement plan contributions.
- The names, addresses, telephone numbers and credentials of all medical professionals and others the child currently sees for this condition.
- All medications the child currently takes, the frequency and dosage, the reason for the medication, and the expected result from the medication.
- All treatments and therapies the child currently receives, including therapies received at home and at school. For each treatment or therapy identify:
  - who does the treatment or therapy
  - who sent the child for the treatment or therapy
  - where the treatment or therapy occurs
  - type of treatment or therapy, frequency and duration of treatment or therapy (e.g. twice a week, 20 minutes each time)
  - how much longer the treatment or therapy is expected to continue (indefinitely, for six months, or some other length)
  - cost of the treatment or therapy
  - how this is paid (private pay, insurance, funding program, grant)
  - uncovered costs of the treatment or therapy
  - incidental costs of the treatment or therapy—transportation, caregiver, supplies, meals, equipment
  - who takes the child to the treatment or therapy.
- The expectations regarding future treatments, therapies, and medications.
- All wait lists the child is on for any treatment, therapy, program, school or funding.
- A detailed itemization of all direct and indirect costs resulting from the child's special needs, including:
  - prescription medications

- ○ non-prescription medications
- ○ supplements
- ○ equipment
- ○ supplies
- ○ caregiver training
- ○ special dietary and nutritional requirements
- ○ special clothing and personal care item requirements
- ○ home modifications
- ○ vehicle modifications
- ○ modifications at school
- ○ non-parental caregiver costs
- ○ transportation
- ○ any other costs applicable in your case.

B. Should you have your child's disability or special need evaluated?

When should you send your child for professional evaluation? Some general warning signs include:

- your child is having ongoing problems at school
- your child is having ongoing run-ins with law enforcement or other authority
- you have difficulty "handling" your child
- your child is frequently sick or misses school
- you or others are concerned that your child is not performing up to your child's abilities—i.e. your child is underachieving
- your child is not developing with his peers—including physical, emotional, academic, and skills development
- you, your lawyer, your child's teacher, or a significant caregiver express concern that "something is not quite right."

C. Information you will need for your first meeting with your lawyer

Information about you that you will need for your lawyer:

- your name and any maiden and former names you have used
- your current address
- how long you have lived at this address
- how long you have lived in your county and state
- a secure mailing address for your lawyer to send you mail
- a secure email address your lawyer can use to contact you
- whether you want maiden/former name back
- your social security number
- the date of this marriage

- city, county, and state where you got married
- the date you and your spouse separated
- your home phone, cell phone, work phone, and any other phone
- where your lawyer can call you, and where she can leave messages
- your date of birth
- your place of birth—city, county, state, and country
- your years of education and your race (required for Bureau of Vital Statistics form)
- your employer, job title, annual gross income, and bonuses
- whether you want maintenance and if so, how much
- whether you been married before. If so, how many times, and when, where, and how each previous marriage ended (death, dissolution, annulment)
- whether you are on active military duty
- whether you are pregnant. If so, if it is of this marriage and your due date.

Information your lawyer will need about your spouse:
- your spouse's name and any maiden and former names used
- your spouse's current address
- how long your spouse has lived at this address
- how long your spouse has lived in his/her county and state
- a mailing address for your spouse
- a secure email address for your spouse
- whether your spouse wants maiden/former name back
- your spouse's social security number
- your spouse's home phone, cell phone, work phone, and any other phone
- your spouse's date of birth
- your spouse's place of birth—city, county, state, and country
- your spouse's years of education and race (required for Bureau of Vital Statistics form)
- your spouse's employer, job title, annual gross income, and bonuses
- whether your spouse wants maintenance and if so, how much
- whether your spouse has been married before. If so, how many times, and when, where, and how each previous marriage ended (death, dissolution, annulment)
- whether your spouse is on active military duty
- whether your spouse is pregnant. If so, if it is of this marriage and her due date.

Other information your lawyer will need:
- reason for the divorce
- was there a prenuptial agreement?
- are there any pending lawsuits?
- do either of you receive goverment support?

- are either of you in counseling?
- have either of you had any restraining orders?
- has your spouse already filed for divorce?
- for all children of this marriage: name, date of birth, social security number, age, and whether they have any disabilities or special needs
- current custody arrangements: physical custody and legal custody
- your wishes as to custody: physical custody and legal custody
- is child support being paid currently?
- if so, how much is being paid, and by whom?
- who carries the health insurance on the children?
- do you or your spouse have other children?
- are either of you paying or receiving child support or maintenance not related to these parties?
- contact person (emergency).

If any of the children have special needs, detail:
- which child(ren)
- what type(s) of special needs
- doctors, therapists
- date of diagnosis
- types of therapy
- costs—direct and indirect
- schedule
- prognosis
- short-term and long-term plans
- regular caregiver(s)
- respite care
- educational situation including IEPs and 504 Plans
- medications
- effects on primary caregiver parent—job, stress, career, retirement savings program
- specific needs of the child(ren)
- sensory issues
- transition and adjustment issues

D. Financial information to collect for your lawyer

- Name and address of your employer.
- Gross wages or salary and commission each pay period.
- Pay period: weekly, biweekly, semimonthly, monthly.
- Number of dependents claimed.
- Payroll deductions:

- ○ FICA (Social Security tax)
- ○ federal withholding tax
- ○ state withholding tax
- ○ city earnings tax (if applicable)
- ○ union dues
- ○ other deductions
- ○ total deductions each pay period
- ○ net take home pay each pay period.
- Additional income from rentals, dividends and business enterprises, Social Security, A.F.D.C. (Aid to Families with Dependent Children), V.A. (Veterans Administration) benefits, pensions, annuities, bonuses, "commissions and all other sources" (give monthly average and list sources of income).
- Average monthly total.
- Total average net monthly income.
- Your share of the gross income shown on last year's federal income tax return.

Your lawyer may also need information on your expenses. Be prepared to provide information on your monthly expenses for:

- rent or mortgage payments
- utilities: gas, water, electricity, telephone, trash service
- automobiles: gas, routine maintenance, taxes and license, payment on the auto loan
- insurance: life, health & accident, disability, homeowners, automobile
- total payment installments contracts
- child support paid to others for children not in your custody (excluding children of this marriage)
- maintenance or alimony (excluding your current spouse)
- church and charitable contributions
- other living expenses: food, clothing, medical care, dental care, medication, recreation, laundry and cleaning, barber shop or beauty shop, school and books
- daycare center or babysitter
- all other expenses
- special needs expenses: medical treatment, doctors, therapy, other medical expenses, equipment, supplies, training, transportation, caregiver, companion, professionals, medication, supplements, dietary modifications, household modifications, daily/personal care items, respite care, activities, meals, sensory items, other special needs items
- total special needs items.

E. SPECIAL NEEDS ISSUES FOR ANSWER AND COUNTER PETITION

When you are working with your lawyer on the Answer and Petition, consider including the following items if they are relevant in your case:

- a statement of your child's special needs, if the child's special needs have not been recited in the Petition

- a correction about your child's special needs if they have been inaccurately alleged in the Petition

- the need to use a different child support amount, if appropriate but not stated in the Petition

- the need to use a different Parenting Plan, if appropriate but not stated in the Petition

- physical custody, legal custody, visitation, and the need for maintenance.

F. DISCOVERY SUMMARY LIST

- Do any of your children have any physical, mental or emotional disability, learning disability, behavior or mood disorders? Sign releases so your lawyer can get records for this and all categories in this summary list.

- Do any of your children receive special assistance at school?

- Do any of your children have an IEP or 504 Plan at school? You may need to sign two releases, one for the general education program and one for the department that provides the special education/therapy at the school.

- Are any of your children on medication?

- Are any of your children in counseling, physical therapy, behavior therapy, or psychological counseling?

- What is the official diagnosis?

- Who made the diagnosis and when was it made?

- When did the first symptoms appear? You may need records from preschools, babysitters, pediatricians, emergency room personnel, law enforcement personnel, relatives of the child, Parents As Teachers, or other early childhood programs.

- What testing was done to evaluate your child's condition, and why was your child seen by the person who made the diagnosis?

- Has any other professional confirmed the diagnosis?

- Find out about your child's current condition. Do research on your child's actual condition. Get authoritative and scholarly materials on your child's particular condition.

- Find out about your child's prognosis. Get authoritative and scholarly materials on your child's particular prognosis.

- Is your child's condition curable, treatable, or terminal? Get authoritative and scholarly materials on the curability, treatment, and terminal nature of your child's particular condition.

- Find out if your child is expected ever to be able to get a high school diploma, get a college degree, live on her own, hold a regular job, live completely independently, marry, or have children. Get authoritative and scholarly materials on the lifetime implications of the child's particular condition.

- Find out about your child's life expectancy. Get authoritative and scholarly materials on the life expectancy of your child's particular condition.

- Find out about how this condition impacts your child's life now, how it is expected to impact your child's life in the future, how this condition impacts siblings' lives now and how it is expected to impact siblings' lives in the future. Get authoritative and scholarly materials on the impact of the child's particular condition.

- How does this condition impact the lives of you and your spouse now and how is it expected to impact your lives in the future? Get authoritative and scholarly materials on the future impact of the child's particular condition on parents.

- Who is the primary caregiver? Outline how the condition has impacted the careers of you and your spouse and how it is expected to impact your career advancement and retirement plan contributions in the future. Get employer and retirement account records from three time periods: prior to your child's special need; the time your child's special need occurred; and the current time. Get authoritative and scholarly materials on the impact of the child's particular condition on career advancement and retirement plan contributions of parents.

- Provide the names, addresses, telephone numbers, and credentials of all persons your child currently sees for this condition.

- List all medications your child currently takes, the frequency and dosage, the reason for the medication and the expected result from the medication.

- Detail all therapies and treatments your child currently receives, including therapies at home and at school. Get authoritative and scholarly materials on each of the child's particular treatments and therapies. Collect billing, invoices, and receipts. *For each treatment or therapy provide details about:*

  o who provides the treatment or therapy

  o who referred your child to that person or organization

  o where the treatment or therapy is received

  o the type of treatment or therapy and method used

  o the frequency and duration of treatment or therapy (for example: two times a week, one hour each time)

  o how long the treatment or therapy is expected to continue

  o cost of the treatment or therapy

  o how this is paid (private pay, insurance, grant, funding program)

  o amount of uncovered costs and incidental costs of this treatment or therapy—transportation, caregiver, supplies, meals, equipment

  o who takes your child to the therapy

  o what the expectations are for future therapies and medications.

- Is your child is on a waiting list for any therapy, program, school, or funding?

- Keep an itemization of all direct and indirect costs resulting from the child's special needs, including therapy, doctors, other practitioners, medications, supplements, equipment, supplies, caregiver training, special nutritional requirements, special clothing and personal care item requirements, home modifications, vehicle modifications, modifications at school, non-parental caregiver costs, transportation, and any other costs.

- Your lawyer's special needs discovery file should contain: medical reports, test results, diagnoses, evaluations, treatment plans, therapy plans, medication plans, child's safety plans for home, school, and away, medical bills, documentation of all costs, IEPs, 504 Plans current and previous, information on every treating professional, copies of articles or book excerpts providing information on your child's particular condition, detailed therapy and treatment schedule, and your child's detailed daily schedule.

G. COSTS OF DISABILITY AND SPECIAL NEEDS

Additional costs of raising a child with special needs:

- increased health insurance premiums
- co-pays and deductibles, which are often at a higher rate due to more specialists and some out-of-network providers
- medications
- treatments
- therapies
- equipment
- supplements
- dietary costs and specific nutritional regimens
- sensory therapy items, special clothing due to sensory issues, and other sensory items
- respite care
- professionals
- modifications to the home environment
- modifications to transportation, handicap van, etc.
- seminars and conferences
- travel to out-of-local-area for medical care and treatment
- lodging and meals at nonlocal hospitals and other sources of medical care and treatment
- meals when your child is hospitalized locally
- childcare for your other children when you need to be with your disabled or special needs child within or outside of the home, doing therapy, taking the child for treatments, staying with the child at the hospital, etc.
- extra laundry, if the child has vomiting or diarrhea, is incontinent or is bleeding on clothing, sheets, blankets, and towels
- other costs caused by the constantly changing needs of the child.

Sample Documents

A. Petition

B. Answer

C. Counter Petition

D. Parenting Plan

E. Settlement Agreement

F. Judgment of Dissolution

G. Guardian-ad-Litem Motion

H. Guardian-ad-Litem Order

I. Affidavit for Judgment

J. Motion to Modify

A. PETITION

IN THE FAMILY COURT FOR THE COUNTY OF SOMEWHERE
STATE OF YOURSTATE

PAUL JONES, Petitioner,	))
	) Case Number _____
v.	)) Division _____
RITA JONES, Respondent.	))

PETITION FOR DISSOLUTION OF MARRIAGE

COMES NOW Petitioner, Paul Jones, and for his Petition for Dissolution of Marriage hereby states to the Court as follows:

1. Petitioner, Paul Jones, has been a resident of the state of Yourstate for more than ninety (90) days immediately preceding the filing of this Petition, and is now residing at 123 Oak Street, Hometown, Somewhere County, Yourstate, 11111.

2. Respondent, Rita Jones, has been a resident of the state of Yourstate for more than ninety (90) days immediately preceding the filing of this Petition, and is now residing at 456 Elm Street, Hometown, Somewhere County, Yourstate, 11111.

3. Petitioner is self-employed as an accountant. His social security number is xxx-xx-xxxx.

4. Respondent is not employed, and is a homemaker. Her social security number is xxx-xx-xxxx.

5. Petitioner and Respondent were married on January 1, 1990 in Honolulu, Hawaii, and said marriage is registered in Honolulu, Hawaii.

6. Petitioner and Respondent separated on or about July 4, 2010.

7. There was one child born of the marriage, namely Brian Peter Jones, born January 1, 2000, having the social security number xxx-xx-xxxx. Said child is not emancipated.

8. Said minor child Brian Peter Jones has SPECIAL NEEDS in that he has been diagnosed with autism.

9. As a result of the minor child's special needs, it is necessary to deviate from the usual child support calculations.

10. As a result of the minor child's special needs, it is necessary to deviate from the standard Parenting Plan, in the areas of physical custody, legal custody and visitation, among others.

11. To the best of Petitioner's knowledge, Respondent is not now pregnant.

12. Neither Petitioner nor Respondent are members of the armed services of the United States, and neither Petitioner nor Respondent are entitled to the protections and immunities of the Servicemembers Civil Relief Act.

13. The parties possess certain marital and separate property.

14. There is no reasonable likelihood that the marriage of the parties can be preserved, and therefore, the marriage is irretrievably broken.

15. The minor child has lived with Petitioner and Respondent at 456 Elm Street, Hometown, Somewhere County, Yourstate, 11111 continuously for a period of more than six months immediately preceding the filing of this Petition.

16. Petitioner has not participated in any capacity in any other litigation concerning the custody of the minor child in this or any other state. Petitioner does not know of any other person not a party to these proceedings who has physical custody of said minor child or who claims to have custody or visitation rights with respect to such minor child.

17. Petitioner further states that it is in the best interest of the minor child that custody and visitation be ordered pursuant to the Parenting Plan to be filed by Petitioner in this case.

WHEREFORE, Petitioner respectfully prays that the marriage of the parties be dissolved; that the Court award the care, custody and control of the parties' minor child pursuant to Petitioner's Parenting Plan; that the child support calculation include additional costs as a result of the minor child's special needs; that the Court apportion the marital property of the parties in a fair and equitable manner; that the Court set aside to Petitioner his separate property; that the Court order Petitioner and Respondent to each pay their own attorney's fees herein; that the Court costs be split equally between the parties; and for such other and further orders as this Court shall deem just and appropriate.

> Ima Lawyer, Bar No. xxxxx
> 123 Courthouse Road
> Hometown, Yourstate 11111
> (111) 111–1111 tel
> (111) 111–1112 fax
> ima@imalawyer.com

STATE OF YOURSTATE)
) SS

COUNTY OF SOMEWHERE)

PAUL JONES, being first duly sworn upon his oath, of lawful age and competent to testify herein, states that he is the Petitioner above named and that the facts contained herein are true according to his best knowledge, information and belief.

_____
PAUL JONES, Petitioner

Sworn and subscribed before me, a Notary Public, this ___ day of ____, 20___.

_____
Notary Public

My commission expires: _____

B. ANSWER

IN THE FAMILY COURT FOR THE COUNTY OF SOMEWHERE
STATE OF YOURSTATE

PAUL JONES, Petitioner,	))) Case Number _____
v.	)) Division _____
RITA JONES, Respondent.	))

ANSWER TO PETITION FOR DISSOLUTION OF MARRIAGE

COMES NOW Respondent, Rita Jones, and for her Answer to the Petition for Dissolution of Marriage hereby states to the Court as follows:

1. Respondent admits the allegations contained in paragraphs 1 through and including 16 of Petitioner's Petition for Dissolution of Marriage.

2. Respondent denies the allegations contained in paragraph 17 of the Petition. By way of further Answer, Respondent states that it would be in the best interest of the minor child that custody and visitation be ordered pursuant to the Parenting Plan to be filed by Respondent in this case.

3. Respondent is without sufficient resources to pay for living expenses, the living expenses of the minor child, or Respondent's attorney fees and costs of this action without contribution from Petitioner. Petitioner is gainfully employed and earns a substantial wage, sufficient to meet his own needs and contribute to the payment of Respondent's living expenses, the living expenses of the minor child, and Respondent's attorney fees and costs of this action.

WHEREFORE, having fully answered, Respondent respectfully prays that the marriage of the parties be dissolved; that the Court award the care, custody and control of the parties' minor child pursuant to Respondent's Parenting Plan; that the child support calculation include additional costs as a result of the child's special needs; that the Court apportion the marital property of the parties in a fair and equitable manner; that the Court set aside to Respondent her separate property; that the Court order Petitioner to pay a reasonable sum of maintenance to Respondent; that the Court order Petitioner to pay the attorney's fees of Respondent herein; that Petitioner be ordered to pay the Court costs herein; and for such other and further orders as this Court shall deem just and appropriate.

> Ura Turney, Bar No. xxxxx
> 456 Courthouse Road
> Hometown, Yourstate 11111
> (111) 111–2222 tel
> (111) 111–2223 fax
> ura@uraturney.com

STATE OF YOURSTATE   )
) SS

COUNTY OF SOMEWHERE   )

RITA JONES, being first duly sworn upon her oath, of lawful age and competent to testify herein, states that she is the Respondent above named and that the facts contained herein are true according to her best knowledge, information and belief.

_____

RITA JONES, Respondent

Sworn and subscribed before me, a Notary Public, this ___ day of ____, 20___.

_____

Notary Public

My commission expires: _____

C. COUNTER PETITION

IN THE FAMILY COURT FOR THE COUNTY OF SOMEWHERE
STATE OF YOURSTATE

PAUL JONES, Petitioner/Counter Respondent, v. RITA JONES, Respondent/Counter Petitioner.	))) Case Number _____)) Division _____)))

COUNTER PETITION FOR DISSOLUTION OF MARRIAGE

COMES NOW Respondent/Counter Petitioner, Rita Jones, and for her Counter Petition for Dissolution of Marriage hereby states to the Court as follows:

1. Petitioner, Paul Jones, has been a resident of the state of Yourstate for more than ninety (90) days immediately preceding the filing of the original Petition, and is now residing at 123 Oak Street, Hometown, Somewhere County, Yourstate, 11111.

2. Respondent, Rita Jones, has been a resident of the state of Yourstate for more than ninety (90) days immediately preceding the filing of the original Petition, and is now residing at 456 Elm Street, Hometown, Somewhere County, Yourstate, 11111.

3. Petitioner is self-employed as an accountant. His social security number is xxx-xx-xxxx.

4. Respondent is not employed, and is a homemaker. Her social security number is xxx-xx-xxxx.

5. Petitioner and Respondent were married on January 1, 1990 in Honolulu, Hawaii, and said marriage is registered in Honolulu, Hawaii.

6. Petitioner and Respondent separated on or about July 4, 2010.

7. There was one child born of the marriage, namely Brian Peter Jones, born January 1, 2000, having the social security number xxx-xx-xxxx. Said child is not emancipated.

8. Said minor child Brian Peter Jones has SPECIAL NEEDS in that he has been diagnosed with autism.

9. As a result of the minor child's special needs, it is necessary to deviate from the usual child support calculations.

10. As a result of the minor child's special needs, it is necessary to deviate from the standard Parenting Plan, in the areas of physical custody, legal custody and visitation, among others.

11. Respondent is not now pregnant.

12. Neither Petitioner nor Respondent are members of the armed services of the United States, and neither Petitioner nor Respondent are entitled to the protections and immunities of the Servicemembers Civil Relief Act.

13. The parties possess certain marital and separate property.

14. There is no reasonable likelihood that the marriage of the parties can be preserved, and therefore, the marriage is irretrievably broken.

15. The minor child has lived with Petitioner and Respondent at 456 Elm Street, Hometown, Somewhere County, Yourstate, 11111 continuously for a period of more than six months immediately preceding the filing of this Petition.

16. Respondent has not participated in any capacity in any other litigation concerning the custody of the minor child in this or any other state. Respondent does not know of any other person not a party to these proceedings who has physical custody of said minor child or who claims to have custody or visitation rights with respect to such minor child.

17. Respondent further states that it is in the best interest of the minor child that custody and visitation be ordered pursuant to the Parenting Plan to be filed by Respondent in this case.

18. Petitioner is gainfully employed and earns a substantial wage, sufficient to provide for his own living expenses, pay child support to Respondent and contribute to the living expenses of Respondent.

19. Respondent is not employed, and is a homemaker. Respondent lacks sufficient income or other financial resources to provide for her own living expenses or the living expenses of the minor child without contribution from Petitioner. Respondent lacks sufficient income or other financial resources to pay her attorney fees or costs of this action without contribution from Petitioner.

WHEREFORE, Respondent respectfully prays that the marriage of the parties be dissolved; that the Court award the care, custody and control of the parties' minor child pursuant to Respondent's Parenting Plan; that the child support calculation include costs caused by the minor child's special needs; that the Court order Petitioner to pay child support to Respondent pursuant to such calculation, retroactive to the date of filing of the original Petition; that the Court order Petitioner to pay maintenance to Respondent; that the Court apportion the marital property of the parties in a fair and equitable manner; that the Court set aside to Respondent her separate property; that the Court order Petitioner to pay the attorney's fees and litigation costs of Respondent herein; that the Court assess the court costs against Petitioner; and for such other and further orders as this Court shall deem just and appropriate.

> Ura Turney, Bar No. xxxxx
> 456 Courthouse Road
> Hometown, Yourstate 11111
> (111) 111–2222 tel
> (111) 111–2223 fax
> ura@uraturney.com

STATE OF YOURSTATE   )
) SS

COUNTY OF SOMEWHERE   )

RITA JONES, being first duly sworn upon her oath, of lawful age and competent to testify herein, states that she is the Counter Petitioner above named and that the facts contained herein are true according to her best knowledge, information and belief.

_____
RITA JONES, Counter Petitioner

Sworn and subscribed before me, a Notary Public, this ___ day of ____, 20___.

_____
Notary Public

My commission expires: _____

D. PARENTING PLAN

IN THE FAMILY COURT OF THE COUNTY OF SOMEWHERE
STATE OF YOURSTATE

PAUL JONES,   )
Petitioner,   )
) Case Number _____
v.   )
) Division _____
RITA JONES,   )
Respondent.   )

CONSENT PARENTING PLAN FOR SPECIAL NEEDS

Mother and Father shall have joint legal custody and Mother shall have sole physical custody of said minor child. Mother's residence shall be designated as the primary residence of the minor child for mailing and educational purposes.

Due to the special needs of the child, the standard visitation schedule is not in the best interests of the child. The child has autism. He receives intensive therapy for many hours every week, and because of his special needs, his life is extremely structured.

The two most important aspects of this Parenting Plan are:

- the best interests of the child, and
- cooperation of the parents.

CUSTODY, VISITATION AND RESIDENTIAL TIME FOR THE CHILD WITH EACH PARENT SHALL BE AT SUCH TIMES AS THE PARTIES SHALL AGREE. The parties are strongly encouraged to work together cooperatively and flexibly to reach by amicable agreement such custody, visitation and residential times as shall be in the best interests of the child and keeping in mind his special needs. In the event the parties cannot agree, Father shall have custody, visitation or residential time as set forth below and Mother shall have all other time as her custody, visitation or residential time.

EACH PARENT IS STRONGLY ENCOURAGED TO PUT THE CHILD FIRST AND TO MAKE EVERY REASONABLE EFFORT TO MEET THE UNIQUE NEEDS OF THE SPECIAL NEEDS CHILD.

WEEKDAY VISITATION

Father may come to Mother's house to visit the child during the evenings whenever his schedule permits, as long as the parties shall so agree. In the event the parties cannot agree upon the night or nights of this visitation, Father shall visit the child at Mother's house or pick him up at Mother's house on Wednesday evenings. Father shall visit/pick up child at 6:00 pm and return him to Mother's house by 7:30 pm, when he is welcome to participate in his bedtime routine, which usually lasts until 8:30 pm. Father may extend this weekday visitation to overnight visitation. In the event the parties agree upon overnight visitation during the week, Father shall either return the child to Mother's house the next morning or take him to his morning activity, as agreed to by the parties.

WEEKENDS

The child is involved in many activities due to his special needs. These activities require great flexibility and cooperation by the parents regarding the weekend visitation. The general goal is that Father shall have the child for approximately half of the weekends, although this will often not be every other weekend. The parties shall frequently consult each other regarding the scheduled activities and arrange the weekend visitation around the schedule and best interests of the child.

If the parties cannot agree, Father shall have visitation of the child every other weekend beginning at 6:00 pm on Friday through and ending at 6:00 pm on Sunday, beginning the weekend following the date of the judgment.

SUMMER

The child attends summer school for six weeks every year. This usually runs between June and August. There is usually a week or two between the regular school year letting out and the start of summer school, and there is a week or two between the end of summer school and the beginning of the next school year. During these weeks, the child usually attends a special needs summer day camp. It is important for the child to attend summer school. If he is registered for summer school but does not attend consistently, he will not be eligible to attend in subsequent years.

Father may exercise periods of summer visitation during the summer regardless of whether it is during the weeks of summer school, as long as he shall take the child to summer school if his time periods fall during those weeks. Since these arrangements must be made well in advance, Father shall notify Mother of his choice in writing by February 1 every year.

Father may have liberal summer visitation as the parties shall agree. In the event the parties cannot agree, subject to the above provisions, Father shall have three weeks each summer (to be divided into three 7 consecutive day periods) to coincide with the child's school summer vacation. Father may select the first week of this summer vacation by notifying Mother of same (each notification herein to be in writing) by February 1 of each year, one week may then be excluded by Mother by February 15 and then the next week may be selected by Father by March 1, one more week may then be excluded by Mother by March 15, the final week may be selected by Father by April 1. Mother's excluded weeks shall prevail over Father's weekend and weekday periods set forth above.

HOLIDAYS AND SPECIAL DAYS

1. Holiday and special day custody shall prevail over weekend, weekday and summer vacation set forth above. Birthday periods shall not prevail when in conflict with other Holidays and Special Days.

2. Mother shall have the minor child on her birthday and on Mother's Day of each year from 9:00 am to 9:00 pm; plus "Holiday Group A" in even-numbered years and "Holiday Group B" in odd-numbered years.

3. Father shall have the minor child on his birthday and on Father's Day of each year from 9:00 am to 9:00 pm; plus "Holiday Group A" in odd-numbered years and "Holiday Group B" in even-numbered years.

4. Mother and Father are encouraged to communicate to attempt to arrange a combined event/activity for the child's birthday. In the event they cannot agree, the following provisions regarding the child's birthday shall apply.

5. Due to the serious special needs of the child, the conditions stated in the above paragraphs concerning WEEKDAY, WEEKEND and SUMMER visitation shall apply to HOLIDAY GROUPS A & B.

HOLIDAY GROUP A

1. PRESIDENT'S DAY/WASHINGTON'S BIRTHDAY (OBSERVED) weekend from 5:00 pm the Friday prior to 8:00 am the following Tuesday.

2. A period of 7 (seven) days during the child's school Spring break, the exact days to be selected and notice given in writing to the other parent by February 1.

3. INDEPENDENCE DAY If July 4 falls on a: (a) Tuesday, Wednesday or Thursday from 5:00 pm on July 3 until 9:00 am on July 5, (b) Friday or Saturday from 5:00 pm on the Thursday before until 9:00 am on the following Monday, (c) Sunday or Monday from 5:00 pm on the Friday before until 9:00 am on the following Tuesday.

4. HALLOWEEN (October 31) night from 4:00 pm until 9:00 am the following day.

5. CHRISTMAS VACATION from December 25 beginning at 10:00 am through 9:00 am on December 31.

6. The child's birthday from 9:00 am until 9:00 am the following day.

HOLIDAY GROUP B

1. MARTIN LUTHER KING weekend from 5:00 pm the Friday prior through 8:00 am the following Tuesday.

2. MEMORIAL DAY weekend from 5:00 pm the Friday prior through 8:00 am the following Tuesday.

3. LABOR DAY weekend from 5:00 pm the Friday prior through 8:00 am the following Tuesday.

4. THANKSGIVING weekend from 5:00 pm the Wednesday prior through 8:00 am the following Monday.

5. CHRISTMAS VACATION from 5:00 pm the day the child's school Christmas vacation begins through 10:00 am on December 25 and December 31 beginning at 9:00 am through 8:00 am the day the child's school Christmas vacation ends.

6. The day prior to the child's birthday beginning at 9:00 am through 9:00 am the day of the birthday.

The serious special needs of the child require that Mother and Father be far more cooperative and flexible than the parents of a child without special needs.

EXCHANGES

Exchanges of the child shall occur at the residence of Mother or at school or summer camp, unless otherwise agreed. If an exchange occurs at a location other than a parent's residence, the parent scheduled to have time with the child shall pick up and return the child to the specified location and the other parent shall be responsible for assuring the child is at the specified location for pick up, unless other arrangements are described.

TRANSPORTATION

Transportation arrangements for the child for all scheduled parenting times including weekdays, weekends, holidays and vacation times, shall be as follows:
Father shall be responsible for transportation of the child at the beginning and end of the visit.

CHANGES

The parents' schedules and commitments may require occasional changes in the parenting time schedule. Parents shall attempt to agree on any changes, but the parent receiving a request for a change shall have the final decision on whether the change shall occur. The parent making the request may make such request in person, by phone, in writing to the other parent, by text message or by email. The request for change shall be made no later than one week prior to the date of the requested change. The parent receiving the request shall respond no later than 24 hours after receiving the requested change. The response to the request may be made in person, by phone, in writing to the other parent, by text message or by email. Any parent requesting a change of schedule shall be responsible for any additional childcare or transportation costs resulting from the change. Mother and Father shall cooperate to allow the child to meet their therapeutic, school and social commitments.

ELECTRONIC CONTACTS

Each parent shall have reasonable access to the child by telephone, text message, email or social media during any period in which the child is with the other parent, unless otherwise specified.

RELOCATION

Absent exigent circumstances as determined by a Court with jurisdiction, you, as a party to this action, are ordered to notify, in writing by certified mail, return receipt requested, and at least 60 days prior to the proposed relocation, each party to this action of any proposed relocation of the principal residence of the child, including the following information: (1) The intended new residence, including the specific address and mailing address, if known, and if not known, the city; (2) The home telephone number of the new residence, if known; (3) The date of the intended move or proposed relocation; (4) A brief statement of the specific reasons for the proposed relocation of the child; and (5) A proposal for a revised schedule of custody or visitation with the child. Your obligation to provide this information to each party continues as long as you or any other party by virtue of this order is entitled to custody of a child covered by this order. Your failure to obey the order of this Court regarding the proposed relocation may result in further litigation to enforce such order, including contempt of court. In addition, your failure to notify a party of a relocation of the child may be considered in a proceeding to modify custody or visitation with the child. Reasonable costs and attorney fees shall be assessed against you if you fail to give the required notice.

LEGAL CUSTODY

Legal custody: The parties shall agree before making any final decisions on issues affecting the growth and development of the child; including, but not limited to, choice of religious upbringing, choice of childcare provider, choice of school, course of study, special tutoring, extracurricular activities, including but not limited to, music, art, dance and other cultural lessons or activities and gymnastics or other athletic activities, choice of camp or other comparable summer activity, non-emergency medical and dental treatment, psychological, psychiatric or like treatment or counseling, the choice of particular healthcare providers, the extent of any travel away from home, part or full-time employment, purchase or operation of a motor vehicle, contraception and sex education, and decisions relating to actual or potential litigation on behalf of the child. However, each parent may make decisions regarding the day-to-day care and control of the child and in emergencies affecting the health and safety of the child while the child is residing with him or her. The parents shall endeavor, whenever reasonable, to be consistent in such day-to-day decisions.

Communication: Each parent shall ensure that the other parent is provided with copies of all communications or information received from the child's school, and if a second copy of the communication is not provided by the school, shall make a copy for the other parent. Each parent shall notify the other of any activity such as school conferences, programs, sporting and other special events etc., where parents are invited to attend and each shall encourage and welcome the presence of the other.

Child not involved in court or financial communications: The parties shall not talk about adult issues, parenting matters, financial issues, and other court-related topics, when the child is present. Such discussions shall not be had during custody exchanges of the child or during electronic visits. The child shall not be used to carry such messages, written communication or child support payments between the parents.

Medical care information: Each parent shall have the authority to seek any emergency medical treatment for the child when in his or her custody. Each shall advise the other of any medical emergency or serious illness or injury suffered by the minor child as soon as possible after learning of the same, and shall give the other parent details of the emergency, injury or illness and the name and telephone numbers of all treating doctors. Each parent shall inform the other before any routine medical care, treatment or examination by a healthcare provider including said provider's name and telephone number. Each party shall direct all doctors involved in the care and treatment of the minor child to give the other parent all information regarding any injury or illness and the medical treatment or examination, if requested. For purposes of this paragraph, a serious injury or illness is one which requires the child (1) to be confined to home for more than 48 hours, or (2) to be admitted to, or treated at, a hospital or surgical facility, (3) to receive any type of general anesthesia or invasive surgical procedure or test, or (4) to miss school.

Childcare provider: If both parents will need to use a childcare provider during periods of custody or visitation they shall use the same childcare provider, unless the distances between their residences or places of employment make the use of the same childcare provider unreasonable.

Access to records: Each parent shall be entitled to immediate access from the other or from a third party to records and information pertaining to the child including, but not limited to, medical, dental, health, childcare, school or educational records; and each shall take whatever steps are necessary to ensure that the other parent has such access.

Activities to not conflict with custody or visitation: The parties shall enroll the child in activities, particularly outside of school, which, to the extent possible, are scheduled at times and places which avoid interruption and disruption of the custody or visitation time of the other party unless consented to by that parent. The special needs of the child requires far greater cooperation and flexibility by the parents than is required of the parents of a child without special needs.

Resolution of disputes: If the parties fail to agree on the interpretation of the Parenting Plan, or are unable to agree upon a final decision on issues affecting the growth and development or health and safety of the child, they shall submit the dispute to a mutually agreed-upon Special Needs Coordinator who shall hear and arbitrate the issue. In the event they are not able to agree on a Special Needs Coordinator they shall each select a Special Needs Coordinator from the list of approved Special Needs Coordinators maintained by the Somewhere County Family Court and the two Special Needs Coordinators shall determine who shall mediate the case. The Special Needs Coordinator shall be a quick and informal tribunal to arbitrate issues which may arise in the future, including but not limited to: increasing or decreasing child support, changes in therapy, treatment, education, custody and/or visitation, and issues relating to expenses.

CHILD SUPPORT AND OTHER EXPENSES

Due to the special needs of the child, the application of Standard Child Support Guidelines would be inappropriate and/or unjust. The initial amount of child support shall be $_____ per month, payable by Father to Mother. This amount shall be modifiable. This is the base amount, which DOES include the current amount for nutritional supplements/regimens, and DOES NOT include additional support for therapy, activities, camps, or other expenses necessitated by the child's special needs. Parents shall pay for these additional items based upon their proportional share of income. Parents acknowledge that future nutritional supplements/ regimens may involve an increased cost, and parents agree to pay such increased cost based upon their proportional income.

The Parties recognize that due to the special needs of the minor child, child support may not terminate at age 18 or at any particular age and may continue if the child is physically or mentally incapacitated from supporting himself and insolvent and unmarried as per § _____ [Statutes of state of Yourstate].

In addition, each party will continue to contribute to child support as long as they are able to provide child support.

The child support shall be paid 50% on the first and 50% on the 15th day of each month.

HEALTHCARE COSTS

The child is currently covered by medical insurance through Father's employer. Both parents shall cooperate to keep the child covered under this insurance or under another plan. In the event it becomes appropriate to obtain other health insurance for the child, the parents shall pay the expense of such coverage based upon their proportionate share of income. Both parents shall cooperate to provide insurance ID cards to the other parent as applicable, and to complete all forms required by the coverage.

Unless both parties have agreed to use a healthcare provider that is not covered by the health benefit plan, if a parent incurs an expense to a healthcare provider that is not covered by the health benefit plan that would have been covered, or covered at a more favorable rate, if a provider included in the plan had been used, then that parent shall pay seventy-five percent (75%) and the other parent shall pay twenty-five percent (25%) of the uncovered expenses.

"Health expenses" shall be defined in accordance with Internal Revenue Code (1987) §213 "Medical, Dental, etc., Expenses" or any other section enacted in replacement, in addition or in substitution thereof, and/or any Internal Revenue Regulation including, but not limited to, §1.213–1 or any relevant Regulation enacted in replacement, in addition or in substitution thereof, or any relevant Treasury Decision, Regulation or any Revenue Ruling defining those types or kinds of medical costs that are deductible under the Internal Revenue Code, and shall also include orthodontic and optical care (including, but not limited to, prescription eyeglasses or contact lenses and eye examinations conducted by an optician, optometrist or ophthalmologist), treatment and appliances. Psychological and counseling expenses shall be paid as the parties agree, or absent agreement to the extent they are included as "Health Expenses" defined above or are determined by the child's case manager to be in the best interests of the child.

All health expenses incurred on behalf of the child and not paid by the health benefit plan shall be paid based upon each parent's proportionate share of income.

The health expenses covered by this paragraph are not limited to just the usual medical, dental, orthodontic, optical and psychological expenses of a child without special needs. Due to the special needs of the child, they have and are expected to continue to have extraordinary medical, therapeutic and other expenses, which shall be paid by the parents based upon proportionate share of income, in addition to the base amount of child support.

The Parties recognize that due to the special needs of the child, the duty to provide health insurance and to pay medical and dental expenses may not terminate at age 18 or at any particular age and may continue if the child is physically or mentally incapacitated from supporting himself and insolvent and unmarried as per § _____ [Statutes of state of Yourstate].

In addition, each party will continue to contribute to healthcare as long as they are able to provide healthcare.

AN EXHIBIT SHALL BE ATTACHED CONTAINING A SUMMARY OF:

[ ] Child's diagnosis

[ ] Doctors, therapists and other professionals

[ ] Child's current daily schedule and routine

[ ] Child's current therapy plan

[ ] How special needs affect the child's daily life

[ ] Itemization & explanation of the costs involved in or caused by the special needs

[ ] Who the primary caregiver of the child is

[ ] Primary caregiver's daily schedule

[ ] Statement as to the impact of transitions and schedule changes on the child

[ ] List of equipment and special items needed by the child and the location of such items

[ ] Suggested physical custody arrangement

[ ] Suggested legal custody arrangement

[ ] Suggested visitation—daily, weekly, weekends, holidays, summers & special days

EDUCATION AND EXTRAORDINARY EXPENSES

Due to the special needs of the child, he currently incurs and is expected to continue to incur extraordinary educational and other expenses. These shall be paid by the parties based upon their proportionate share of income. If the parties cannot agree on the extraordinary expenses for education, therapy, activities, equipment, supplements and/or other items, the parties agree to pay (based upon their proportionate share of income) for the items determined by the child's Special Needs Coordinator to be in the best interest of the child.

_____	_____
Petitioner	Respondent
_____	_____
Attorney for Petitioner	Attorney for Respondent

(Adapted from Special Needs Parenting Plan co-written with Kieran Coyne, attorney in St. Louis, Missouri.)

E. SETTLEMENT AGREEMENT

IN THE FAMILY COURT OF THE COUNTY OF SOMEWHERE
STATE OF YOURSTATE

PAUL JONES,   )
Petitioner,   )
) Case Number _____
v.   )
) Division _____
RITA JONES,   )
Respondent.   )

MARITAL SETTLEMENT AGREEMENT

This Marital Separation Agreement (hereinafter the "Agreement") is made on the _____ day of _____, 20___, between _____ (hereinafter the "Wife"), and _____ (hereinafter the "Husband"), and collectively referred to as the "Parties."

WHEREAS, the Parties to this Agreement were married on the 1st day of January, 1990, and because of irreconcilable differences which have arisen between them, which render it impossible for them to live together as husband and wife, and

WHEREAS, the Parties believe there is no reasonable likelihood that the marriage of the Parties can be preserved, and that the marriage is irretrievably broken, and WHEREAS, there was one child born of the marriage, namely: Brian Peter Jones, born January 1, 2000 (hereinafter the "Minor Child"), and

WHEREAS, there is now pending an action in the Family Court of the County of Somewhere, State of Yourstate praying that the marriage of the Parties be dissolved, and

WHEREAS, the Parties hereby desire to fully and finally settle all property rights, and claims between them and make provisions regarding the disposition of their property, maintenance, child support, child custody, attorneys' fees and the costs of these proceedings;

NOW, THEREFORE, for valuable consideration, each received by the other and for mutual promises herein contained, it is agreed as follows:

I. AGREEMENT CONTINGENT UPON COURT REVIEW

All of the stipulations, conditions and Agreements hereinafter contained are contingent upon the Family Court of the County of Somewhere, State of Yourstate, entering an order and judgment dissolving the marriage of the Parties and are contingent upon the Court's determination that this Agreement is not unconscionable.

II. CHILD CUSTODY AND SUPPORT MATTERS

The Parties agree that the provisions of the Parenting Plan (hereinafter the "Plan") attached as Exhibit 'A' shall govern the terms of the Minor Child's custody, visitation, and support arrangements. The Parties agree that they will abide by the terms of the Plan. (Father shall pay Mother the sum of $_____ per month in child support.)

III. DIVISION OF PROPERTY

A. NON-MARITAL PROPERTY

The Parties agree that there is non-marital property to be set apart by the Court, which property is divided as indicated on Exhibit "B" attached.

B. MARITAL PROPERTY

1. PERSONAL PROPERTY

a) Division of personal property

The Parties make specific reference to the division of personal property identified on Exhibit "B" attached, with the property being awarded to the Party indicated. Any household goods and personal effects not identified on said exhibit or awarded by this Agreement are awarded to the party who has possession or control of such unidentified goods or personal effects. Each Party is to be responsible for the payment of personal property taxes, if any, that are due for the personal property they are awarded by this agreement.

Vehicles

The Parties agree that Husband is awarded the _____ as his sole and separate property. Further, Husband shall pay and be responsible for any loan or obligation secured by said vehicle, any personal property tax obligations for said vehicle, any leases for said vehicle, and the cost of insuring and operating said vehicle and shall indemnify and hold harmless Wife for such debts.

The Parties agree that Wife is awarded the _____ as her sole and separate property. Further, Wife shall pay and be responsible for any loan or obligation secured by said vehicle, any personal property tax obligations for said vehicle, any leases for said vehicle, and the cost of insuring and operating said vehicle and shall indemnify and hold harmless Husband for such debts.

Joint bank account

The Parties agree that the parties will close this account and share the proceeds from this account equally.

Individual bank accounts

The Parties agree that Husband is awarded all checking and savings accounts in his name as his sole and separate property.
The Parties agree that Wife is awarded all checking and savings accounts in her name as her sole and separate property.

Pensions and IRAs

The Parties acknowledge that Wife is currently receiving retirement and/or disability benefits as a result of her military service. The Parties agree that Wife shall be awarded 100% of her own retirement/pension/disability benefits as her respective property. The Parties agree that Husband and Wife shall each receive 50% or one-half of the retirement/pension/disability benefits in the name of Husband. Husband is awarded the IRA in his name as his property. Mother is the primary caregiver for the Minor Child, who has Special Needs, and thus is unable to work to her otherwise full ability, thereby decreasing the amount she is able to contribute to a retirement plan for her future benefit; therefore the parties agree that this is a fair and equitable distribution of the pensions, retirement accounts and IRAs.

Life insurance

The Parties are each awarded the life insurance policies in their respective names (on their respective lives) as their property. The Parties agree that they will continue to maintain their child as the sole beneficiary on the existing life insurance policies until the child is actually emancipated as defined within the Parenting Plan. Further, each Party shall provide the other Party documentation regarding the terms of the Policy and its current status, upon the other Party's request. Further, the Parties consent to the insurance company issuing, and/or managing, such Policy providing to the Other Party such information about the Policy that is reasonably necessary to determine the existence, terms, beneficiaries, and status of the Policy.

Additionally, the Parties agree that there is a life insurance policy insuring their child, and the Parties agree to maintain such insurance Policy and to each pay one-half of the insurance premiums for said Policy until the insured minor child is emancipated. The Parties further agree that they will each be designated as equal co-beneficiaries on such Policy, and in the event of the death of the insured minor child, the insurance proceeds will be used to satisfy the burial costs of the child, the child's outstanding uninsured medical bills, if any, the child's outstanding educational expenses, and thereafter such remaining proceeds shall be shared equally between the Parties.

b) Titles and papers

Each Party shall promptly deliver to the other all property or documents evidencing ownership of property which by the terms of this Agreement is to remain or become the property of the other. Each Party shall execute and deliver to the other Party such Affidavits of Gift and Limited Powers of Attorney that are reasonably required to transfer each Party's interest in the cars, automobiles, and vehicles awarded the other Party and to permit the other Party to act as attorney in fact for the sole purpose of transferring title of the car, automobile or vehicle awarded by this Agreement.

Further, each party agrees to keep all property, and documents evidencing ownership of property, which by the terms of this Agreement is to remain or become the property of the other in good condition, normal wear and tear excepted, until such time as delivery of such property and documentation to the other Party has occurred. The Parties agree that neither Party shall be obligated to store or keep the property or documentation of ownership of such property, which by the terms of this Agreement, is to remain or become the property of the other, for more than 30 days after written notice of a request to pick up such property and documentation has been mailed by certified mail, return receipt requested, to the Party to whom such property and documentation is awarded by this Agreement. (Such notice to pick up property shall be addressed to the last known mailing address of the recipient Party and shall specify a date, time and place, where the property and documentation in question is to be picked up, which date and time shall be reasonable, and not sooner than five days from the date of mailing of such notice.)

2. REAL PROPERTY

a) Identification of real property

The Parties acknowledge that they now own or have a marital interest in the following real property:

i) 123 Oak Street, Hometown, located in the County of Somewhere, State of Your-State, with the legal description contained on Exhibit ___ attached (hereinafter the "Marital Residence") which real property is security for an obligation, evidenced by a Deed of Trust, in favor of XYZ Bank (hereinafter the "Mortgagee for Marital Residence").

b) Division of real property

The Parties agree that the real property in which they have a marital interest shall be disposed of as follows:

i) Marital Residence

The Parties agree that the Marital Residence is awarded to Wife as her sole and exclusive property.

Wife shall assume and pay the unpaid balance of approximately $_____, owing on the Marital Residence. Wife shall also assume and pay the unpaid balance of any other obligation or line of credit that is secured by the Marital Residence and shall indemnify and hold Husband harmless for such other obligations, if any.

Wife shall indemnify and hold Husband harmless should the Mortgagee for the Marital Residence, or its assigns or successors, proceed against Husband upon Wife's failure to assume or pay the obligation owed to the Mortgagee for the Marital Residence, or upon Wife's default under any provision of the loan instruments, promissory notes, or Deed of Trust evidencing or securing the obligation to the Mortgagee for the Marital Residence.

Wife shall also be responsible for any obligation for taxes, subdivision dues, insurance costs, repair costs and utility costs, and any other costs, associated with the ownership, possession or use of the Marital Residence. Wife shall indemnify and hold Husband harmless on such costs.

Wife agrees to take such reasonable action as is necessary to remove Husband's name from the obligation to the Mortgagee for the Marital Residence, including but not limited to, refinancing the obligation. Husband's name shall be removed from the obligation within six months of the date of a Judgment of Dissolution of Marriage between the parties.

Husband shall deliver a Quitclaim Deed, transferring his interest in the Marital Residence to Wife concurrently with the removal of his name from the mortgage obligation.

Husband does herewith assign, transfer and set over to the Wife all of interest in the Escrow fund, if any, held on the Marital Residence and further the Husband assigns, transfers and sets over to the Wife all of Husband's interest in all existing insurance on the Marital Residence.

Husband waives any interest in any deposit previously paid to any utility service providers, whether for phone, water, trash, electric, gas, and sewer service, for service to the Marital Residence. Husband agrees to cooperate with Wife and to do all things reasonably necessary to have the water, phone, electric, gas, sewer, and trash utilities for the Marital Residence put in the name of the Wife.

c) Other real property

The Parties each acknowledge and represent to the other that neither party has any interest in any real property in the State of YourState or elsewhere, whether in their names alone or with others, except as identified above.

3. NATURE OF PROPERTY DIVIDED

The Parties agree that all of the property divided by Section B above is marital property (except for property listed on Petitioner's Statement of Property filed with the Court as being separate/non-marital property). The transfers represent fair and equitable divisions of property after consideration of the other financial provisions of this Agreement.

4. TRANSFERS OF PROPERTY INTEREST

The Parties stipulate and agree that the transfers of property interests, which take place in order to satisfy the terms of this Agreement, shall be transfers pursuant to Section 1041 of the Internal Revenue Code, and the Parties agree to execute any forms or other documents as might be necessary to establish this intent.

IV. MAINTENANCE

The Parties agree, after examining all relevant factors, including the factors specified under Section _____ (statutes of state of _____), that Husband shall pay to Wife the sum of $_____ per month as and for maintenance, such payments are due on the first day of each month, beginning on first of _____, 20___. The Parties agree that this provision as to maintenance shall be modifiable. Maintenance shall automatically terminate upon the first of the following to occur: Husband's death, Wife's death, Wife's remarriage. The Parties agree that no wage withholding orders are required at this time, although the Parties understand that in the event maintenance or child support is not paid in a timely fashion, then a wage withholding order may be applied for by Wife.

V. DEBTS

a) Assumption of debts and liabilities: From and after the date the Petition in this cause was filed, each Party will be solely liable for the debts acquired by him or her.

b) Terms of payments: The Parties' debts and liabilities will be assumed and paid as provided on the exhibits attached hereto (i.e. Exhibit "B") and incorporated herein by reference. Each Party is responsible for any debt or obligation that is incurred in connection with the ownership, possession or use of an asset of property, whether real or personal, unless specifically indicated otherwise in this Agreement.

c) Indemnification: The Parties agree to indemnify and hold harmless each other and defend the other from and against all claims and liabilities and will reimburse the other for any and all expenses made or incurred by the other, either directly or indirectly, including reasonable attorney's fees, as a result of his or her failure to pay or otherwise satisfy the debts and liabilities assumed by each in this Agreement.

d) No undisclosed debts: The Parties warrant to each other that he or she has not incurred any debt or obligation which is either (1) an obligation on or for which the other Party is or may become personally liable, or (2) an obligation that could be enforced at any time against an asset held or to be received under this Agreement by the other Party, except as disclosed on attached Exhibit "B". Each Party covenants not to incur any such obligations or debts on or after the execution of this Agreement.

VI. INCORPORATION IN DECREE

It is the intent of the Parties that the terms of this Agreement be incorporated and fully set forth in any Decree of Dissolution of Marriage entered by the Court, and the Parties shall be ordered to perform the terms thereof.

VII. SEVERABILITY OF PROVISIONS

In the event that any provision of the Agreement is unenforceable when incorporated as part of the Court's judgment, it shall be considered severable and enforceable by an action based on contractual obligation, and it shall not invalidate the remainder of this Agreement as incorporated in any Decree.

VIII. PROVISIONS FOR FAILURE TO PERFORM
WITH NOTICE REQUIRED

In the event that either Party brings an action for failure to perform any of the obligations imposed by the Agreement due him or her, or for enforcement or clarification of the Agreement, the prevailing Party in such action shall have the right to recover his or her reasonable attorney's fees and litigation costs reasonably expended in prosecuting or defending the action. However, no attorney fees shall be so recovered by a Party filing an action unless the Party seeking to recover said attorney fees and costs shall have mailed to the other Party written notice of the alleged failure to perform and said alleged failure was not cured within ten (10) days after the date of mailing of said notice by certified mail to the alleged breaching Party's residential address. Provided further, that no such notice shall be necessary as to any periodic child support obligation which Petitioner has failed to perform in a timely fashion in accordance with this Agreement on more than two occasions. Provided further, that no such notice shall be necessary as to any periodic maintenance obligation which wife has failed to perform in a timely fashion in accordance with this Agreement on more than two occasions.

No fees or costs authorized by this paragraph shall be recovered except as determined and awarded by the Court in an action brought for enforcement, breach or clarification of the Agreement.

IX. MODIFICATION AND APPROVAL

The terms of this Agreement shall be subject to modification or change only by a mutual agreement of the Parties in writing. It is understood that this provision is not applicable to the terms of the Agreement dealing with child custody, visitation, and child support. The Parties recognize that the provisions relating to custody, visitation, and child support are subject to the approval of the Court, and may be modified by the Court regardless of this paragraph.

X. MUTUAL RELEASE

Subject to the provisions of the Agreement, each Party has remised, released and forever discharged and, by these presents, does himself or herself and his or her heirs, legal representatives, executors, administrators and assigns remise, release and forever discharge the other Party, and the other Party's family, employees, agents and attorneys, of and from all cause or causes of action, claims, rights or demands whatsoever in law or equity, which either Party hereto ever had or now has against the other, except any and all cause or causes of action for dissolution of marriage or rights arising from this Agreement or subsequent Court Order.

XI. MUTUAL WAIVER OF RIGHTS IN ESTATES

Except as otherwise provided in this Agreement, each Party shall have the right to dispose of his or her property of whatsoever nature, real or personal, and each Party, for himself or herself, respectively, and for their respective heirs, legal representatives, executors, administrators, personal representatives and assigns, hereby waives any right of election which he or she may have or hereafter acquire regarding the estate of the other or to take against any Last Will and Testament of the other or any codicil thereto, whether heretofore or hereafter executed, as provided for in any law now or hereinafter effective of this state or any other state or territory of the United States or any foreign country and renounces and releases all interest, right or claim of distributive share or interstate succession or dower or courtesy, or community property or statutory exemption or allowance or otherwise, that he or she now has or might otherwise have against the other or the estate of the other, or the property of whatsoever nature, real or personal, of the other Party under or by virtue of the laws of any state or country. Nothing contained in this particular paragraph, however, shall affect any obligation undertaken in the other paragraphs of the Agreement by either Party.

XII. DISPOSAL OF PROPERTY

Except as set forth in this agreement, each of the Parties shall, from the date of the execution of this Agreement, have the right to dispose of his or her property by *intervivos* conveyance, gift, Last Will or otherwise, as though a single person.

XIII. EXECUTION OF PAPERS

The Parties agree that they shall take any and all steps to execute, acknowledge and deliver to the other any and all instruments, assurances and affidavits that the other Party may reasonably require or find convenient, expedient or businesslike for the purpose of giving full force and effect to the provisions of this Agreement.

XIV. PERFORMANCE OF ACTS REQUIRED IN AGREEMENT

Where acts and things are required to be performed under the terms of this Agreement and no time is specified for their performance, they shall be done as soon as practical after a Judgment of Dissolution of marriage is entered between the Parties, or within 15 days of the date the Judgment of Dissolution of marriage is entered between the Parties, whichever is sooner.

XV. VOLUNTARY AGREEMENT AND INVESTIGATION AND DISCLOSURE

Each of the Parties hereby affirms that they each are entering into this Agreement freely and voluntarily; that they have ascertained and weighed all the facts and circumstances likely to influence his or her judgment herein; that they have given due consideration to such provisions in question; that they have sought independent advice of counsel in regard to all details and particulars of the Agreement (or, they had an opportunity to seek independent advice of counsel) and the underlying facts; and that they clearly understand and assent to all the provisions hereof.

Each Party further warrants that they have each disclosed to the other the full extent of their respective properties and income, either on the Statements of Property and/or Statements of Income and Expenses filed with the Court, or on the attachments to this Agreement. Each Party further warrants that they have not secreted, hidden, transferred, or disposed of any assets that either Party may have an interest in. Each Party warrants that neither Party has since the ___ day of _____, 20___ withdrawn, consumed or borrowed, except for ordinary, regular and normal living expenses, funds from the bank accounts, stock holdings, retirement plans, 401k plans, pension plans, and Thrift Savings Plans, in their respective names or control. Each Party warrants that the equity values or balances of the bank accounts, stock holdings, retirement plans, 401k plans, pension plans, and Thrift Savings Plans, except as values fluctuate with the market or accounts are subject to third party charges, are as disclosed on each Party's Statements of Property filed with the Court, or as disclosed on the account statements or documentation provided the other Party in response to Requests for the Production of Documents, whichever documentation contains the most current information.

Each Party agrees that in the event property, assets or interests are discovered that have not been disclosed on their Statements of Property or on attachments to this Agreement, and which property, assets or interests were acquired in whole or in part during the marriage and not by way of inheritance or gift or in exchange for non-marital property, that such property, assets or interests shall be divided equally between the Parties promptly after the discovery of the same.

XVI. WAIVER OF DISCOVERY

Each party acknowledges that he or she has had the opportunity to complete the discovery each as Interrogatories, Request for Production of Documents, appraisals, real estate and other property, and depositions, and has chosen not to do same. Each party acknowledges the risks of proceeding without completion of such discovery. Each party has, nevertheless, directed his or her attorneys to proceed without completion of such discovery. Each party acknowledges that without such completed discovery, his or her counsel has not conducted any investigation or analysis that would permit his or her counsel to determine the full extent and value of the parties' marital property, debts, income and expenses, and whether there is any marital component in any non-marital property. The settlement has been based on the personal knowledge of each party, and the review of limited documents exchanged between the parties and Statement of Income and Expenses and Statement of Property filed by each party herein.

XVII. RIGHTS TO TRIAL

Both Parties understand they have a right to trial. The Parties agree and stipulate, having been fully advised by their respective attorneys of the consequences and considerations that could result if fully litigated and that trying the case could be more favorable or could be less favorable than the terms of this Property Settlement and Separation Agreement. Nevertheless, the Parties have agreed it is in their respective best interests to waive any trial of this matter and settle the case.

XVIII. LIVING APART

The Parties shall continue to live separate and apart and from the date of the execution of this Agreement, free from any interference by the other, as if fully unmarried, and further, neither will molest, malign, annoy or trouble the other in any manner.

XIX. JOINT INCOME TAX RETURNS

The Parties agree to file joint income tax returns for the tax year ending December 31, 20 ___, and each shall be entitled to one-half (1/2) of any refund on any joint returns filed for said tax year and will likewise be responsible for one-half (1/2) of any taxes, interest and penalties on returns which are jointly filed.

The Parties agree that in the event any jointly filed income tax return is audited by the appropriate taxing authorities, they will cooperate with each other and their respective attorneys, and accountants, to investigate, respond to or comply with such audit. Any non-cooperating Party shall indemnify and hold harmless the other Party for failure to perform any reasonable request to assist the attorney/accountants in investigating, responding to or complying with said audit.

The Parties agree that in the event either Party receives any notice or documentation from the Internal Revenue Service, or any state taxing authority, that references or involves an income tax return that was filed by either Party, or the Parties jointly, during the course of the marriage, they shall promptly forward a copy of such notice or documentation to the other Party at their last known mailing address. In the event a Party fails to promptly forward a copy of such notice or documentation to the other Party and additional taxes, interest or penalties are assessed against the other Party after the date of receipt of such notice or documentation by the non-forwarding Party, then the non-forwarding Party shall indemnify and hold harmless the other Party for such additional taxes, interest and penalties.

XX. PAYMENT OF ATTORNEY'S FEES

The Parties agree that Husband shall pay his own respective attorney fees and costs incurred in this cause, and that Husband shall pay $5,000.00 to Wife's attorney as and for her attorney fees incurred in this cause.

XXI. PAYMENT OF COURT COSTS

The Parties agree that the court costs, excluding deposition costs, of this proceeding shall be equally shared between the Parties. Any deposition costs shall be borne solely by the Party taking the deposition. In the event the Court orders court costs paid from any deposits already on hand with the Court, then the Respondent shall indemnify, hold harmless, and reimburse Petitioner for Respondent's share of court costs as agreed to in this paragraph.

XXII. BINDING EFFECT

This Agreement shall be binding on the heirs, representatives and assigns of the Parties hereto except as to the specific paragraphs which contain provisions for termination of obligations on the death of one or both of the Parties.

XXIII. EXECUTION

Each Party hereto acknowledges that each of them is making this Agreement of his or her own free will and volition and acknowledges that no coercion, force, pressure or undue influence has been used against either Party in the making of this Agreement or by any other person or persons.

XXIV. STATUTORY COMPLIANCE

The validity and construction of this Agreement shall be determined in accordance with the laws of the State of YourState.

XXV. SIGNATURES

IN WITNESS WHEREOF, the Parties set their signatures to this document hereafter.

STATE OF _____   )
) SS
COUNTY OF _____   )

_____, of lawful age, being first duly sworn on his oath, states that he is the Petitioner (and Husband) named herein and that he has read the above and foregoing Agreement; he further states that the facts and matters contained therein are true and correct to the best of his knowledge, information and belief and he has executed this document voluntarily and of his free will.

_____
                                              Petitioner

On this _____ day of _____, 20___ before me a Notary Public in and for said State personally appeared _____to me known to be the person described in and who executed the foregoing instrument, and acknowledged and stated under oath and/or affirmed that he executed the same as his free act and deed, and that the facts and matters contained therein are true and correct to the best of his knowledge, information and belief.

IN TESTIMONY WHEREOF, I have hereunto set my hand and affixed my official seal in the County and State aforesaid, the day and year first above written.

_____
                                              Notary Public

My Commission expires: _____

STATE OF _____   )
) SS

COUNTY OF _____   )

_____, of lawful age, being first duly sworn on her oath, states that she is the Respondent (and Wife) named herein and that she has read the above and foregoing Agreement; she further states that the facts and matters contained therein are true and correct to the best of her knowledge, information and belief and she has executed this document voluntarily and of her free will.

_____

                Respondent

On this _____ day of _____, 20___ before me a Notary Public in and for said State personally appeared _____ to me known to be the person described in and who executed the same as her free act and deed, and that the facts and matters contained therein are true and correct to the best of her knowledge, information and belief.

IN TESTIMONY WHEREOF, I have hereunto set my hand and affixed my official seal in the County and State aforesaid, the day and year first above written.

_____

             Notary Public

My Commission expires: _____

EXHIBIT "A"
Parenting Plan

EXHIBIT "B"
Division of Property

EXHIBIT "C"
Legal Description for Marital Residence

(Adapted from Settlement Agreement co-written with Kieran Coyne, an attorney in St. Louis, Missouri.)

F. JUDGMENT

IN THE FAMILY COURT OF SOMEWHERE COUNTY
STATE OF YOURSTATE

In Re the Marriage of:

PAUL JONES,)
Petitioner,)
) Case Number _____

v.)
) Division _____

RITA JONES,)
Respondent.)

JUDGMENT OF DISSOLUTION

Now on this ____ day of _____, 20__ this cause comes on for hearing; Petitioner, Paul Jones, appearing in person and with his attorney, (name). Respondent, Rita Jones, appearing in person and with her attorney, (name).

Whereupon, all matters contained in the Petition are submitted to the Court for trial. All parties announce ready for hearing. After hearing all the evidence, reviewing the Property Settlement Agreement and being fully advised in the premises, the Court finds that Petitioner has been a resident of the State of _____ for more than ____ days next preceding the commencement of this proceeding and that more than ___ days have elapsed since the filing of the Petition. The Court finds that the Respondent, Rita Jones, is not now pregnant. The Court finds that there remains no reasonable likelihood that the marriage can be preserved and that the marriage is irretrievably broken.

IT IS THEREFORE ORDERED, ADJUDGED AND DECREED by the Court that the parties hereto be and they are hereby granted the dissolution of their marriage and restored to all rights and privileges of single and unmarried persons.

The Court finds that the Property Settlement Agreement is presented to the Court and after being duly examined is found not to be unconscionable, and is to be made a part of the Judgment. The Court finds that said agreement disposes of all marital and non-marital property and debt.

The Court finds that there was one child born of the marriage, namely: Brian Peter Jones, born January 1, 2000.

THE COURT FINDS THAT SAID MINOR CHILD HAS A SPECIAL NEED, NAMELY AUTISM, WHICH SPECIAL NEED HAS BEEN COMPLETELY ADDRESSED IN THE SETTLEMENT AGREEMENT, PARENTING PLAN AND PROPOSED JUDGMENT. THESE DOCUMENTS HAVE BEEN APPROVED BY THE SPECIAL NEEDS COORDINATOR ASSIGNED TO THIS CASE.

The Court finds that it is in the best interests of the child for the parents to be awarded joint physical and joint legal custody of the child.

In determining the custody of the child, the Court has considered the wishes of the child's parents as to custody and the proposed Parenting Plan submitted by both parties; the needs of the child for a frequent, continuing and meaningful relationship with both parents and the ability and willingness of parents to actively perform their function as mother and father for the needs of the child; the interaction and interrelationship of the child with parents, siblings, and any other person who may significantly affect the child's best interests; which parent is more likely to allow the child frequent, continuing and meaningful contact with the other parent; the child's adjustment to the child's home, school, community; the mental and physical health of all individuals involved, including any history of abuse of any individuals involved; the intention of either parent to relocate the principal residence of the child; and the wishes of a child as to the child's custodian.

In the event either party relocates their principal residence, then you are advised pursuant to Section _____ of the Statutes of the State of YourState as follows: Absent exigent circumstances as determined by a Court with jurisdiction, you, as a party to this action, are ordered to notify, in writing by certified mail, return receipt requested, and at least 60 days prior to the proposed relocation, the other party of any proposed relocation of the principal residence of the child, including the following information:

1. The intended new residence, including the specific address and mailing address, if known, and if not known, the city;

2. The home telephone number of the new residence, if known;

3. The date of the intended move or proposed relocation;

4. A brief statement of the specific reasons for the proposed relocation of the child; and

5. A proposal for a revised schedule of custody or visitation with the child.

Your obligation to provide this information to each party continues as long as you or any other party by virtue of this order is entitled to custody of a child covered by this order. Your failure to obey this order of this court regarding the proposed relocation may result in further litigation to enforce such order including contempt of court. In addition, your failure to notify a party of a relocation of the child may be considered in a proceeding to modify custody or visitation with the child. Reasonable costs and attorney fees may be accessed against you if you fail to give the required notice.

The Court orders that each party pay their respective pro rata share of the 20__ personal property taxes based upon the assessed value of the vehicles awarded to each party. Each party shall pay their share prior to December 31, 20__.

The Court orders the Sheriff or other Law Enforcement Officer to enforce visitation or custody rights.

The Court orders Petitioner to pay to Respondent the sum of $_____ per month as and for Respondent's maintenance until further order of the Court. Said maintenance obligation shall be modifiable.

It is contemplated by and the intention and agreement of the parties that the amounts payable by Petitioner to Respondent under this Section shall be deductible on Petitioner's federal and (state) income tax returns and shall constitute income to Respondent for federal and (state) income tax purposes.

The Court orders Respondent to pay to counsel for Petitioner the sum of $_____ as and for a portion of Petitioner's attorney fees.

The Court orders Petitioner to pay all court costs incurred herein.

The Court finds that this Judgment has disposed of all marital and non-marital property and debts.

IT IS FURTHER ORDERED, ADJUDGED AND DECREED by the Court that the parties shall sign any and all documents necessary to effectuate the terms of this Judgment Entry.

IT IS SO ORDERED.

Dated this _____ day of _____, 20____.

_____

The Honorable _____

Case No. _____

APPROVED AS TO FORM:

_____

Attorney for Petitioner

_____

Attorney for Respondent

G. GUARDIAN-AD-LITEM MOTION

IN THE FAMILY COURT OF SOMEWHERE COUNTY
STATE OF YOURSTATE

In Re the Marriage of:

PAUL JONES, Petitioner,	))
	) Case Number _____
v.	)
	) Division _____
RITA JONES, Respondent.	))

MOTION FOR APPOINTMENT OF GUARDIAN-AD-LITEM

Comes now the Petitioner, Paul Jones, by and through his attorney, _____, and respectfully requests the Court appoint a Guardian-ad-Litem for the minor child(ren): _____ for the following reasons:

_____ credible allegations of child neglect

_____ credible allegations of child abuse

_____ special needs of the child(ren), specifically: _____

      I AM/AM NOT AWARE OF ANY SPECIAL NEEDS OF THE CHILD(REN), SPECIFICALLY: _____

_____ other

This Motion for Appointment of Guardian-ad-Litem is supported by a sworn affidavit, a true and correct copy of which is attached hereto and marked as Exhibit 1.

Respectfully submitted,

_____
Attorney for Respondent

CERTIFICATE OF SERVICE

I hereby certify that a true and correct copy of the foregoing was deposited in the U.S. Mail, postage prepaid to:

Opposing Counsel's Name, Street Address, City, State ZIP

this _____ day of _____, 20___.

_____
Attorney for Respondent

H. GUARDIAN-AD-LITEM ORDER

IN THE FAMILY COURT OF SOMEWHERE COUNTY
STATE OF YOURSTATE

In Re the Marriage of:

PAUL JONES,	)
Petitioner,	)
	) Case Number _____
v.	)
	) Division _____
RITA JONES,	)
Respondent.	)

ORDER APPOINTING GUARDIAN-AD-LITEM

IT IS HEREBY ORDERED that _____ shall be appointed as Guardian-ad-Litem for the minor children: _____ for the following reasons:

_____ credible allegations of child neglect
_____ credible allegations of child abuse
_____ special needs of the child(ren), specifically: _____

THE PARTIES STATE THAT THEY ARE/ARE NOT AWARE OF ANY SPECIAL NEEDS OF THE CHILD(REN), SPECIFICALLY:

_____

_____ other

SO ORDERED:

_____

The Honorable _____

I. AFFIDAVIT FOR JUDGMENT

IN THE FAMILY COURT OF SOMEWHERE COUNTY
STATE OF YOURSTATE

In Re the Marriage of:

PAUL JONES,)
Petitioner,)
) Case Number _____
v.   )
) Division _____
RITA JONES,)
Respondent.)

AFFIDAVIT OF PETITIONER REQUESTING
DISSOLUTION OF MARRIAGE—SPECIAL NEEDS CASE

Petitioner, upon his oath submits the following affidavit pursuant to local rules, to form a basis for the court's entering a judgment in this case upon affidavit and without the necessity of a formal hearing.

1. The Petition in this case was filed on _____, 20___.

2. Respondent was served with summons in this case on _____ (date) and filed a responsive pleading on _____ (date).

3. Respondent is and has been a resident of the State of YourState for more than _____ days/months immediately preceding the filing of the Petition in this case.

4. Both parties are over eighteen years of age.

5. At the time of filing, Petitioner resided at _____ (street address, city, county, state, zip code).

6. At the time of filing, Respondent resided at _____ (street address, city, county, state, zip code).

7. Petitioner's social security number is xxx-xx-xxxx. (if applicable)

8. Respondent's social security number is xxx-xx-xxxx. (if applicable)

9. Petitioner is represented by _____ (attorney name and address).

10. Respondent is represented by _____ (attorney name and address).

11. Petitioner is employed as a _____ (occupation) at _____ (employer name) located at _____ (employer address).

12. Respondent is employed as a _____ (occupation) at _____ (employer name) located at _____ (employer address).

13. Petitioner and Respondent were married on _____(date) at _____ (city, county, state). The marriage was recorded in the County of _____, State of _____.

14. Petitioner and Respondent separated on or about _____, 20___.

15. Petitioner believes that there is no reasonable likelihood that the marriage of Petitioner and Respondent can be preserved and, therefore, believes that the marriage is irretrievably broken.

16. Petitioner is not on active duty with the Armed Forces of the United States of America or its allies.

17. Respondent is not on active duty with the Armed Forces of the United States of America or its allies.

18. Petitioner is not pregnant.

19. The parties have entered into a written agreement for the division of their property which includes all assets and debts and identifies and divides the marital property and debts and sets apart to each party his or her non-marital property. This agreement is attached to this affidavit and incorporated herein by reference.

20. Petitioner and Respondent have agreed that spousal maintenance payable by Respondent to Petitioner in the amount of $ _____ per month as and for Petitioner's maintenance until further order of the Court. Said maintenance obligation shall be modifiable. The parties ask

that the court incorporate this agreed upon spousal maintenance in the Judgment of Dissolution.

21. Petitioner is unaware of any genuine issue as to any material fact in this proceeding.

22. There is one minor, unemancipated child of the marriage, namely: _____ DOB: _____

23. SAID CHILD HAS SPECIAL NEEDS, NAMELY AUTISM, WHICH SPECIAL NEEDS HAVE BEEN COMPLETELY ADDRESSED IN THE SETTLEMENT AGREEMENT, PARENTING PLAN AND PROPOSED JUDGMENT. THESE DOCUMENTS HAVE BEEN APPROVED BY THE SPECIAL NEEDS COORDINATOR ASSIGNED TO THIS CASE.

24. The child has lived with Petitioner and Respondent at _____ (street address, city, county, state) for six months immediately preceding the filing of this Petition.

25. That Petitioner has not participated in any capacity in any other litigation concerning the custody of the child in this or any other state. Petitioner has no information of any custody proceeding concerning the child pending in a court of this or any other state; and knows of no person not a party to these proceedings who has physical custody of the child or claims to have custody or visitation rights with respect to the child.

26. Petitioner and Respondent have entered into a custody agreement, which is attached and incorporated herein by reference. Petitioner and Respondent request that the Court incorporate the terms of the custody agreement in the Judgment of Dissolution.

27. Attached hereto is a special needs child support worksheet which has been agreed to by both parties. Petitioner attests to the truth of the contents of the child support worksheet.

28. The parties agree that the amount of support calculated by the special needs child support worksheet is not rebutted as being unjust or inappropriate and agree that Respondent shall pay $____ per month child support.

29. Costs paid by Petitioner.

30. Petitioner shall pay maintenance to Respondent in the amount of $_____ per month. This maintenance is modifiable.

_____
Petitioner

STATE OF _____   )
)
COUNTY OF _____   )

_____ personally appeared before me on _____, who upon being duly sworn stated that the foregoing statements were true and accurate to their best knowledge and belief.

_____
Notary Public

CERTIFICATE OF MAILING

I hereby certify that a copy of the foregoing was mailed on the ___ day of _____, 20__ by U.S. Mail, postage prepaid to:

_____

(opposing counsel's name, street address, city, state and zip code)

J. MOTION TO MODIFY

IN THE FAMILY COURT OF SOMEWHERE COUNTY
STATE OF YOURSTATE

In Re the Marriage of:

PAUL JONES, Petitioner,	))) Case Number _____
v.	)) Division _____
RITA JONES, Respondent.	))

MOTION TO MODIFY—SPECIAL NEEDS

Comes now the Petitioner, Paul Jones, by and through his counsel,_____, and for his cause of action, alleges and states:

1. On _____ this Court entered a Decree of Dissolution in this matter.
   There was one child born of the marriage, namely:
   _____ born _____
   THE COURT FOUND THAT SAID MINOR CHILD HAS SPECIAL NEEDS, NAMELY AUTISM, AND FOUND THAT THE SPECIAL NEEDS HAD BEEN COMPLETELY ADDRESSED IN THE SETTLEMENT AGREEMENT, PARENTING PLAN AND PROPOSED JUDGMENT. THESE DOCUMENTS WERE APPROVED BY THE SPECIAL NEEDS COORDINATOR ASSIGNED TO THIS CASE.

2. The Decree of Dissolution further awarded Petitioner and Respondent the joint physical and legal custody of the minor child.

3. The Decree of Dissolution awarded Respondent as support for said child the sum of $_____ per month.

4. The Decree of Dissolution further ordered Petitioner to pay maintenance to Respondent.

5. The Decree of Dissolution has not been modified.

6. Since the date of the original Decree of Dissolution was entered, there have been changed circumstances so substantial and continuing as to make the terms of said Decree of Dissolution unreasonable in regard to the children. As a result of such changed circumstances, a modification of the Decree of Dissolution is necessary to serve the best interests of the parties.

7. The changed circumstances include but are not limited to the following:

    _____.

8. Petitioner requests the court award sole physical and legal custody of the minor child to him due to the change of circumstances listed above.

9. Petitioner requests the visitation schedule originally ordered be modified as follows:

    _____.

10. Petitioner is unable to provide the ordered child support originally ordered due to the change of circumstances listed above.

11. Petitioner is unable to provide maintenance to Respondent.

12. Petitioner is presently employed by _____.

13. Respondent is presently employed by _____.

14. As a result of the above, all of which involve a substantial and continuing change of conditions and circumstances, the Petitioner prays that a new Order be entered by this Court.

WHEREFORE, Petitioner prays that the Court enter an Order modifying the Decree of Dissolution to award visitation as stated above to serve the best interests of the minor child; to decrease the child support paid by Petitioner, retroactive to the date of the service of this Motion, to a sum which is reasonable in light of the above-described changes in conditions and circumstances; awarding custody of the minor child to Petitioner; to decrease the award of maintenance paid by Petitioner; and further Ordering that in all other respects, the Court's Order entered _____, 20___, shall remain in full force and effect; and for such further Orders as to this Court shall seem just and proper.

_____
Attorney for Petitioner

STATE OF _____   )
) SS
COUNTY OF _____   )

Comes now Paul Jones, Petitioner, being first duly sworn according to law, and states that he has read the foregoing Motion to Modify and states that the facts contained therein are true and correct according to his best knowledge, information and belief.

Subscribed and sworn to before me this _____ day of _____, 20____.

Notary Public

My commission expires: _____

References

American Psychiatric Association (2000) Diagnostic and Statistical Manual of Mental Disorders DSM-IV-TR (4th edn). Washington, DC: American Psychiatric Association.

Ball, S. (2002) *Children with Special Needs in Divorce.* Colorado Springs, CO: Sunni Ball, Domestic Relations Program Manager, CASA of Colorado Springs, 701 S. Cascade Ave., Colorado Springs 80903.

Barham, V., Devlin, R. A. and LaCasse, C. (2000) "Are the new child-support guidelines 'adequate' or 'reasonable'?" *Canadian Public Policy—Analyse de Politiques 26,* 1, 1–15.

Dube, S., Felitti, V., Dong, M., Chapman, D., Giles, W. and Anda, R. (2003) "Childhood abuse, neglect, and household dysfunction and the risk of illicit drug use: The adverse childhood experiences study." *Pediatrics 111,* 3, 564–572.

Hagan, Jr., J. (2001) "Commentary: The new morbidity: Where the rubber hits the road, or the practitioner's guide to the new morbidity." *Pediatrics 108,* 5, 1206–1210.

Hillis, S., Anda, R., Dube, S., Felitti, V., Marchbanks, P. and Marks, J. (2004) "The association between adverse childhood experience and adolescent pregnancy, long-term psychosocial consequences, and fetal death." *Pediatrics 113,* 2, 320–327.

Individuals with Disabilities Education Improvement Act (IDEA) of 1997, amended in 2004 (Pub. L. No. 108–446).

Jennings, S. (2005) "Autism in children and parents: Unique considerations for family court professionals." *Family Court Review 43,* 4, 582–595.

Johnson, B., Grossman, D., Connell, F. and Koepsell, T. (2000) "High-risk periods for childhood injury among siblings." *Pediatrics 105,* 3, 562–568.

Kaufman, F., Halvorson, M. and Carpenter, S. (1999) "Association between diabetes control and visits to a multidisciplinary pediatric diabetes clinic." *Pediatrics 103,* 5, 948–951.

Kraus, M. (2005) "Planning is important even when life doesn't go the way we plan." *Family Court Review 43,* 4, 607–611.

Martinez-Gonzalez, M., Gual, P., Lahortiga, F., Alonso, Y., Irala-Estevez, J. and Cervera, S. (2003) "Parental factors, mass media influences, and the onset of eating disorders in a prospective population-based cohort." *Pediatrics 111,* 2, 315–320.

Meyers, M., Lukemeyer, A. and Smeeding, T. (1996) *Welfare, and the Burden of Disability: Caring for Special Needs of Children in Poor Families. Income Security Policy Series* (Paper no. 12). Syracuse, NY: Center for Policy Research, Maxwell School of Citizenship and Public Affairs, Syracuse University.

Msall, M., Avery, R., Tremont, M., Lima, J., Rogers, M. and Hogan, D. (2003) "Functional disability and school activity limitations and 41,300 school-age children: Relationship to medical impairments." *Pediatrics 111*, 3, 548–553.

Newacheck, P., Strickland, B., Shonkoff, J., Perrin, J. *et al.* (1998) "An epidemiological profile of children with special health care needs." *Pediatrics 102*, 1, 117–123.

O'Connor, T., Davies, L., Dunn, J., Golding, J., the ALSPAC Study Team from the Social Genetic and Developmental Psychiatry Research Centre, Institute of Psychiatry, King's College, London, United Kingdom, and the Institute of Child Health, University of Bristol, Bristol, United Kingdom (2000) "Distribution of accidents, injuries, and illness by family types." *Pediatrics 106*, 5, 68–78.

Perryman, H. (2005) "Parental reaction to the disabled child: Implications for family courts." *Family Court Review 43*, 4, 596–606.

Saposnek, D. (2005) Editorial preface to special issue of *Family Court Review. Family Court Review 43*, 4, 563–565.

Sneed, R., May, W. and Stencel, C. (2000) "Training of pediatricians in care of physical disabilities in children with special health needs: Results of a two-state survey of practicing pediatricians and national resident training programs." *Pediatrics 105*, 3, 554–561.

Tanner, J.L. and Committee of Psychosocial Aspects of Child and Family Health (2002) "Parental separation and divorce: Can we provide an ounce of prevention?" *Pediatrics 110*, 5, 1007–1009.

Title V of the Social Security Act (42 USC 7, Subchapter V §§701–710 (1989).

Wertlieb, D. (2003) "Converging trends in family research and pediatrics: Recent findings for the American Academy of Pediatrics Task Force on the Family, Tufts University Center for Children and the Elliott-Pearson Department of Child Development, Tufts University, Medford, Massachusetts." *Pediatrics 111*, 6, 1572–1587.

Williams, P., Storm, D., Montepiedra, G., Nichols, S. *et al.* for the PACTG (Pediatric AIDS Clinical Trials Group) 219C Team (2006) "Predictors of adherence to antiretroviral medications in children and adolescents with HIV infection." *Pediatrics 118*, 6, 1745–1757.

Bibliography

There are thousands of books on the various types of special needs. Attorneys and judges need to educate themselves properly when handling special needs cases, but they do not have time to read thousands of books. The following is a list of suggested books by subject. This is not an endorsement of any of these books or of the ideas expressed in them. You must evaluate each book and its contents for yourself. This list suggests books on many, but not all of the topics in this book. No slight was intended by not including every subject. There are many more books that can easily be found at the bookstore, library or online.

ADD/ADHD

100 Questions and Answers about Your Child's Attention Deficit Hyperactivity Disorder, Ruth D. Nass, Fern Leventhal, Jones and Bartlett Publishers, Inc. (2005)

Attention Deficits and Hyperactivity in Children and Adults: Diagnosis, Treatment, and Management (2nd edn), Pasquale Accardo, editor, Informa Healthcare (1999)

Driven To Distraction: Recognizing and Coping with Attention Deficit Disorder from Childhood Through Adulthood (Reprint Edition), Edward M. Hallowell, John J. Ratey, Touchstone (1995)

Taking Charge of ADHD: The Complete, Authoritative Guide for Parents (Revised Edition), Russell A. Barkley, The Guilford Press (2000)

Teaching Teens with ADD and ADHD: a Quick Reference Guide for Teachers and Parents, Chris A. Zeigler Dendy, M.D., Woodbine House (2000)

The ADHD Book of Lists: A Practical Guide for Helping Children and Teens with Attention Deficit Disorders, Sandra F. Rief, M.A., Jossey-Bass (2003)

ALLERGIES AND ASTHMA

American Academy of Pediatrics Guide to Your Children's Allergies and Asthma: Breathing Easy and Bringing up Healthy, Active Children, Michael J. Welch, M.D., Villard (2000)

Asthma: the Complete Guide to Integrative Therapies, Jonathan Brostoff, M.D., Linda Gamlin, Healing Arts Press (2000)

Breathe Easy!: A Teen's Guide to Allergies and Asthma, Jean Ford, Mason Crest Publishers (2005)

Understanding and Managing Your Child's Food Allergies (A Johns Hopkins Press Health Book), Scott H. Sicherer, M.D., The Johns Hopkins University Press (2006)

Autism/Asperger's Syndrome

Asperger's Syndrome: A Guide for Parents and Professionals, Tony Attwood, Jessica Kingsley Publishers (1998)

Emergence: Labeled Autistic, Temple Grandin, Margaret M. Scariano, Arena Press, Warner Books (1986)

Overcoming Autism, Lynn Kern, Ph.D., Claire Lazebnik, Penguin (2004)

Raising a Child with Autism: A Guide to Applied Behavior Analysis for Parents, Shira Richman, Jessica Kingsley Publishers (2001)

Bipolar

New Hope for Children and Teens with Bipolar Disorder: Your Friendly, Authoritative Guide to the Latest in Traditional and Complementary Solutions, Boris Birmaher, M.D., Three Rivers Press (2004)

Parenting a Bipolar Child: What to Do and Why, Gianni L. Faedda, Nancy B. Austin, New Harbinger Publications (2006)

The Bipolar Child: The Definitive and Reassuring Guide to Childhood's Most Misunderstood Disorder (3rd edn), Demitri Papolos, M.D., Janice Papalos, Broadway (2007)

The Bipolar Disorder Survival Guide: What You and Your Family Need to Know, David J. Miklowitz, Guilford Press (2002)

The Bipolar Teen: What You Can Do to Help Your Child and Your Family, David J. Miklowitz, Ph.D, Elizabeth L. George, Ph.D., The Guilford Press (2007)

Blindness and Visual Impairment

Blindness and Early Childhood Development, David H. Warren, American Foundation for the Blind (1977)

Children with Visual Impairments: A Guide for Parents (2nd edn), M. Cay Holbrook, editor, Woodbine House (2006)

Cognitive Development in Blind Children, Sara Begum, Discovery Publishing House (2003)

How to Thrive, Not Just Survive: A Guide to Developing Independent Life Skills for Blind and Visually Impaired Children and Youths, Rose-Marie Swallow, author, Kathleen Mary Huebner, editor, American Foundation for the Blind (1987)

Cancer

Childhood Cancer: A Handbook from St. Jude Children's Research Hospital, Joseph Mirro, M.D., R. Grant Steen, Ph.D, Da Capo Press (2000)

Childhood Cancer—A Medical Dictionary, Bibliography, and Annotated Research Guide to Internet References, ICON Health Publications (2004)

Childhood Cancer: A Parent's Guide to Solid Tumor Cancers (2nd edn), Honna James-Hodder, Nancy Keene, Patient Centered Guidance (2002)

Childhood Cancer: Information for the Patient and Family, (2nd edn), Ronald D. Barr, Mary Crockett, Susan Dawson, Marilyn Eves, Anthony Whitton, John Wiernikowski, BC Decker Inc. (2001)

Childhood Cancer: Understanding and Coping, Henry Ekert, Informa Healthcare (1989)

Communication Disorders in Childhood Cancer, Bruce E. Murdoch, editor, Whurr Publishers (1999)

Living with Childhood Cancer: A Practical Guide to Help Families Cope, Leigh A. Woznick, Carol D. Goodheart, American Psychological Association (APA) (2001)

Pediatric Oncology (M. D. Anderson Cancer Care Series), Ka Wah Chan, Jr., editor, R. Beverly Raney, editor, Springer Publishing (2005)

CELIAC DISEASE

Celiac Disease: A Guide to Living with Gluten Intolerance, Sylvia Llewellyn Bower, author, Mary Kay Sharrett, contributor, Steve Plogsted, contributor, Demos Medical Publishing (2006)

Celiac Disease: A Hidden Epidemic, Peter H. R. Green, M.D., Rory Jones, Williams Morrow (2006)

Kids with Celiac Disease: A Family Guide to Raising Happy, Healthy, Gluten-Free Children, Danna Korn, Woodbine House (2001)

The GF Kid: A Celiac Disease Survival Guide, Melissa London, Woodbine House (2005)

CEREBRAL PALSY

Cerebral Palsy: A Complete Guide for Caregiving (A Johns Hopkins Press Health Book) (2nd edn), Freeman Miller, Steven J. Bachrach, The Johns Hopkins University Press (2006)

Children with Cerebral Palsy: A Manual for Therapists, Parents and Community Workers (2nd edn), Archie Hinchcliffe, Sage Publications Pvt. Ltd. (2007)

Children with Cerebral Palsy: A Parents' Guide (2nd edn), Elaine Geralis, editor, Woodbine House (1998)

Handling the Young Child with Cerebral Palsy at Home (3rd revised edn), Nancie R. Finnie, Butterworth-Heinemann (1997)

CHILD ABUSE

A Parent's and Teacher's Handbook on Identifying and Preventing Child Abuse, James A. Montelcone, G.W. Medical Publishing, Inc. (1998)

A Sourcebook on Child Sexual Abuse, David Finkelhor, Sage Publications, Inc. (1986)

Child Abuse and Culture: Working with Diverse Families, Lisa Aronson Fontes, The Guilford Press (2008)

Child Abuse and Neglect: Guidelines for Identification, Assessment and Case Management, Marilyn S. Peterson, editor, Michael Durfee, M.D., editor, Kevin Coulter, editor, Volcano Press (2003)

Child Abuse, Gender and Society (Routledge Research in Gender and Society), Jacqueli Turton, Routledge (2007)

Child Sexual Abuse Curriculum for the Developmentally Disabled, Sol R. Rappaport, Sandra A. Burkhardt, Anthony F. Rotatori, C.C. Thomas Publishing (1997)

Child Sexual Abuse: Disclosure, Delay, and Denial, Margaret-Ellen Pipe, editor, Michael E. Lamb, editor, Yael Orbach, editor, Ann-Christin Cederborg, editor, Lawrence Eribaum Publishing (2007)

Understanding Child Abuse and Neglect (7th edn), Cynthia Crosson-Tower, Allyn & Bacon (2007)

CHRONIC ILLNESS

Chronic Illness in Children: An Evidence-Based Approach, Laura L. Hayman, editor, Margaret M. Mahon, editor, J. Rick Turner, editor, Springer Publishing Company (2002)

Chronic Illness in Children and Adolescents, Ronald T. Brown, Brian P. Daly, Annette U. Rickel, Hogrefe & Huber Publishing (2007)

Cognitive Aspects of Chronic Illness in Children, Ronald T. Brown, editor, The Guilford Press (1999)

Coping With Your Child's Chronic Illness, Alesia T. Singer, Robert D. Reed Publishers (1999)

In Sickness and in Play: Children Coping With Chronic Illness, Cindy Dell Clark, Rutgers University Press (2003)

CROHN'S DISEASE

Learning Sickness: A Year with Crohn's Disease, Jim Lang, Capital Books (2004)

Managing Your Child's Crohn's Disease and Ulcerative Colitis, Keith J. Benkov, M.D., Harland S. Winter, M.D., Mastermedia Publishing Company (1996)

The Angry Gut: Coping with Colitis and Crohn's Disease, W. Grant Thompson, M.D., Da Capo Press (1993)

The First Year—Crohn's Disease and Ulcerative Colitis: An Essential Guide for the Newly Diagnosed, Jill Sklar, Manuel Sklar, Da Capo Press (2007)

CYSTIC FIBROSIS

Cystic Fibrosis: A Guide for Patient and Family, (3d ed), David M. Orenstein, editor, Lippincott Williams and Wilkins (2003)

Cystic Fibrosis: Everything You Need to Know, Wayne Kepron, Firefly Books (2004)

Cystic Fibrosis: The Ultimate Teen Guide, Melanie Ann Apel, The Scarecrow Press, Inc. (2006)

Understanding Cystic Fibrosis, Karen Hopkin, University Press of Mississippi (1998)

DEAFNESS AND HEARING IMPAIRMENT

Deafness in Childhood, Freeman McConnell, University of Illinois Press (1967)

IDEA Advocacy for Children Who Are Deaf or Hard-of-Hearing: A Question and Answer Book for Parents and Professionals, Bonnie P. Tucker, Singular (1997)

Keys to Raising a Deaf Child, Virginia Frazier-Malwald, Lenore M. Williams, Barron's Educational Series (1999)

Raising and Educating a Deaf Child: A Comprehensive Guide to the Choices, Controversies, and Decisions Faced by Parents and Educators (2d ed), Marc Marschark, Oxford University Press, USA (2007)

The Young Deaf or Hard of Hearing Child: A Family-Centered Approach to Early Education, Barbara Bodner-Johnson, editor, Marilyn Sass-Lehrer, editor, Brookes Publishing Company (2003)

Understanding Childhood Deafness, Wilhma Rae Quinn, Thorsons Publishers (1996)

DEPRESSION

Growing up Sad: Childhood Depression and Its Treatment, Leon Cytryn, M.D., Donald H. McKnew, M.D., W.W. Norton & Co. (1998)

Handbook of Depression in Children and Adolescents, John R.Z. Abela, editor, Benjamin L. Hankin, editor, The Guilford Press (2007)

Raising a Moody Child: How to Cope with Depression and Bipolar Disorder, Mary A. Fristad, Ph.D, Jill S. Goldberg Arnold, PhD, The Guilford Press (2003)

Stress and Depression in Children and Teenagers, Vicki Maud, Sheldon Press (2003)

Understanding Teenage Depression: A Guide to Diagnosis, Treatment and Management, Maureen Empfield, Nicholas Bakalar, Owl Books (2001)

DEVELOPMENTAL DISORDERS

A Parent's Guide to Developmental Delays: Recognizing and Coping with Missed Milestones in Speech, Movement, Learning, and Other Areas, Laurie Fivozinsky LeComer, Perigee Trade (2006)

Cognition in Children (Developmental Psychology), Usha Goswami, Psychology Press (1998)

Development and Disabilities: Intellectual, Sensory and Motor Impairments, Robert M. Hodapp, Cambridge University Press (1998)

Developmentally Delayed Children (Child Psychology) (3d ed), Wain K. Brown, William Gladden Press (2008)

Manual of Developmental and Behavioral Problems in Children (Pediatric Habilitation), Vidya Gupta, Informa Healthcare (1999)

Pervasive Developmental Disorders: Diagnosis, Options, and Answers, Mitzi Waltz, Future Horizons (2003)

DIABETES

Growing Up With Diabetes: What Children Want Their Parents to Know, Alicia McAuliffe, Wiley (1998)

Parenting a Child with Diabetes: A Practical, Empathetic Guide to Help You and Your Child Live with Diabetes (2nd edn), Gloria Loring, McGraw-Hill (1999)

Practical Endocrinology and Diabetes in Children, (2nd edn), Joseph E. Raine, Malcolm D.C. Donaldson, John W. Gregory, Martin O. Savage, Raymond L. Hintz, Wiley-Blackwell (2006)

The Everything Parent's Guide to Children with Juvenile Diabetes: Reassuring Advice for Managing Symptoms and Raising a Happy, Healthy Child, Moira McCarthy, author, Jake Kushner, M.D., contributor, Adams Media Corp. (2007)

Type 1 Diabetes in Children, Adolescents, and Young Adults: How to Become an Expert on Your Own Diabetes (3rd edn), Dr. Ragnar Hanas, Class Pub. (2007)

Understanding Insulin-Dependent Diabetes, H. Peter Chase, Childrens Diabetes Foundation (2000)

DOWN SYNDROME

Communication Skills in Children With Down Syndrome: A Guide for Parents, Libby Kumin, Woodbine House (1994)

Fine Motor Skills in Children With Down Syndrome: A Guide for Parents and Professionals, Maryanne Bruni, Woodbine House (1998)

Gross Motor Skills in Children With Down Syndrome: A Guide for Parents and Professionals, Patricia C. Winders, Woodbine House (1997)

Understanding Down Syndrome: An Introduction for Parents, Cliff Cunningham, Brookline Books (1996)

DRUG AND ALCOHOL ABUSE AND ADDICTION

Children of Addiction: Research, Health, and Public Policy Issues, H. Fitzgerald, Garland Science Publishing (2002)

Drug Addiction and Families, Marina Barnard, Fergal Keane, Jessica Kingsley Publishers (2006)

Etiology of Substance Use Disorder in Children and Adolescents: Emerging Findings from the Center for Education and Drug Abuse Research, Center for Education and Drug Abuse Research, corporate author, Ralph E. Tarter, editor, Michael M. Vanyukov, editor, Routledge Publishing (2002)

Impact of Substance Abuse on Children and Families: Research and Practice Implications (Haworth Social Work Practice), Shulamith Lala Ashenberg Straussner, editor, Christine Huff Fewell, editor, Routledge Publishing (2006)

On the Rocks: Teens and Alcohol, David Aretha, Franklin Watts Publishing (2007)

Our Children Are Alcoholics: Coping with Children Who Have Addictions, Sally B. and David B., Islewest Publishing (1997)

DYSLEXIA

How to Reach and Teach Children and Teens with Dyslexia: A Parent and Teacher Guide to Helping Students of All Ages Academically, Socially, and Emotionally, Cynthia M. Stowe, Jossey-Bass Publishing (2000)

Supporting Children with Dyslexia, Learning Service, David Fulton Publishing (2004)

The Everything Parent's Guide to Children with Dyslexia: All You Need to Ensure Your Child's Success (Everything: Parenting and Family) Abigail Marshall, Adams Media Corp. (2004)

The Secret Life of the Dyslexic Child: How she thinks. How he feels. How they can succeed, Robert Frank, Kathryn E. Livingston, Rodale Books (2004)

EATING DISORDERS AND OBESITY

A Parent's Guide to Eating Disorders and Obesity (The Children's Hospital of Philadelphia Series), Martha Moraghan Jablow, C. Everett Koop, Dell Publishing (1991)

Children and Adolescent Obesity: Causes and Consequences, Prevention and Management, Walter Burniat, editor, Tim J. Cole, editor, Inge Lissau, editor, Elizabeth M.E. Poskitt, editor, Cambridge University Press (2006)

Eating Disorders: A Guide for Families and Children (Guide for Families), Valerie Eisbree, author, Sarah Mountbatten-Windsor Duchess of York, Foreword, Merit Publishing International (2007)

Eating Disorders in Children and Adolescents (Cambridge Child and Adolescent Psychiatry), Brett McDermott, author, Tony Jaffa, editor, Cambridge University Press (2006)

Handbook of Childhood and Adolescent Obesity (Issues in Clinical Child Psychology), Elissa Jeialian, editor, Ric G. Steele, editor, Springer Publishing (2008)

EPILEPSY AND SEIZURES

Children with Seizures: A Guide for Parents, Teachers, and Other Professionals, Martin L. Kutscher, M.D., author, Gregory L. Holmes, Foreword, Jessica Kingsley Publishers (2006)

Epilepsy in Childhood and Adolescence (2nd edn), R. E. Appleton, John Gibbs, Taylor & Francis (1998)

Growing Up with Epilepsy: A Practical Guide for Parents, Lynn Bennett Blackburn, Demos Medical Publishing (2003)

Pediatric Epilepsy: Diagnosis and Therapy (3rd edn), John M. Pellock, M.D., editor, Blaise F.D. Bourgeois, M.D., editor, W. Edwin Dodson, editor, Douglas R. Nordill, Jr., M.D., editor, Raman Sankar, editor, Demos Medical Publishing (2007)

Seizures and Epilepsy in Childhood: A Guide, (3rd edn), John H. Freeman, Eileen P.G. Vining, Diana J. Pillas, The Johns Hopkins University Press (2002)

FETAL ALCOHOL SYNDROME

Alcohol, Pregnancy and the Developing Child: Fetal Alcohol Syndrome, Hans-Ludwig Spohr, editor, Hans-Christoph Steinhausen, editor, Cambridge University Press (1996)

Finding Perspective…Raising Successful Children Affected by Fetal Alcohol Spectrum Disorders, Liz Lawryk, OBD Triage Institute Inc. (2005)

Reaching out to Children with FAS/FAE: A Handbook for Teachers, Counselors, and Parents Who Live and Work with Children Affected by Fetal Alcohol Syndrome, Diane Davis, Center for Applied Research in Education (1994)

Recognizing and Managing Children with Fetal Alcohol Syndrome/Fetal Alcohol Effects: A Guidebook, Brenda McCreight, Ph.D., Child Welfare League of America Press (1997)

FRAGILE X SYNDROME

Children with Fragile X Syndrome: A Parents' Guide, Jayne Dixon Weder, editor, Woodbine House (2000)

Educating Children with Fragile X Syndrome: A Multi-Professional View, D. Dew-Hughes, RoutledgeFalmer (2003)

Fragile X Syndrome: Diagnosis, Treatment, and Research (Johns Hopkins Series in Contemporary Medicine and Public Health) (3rd edn), Randi Jenssen Hagerman, editor, Paul J. Hagerman, editor, The Johns Hopkins University Press (2002)

Supporting Children with Fragile X Syndrome, Hull Learning Service, David Fulton Publishing (2004)

HEADACHES AND MIGRAINES

Frequently Asked Questions about Migraines and Headaches (FAQ: Teen Life Set 6), Allan B. Cobb, Rosen Publishing Group (2008)

Headache and your Child: The Complete Guide to Understanding and Treating Migraine and Other Headaches in Children and Adolescents, Seymour Diamond, M.D., Amy Diamond, Fireside (2001)

Headaches and Migraine (Your Child), Maggie Jones, Robson Books Ltd. (2002)

Headaches and Migraines in Childhood, Charles F. Barlow, Cambridge University Press (1991)

HEART DISORDERS AND DISEASE

Encyclopedia of Heart Diseases, M. Gabriel Kahn, Academic Press (2005)

Heart Defects in Children: What Every Parent Should Know, Cheryl J. Wild, Wiley (1998)

The Heart of a Child: What Families Need to Know about Heart Disorders in Children (Johns Hopkins Press Health Book) (2nd edn), Catherine A. Neill, Edward B. Clark, Carleen Clark, The Johns Hopkins University Press (2001)

The Parent's Guide to Children's Congenital Heart Defects: What They Are, How to Treat Them, How to Cope with Them, Gerri Freid Kramer, author, Shari Maurer, author, Sylvester Stallone, Foreword, Three Rivers Press (2001)

HIV/AIDS

Children and HIV/AIDS, Gary Anderson, editor, Constance Ryan, editor, Transaction Publishers (1999)

Children and the HIV/AIDS Crisis: Youth Who Are Infected and Affected, Carrie McVicker, Youth Advocate Program International (1999)

Children, Families, and HIV/AIDS: Psychosocial and Therapeutic Issues, Nancy Boyd-Franklin, editor, Gloria L. Steiner, editor, Mary G. Boland, editor, The Guilford Press (1995)

School Children with HIV/AIDS: Quality of Life Experiences in Public Schools, Jillian Roberts, author, Kathleen Cairns, contributor, Detselig Enterprises Ltd. (1999)

HODGKIN'S DISEASE

Hodgkin Lymphoma, (2nd edn) Richard T. Hoppe, editor, Peter M. Mauch, editor, James O. Armitage, editor, Volker Diehl, editor, Lawrence M. Weiss, editor, Lippincott Williams and Wilkins (2007)

Hodgkin's and Non-Hodgkin's Lymphoma, John P. Leonard, Morton Coleman, Springer (2006)

Hodgkin's Disease (Diseases and Disorders), Sheila Wyborny, Lucent Books (2008)

The Official Parent's Sourcebook on Childhood Hodgkin's Disease: A Revised and Updated Directory for the Internet Age, ICON Health Publications (2002)

INDIVIDUALIZED EDUCATION PLANS

IEP and Inclusion Tips for Parents and Teachers Handout Version, Anne I. Eason, Kathleen Whitbread, IEP Resources, Attainment Company (2006)

Nolo's IEP Guide: Learning Disabilities (3rd edn), Lawrence M. Siegel, NOLO (2007)

The Complete IEP Guide: How to Advocate for Your Special Ed. Child (5th edn), Lawrence M. Siegel, NOLO (2007)

Understanding, Developing, and Writing Effective IEPs: A Step-by-Step Guide for Educators, Roger Pierangelo, George A. Guiliani, Corwin Press (2007)

INTELLECTUAL DISABILITY

Educating Mentally Retarded Children, R. K. Shah, Aavishkar Publishers and Distributors (2004)

Mental Retardation and Developmental Delay: Genetic and Epigenetic Factors (Oxford Monographs on Medical Genetics), Moyra Smith, Oxford University Press, USA (2005)

Teacher of Children with Retarded Mental Development, Jack Rudman, National Learning Corp. (1997)

The Mentally Retarded Child, Abraham Levinson, Greenwood Press Reprint (1978)

KIDNEY AND LIVER DISEASE

ABC of Kidney Disease (ABC Series), David Goldsmith, editor, Satish Jayawardene, editor, Penny Ackland, editor, BMJ Books (2007)

A Parent's Guide to Kidney Disorders (University of Minnesota Guides to Birth and Childhood Disorders), Glenn H. Bock, M.D., Edward J. Ruley, M.D., Michael P. Moore, University Of Minnesota Press (1993)

Kidney Disorders in Children and Adolescents: A Practical Handbook, Ronald J. Hogg, editor, Informa Healthcare (2006)

Liver Disease in Children (3rd edn), Frederick J. Suchy, editor, Ronald J. Sokol, editor, William F. Balistreri, editor, Cambridge University Press (2007)

Pediatric Nephrology (Avner, Pediatric Nephrology), Ellis D. Avner, editor, William E. Harmon, editor, Patrick Niaudet, editor, Lippincott Williams and Wilkins (2003)

LEARNING DISABILITIES

College and Career Success for Students with Learning Disabilities, Roslyn Dobler, McGraw-Hill (1996)

Learning Disabilities: A to Z: A Parent's Complete Guide to Learning Disabilities from Preschool to Adulthood, Corinne Smith, Lisa Strick, Free Press (1999)

Learning Disabilities: From Identification to Intervention, Jack M. Fletcher, G. Reid Lyon, Lynn S. Fuchs, Marcia A. Barnes, The Guilford Press (2006)

Learning Disabilities Information for Teens, Sandra Augustyn Lawton, Omnigraphics, Inc. (2005)

Parenting Children with Learning Disabilities, Jane Utley Adelizzi, Diane B. Goss, Bergin and Garvey Trade (2001)

Surviving Learning Disabilities Successfully: 16 rules For Managing a Child's Learning Disabilities, Nancy E. Graves, Danielle E. Graves, iUniverse, Inc. (2007)

The Misunderstood Child: Understanding and Coping with Your Child's Learning Disabilities, Larry B. Silver, M.D., Three Rivers Press (1998)

Leukemias, Lymphomas and Myelomas

100 Q & A About Leukemia (2nd edn), Edward D. Ball, Jones and Bartlett Publishers, Inc. (2007)

Childhood Leukemia: A Guide for Families, Friends and Caregivers (3rd edn), Nancy Keene, Patient Centered Guides (2002)

Childhood Leukemias (2nd edn), Ching-Hon Pui, editor, Cambridge University Press (2006)

Pediatric Lymphomas (Pediatric Oncology), Howard J. Weinstein, editor, Melissa M. Hudson, editor, Michael P. Link, editor, Springer Publishing (2007)

Understanding Leukemias, Lymphomas and Myelomas, Tarig Mughal, John M. Goldman, Sabena Mughal, Informa Healthcare (2005)

Multiple Disabilities

Including Children with Severe and Multiple Disabilities in Typical Classrooms: Practical Strategies for Teachers (2nd edn), June Downing, Joanne Eichinger, Maryann Demchak, Paul H. Brookes Publishing Company (2001)

Supporting the Children with Multiple Disabilities (2nd edn), Michael Mednick, Continuum International Publishing Group (2007)

Teaching Individuals with Physical or Multiple Disabilities (5th edn), Sherwood J. Best, Kathryn W. Heller, June L. Bigge, Prentice-Hall (2004)

Understanding Physical, Health, and Multiple Disabilities (2nd edn), Kathryn Wolff Heller, Paula E. Forney, Paul A. Alberto, Sherwood J. Best, Morton N. Schwartzman, Prentice Hall (2008)

Multiple Sclerosis

Multiple Sclerosis: A Guide for Families (2nd edn), Rosalind C. Kalb, Ph.D., Demos Medical Publishing (1998)

Multiple Sclerosis: Diagnosis, Medical Management, and Rehabilitation, Jack S. Burks, M.D., Kenneth P. Johnson, M.D., Demos Medical Publishing (2000)

Multiple Sclerosis Q & A: Researching Answers to Frequently Asked Questions, Beth Ann Hill, Avery (2003)

The First Year: Multiple Sclerosis: an Essential Guide for the Newly Diagnosed, Margaret Blackstone, author, Sadiq A. Saud, M.D., Foreword, Marlowe & Co. (2002)

Muscular/Neuromuscular

Muscular Dystrophy in Children: A Guide for Families, Irwin M. Siegel, Demos Medical Publishing (1999)

Neuromuscular Diseases of Infancy, Childhood, and Adolescence (A Clinician's Approach), H. Royden Jones, Darryl De Vivo, Basil T. Darras, Butterworth-Heinemann (2002)

Occupational Therapy and Duchenne Muscular Dystrophy, Kate Stone, Claire Tester, Joy Blakeney, Alex Howarth, Heather McAndrew, Nicola Traynor, Mary McCutcheon, Ruth Johnston, Wiley (2007)

Raising a Child with a Neuromuscular Disorder: A Guide for Parents, Grandparents, Friends and Professionals, Charlotte Thompson, M.D., Oxford University Press (1999)

PREGNANCY

Books, Babies, and School-Age Parents: How to Teach Pregnant and Parenting Teens to Succeed, Jeannie Warren Lindsay, Ph.D., Sharon Githens Enright, Morning Glory Press (1997)

Preteen and Teenage Pregnancy: A Twenty-First Century Reality, June L. Leishman, M&K Publishing (2007)

The Unplanned Pregnancy Book for Teens and College Students, Dorrie Williams-Wheeler, Sparkledoll Productions (2004)

Your Pregnancy & Newborn Journey: A Guide for Pregnant Teens (2nd edn), Jeannie Warren Lindsay, Ph.D., Jean Brunelli, Morning Glory Press (2004)

PSYCHIATRIC/PSYCHOLOGICAL

Childhood Schizophrenia, Sheila Cantor, The Guilford Press (1988)

Helping Your Troubled Teen: Learn to Recognize, Understand, and Address the Destructive Behavior of Today's Teens and Preteens, Cynthia Kaplan, Ph.D., Blaise Aguirre, M.D., Michael Rater, M.D., Fair Winds Press (2007)

Should I Medicate My Child? Sane Solutions for Troubled Kids with—and without—-Psychiatric Drugs, Lawrence H. Diller, M.D., Basic Books (2003)

The American Psychiatric Publishing Textbook of Child and Adolescent Psychiatry (3rd edn), Jerry M. Wiener, Mina K. Dulcan, American Psychiatric Publishing, Inc. (2003)

The Handbook of Psychiatric Drug Therapy for Children and Adolescents, Karen A. Theesen, PharmD., Haworth Press (1997)

SENSORY

Raising a Sensory Smart Child: The Definitive Handbook for Helping Your Child with Sensory Integration Issues, Lindsey Biel, Nancy Peske, Penguin (2005)

Sensory Integration and the Child: 25th Anniversary Edition, A. Jean Ayres, Western Psychological Services (2005)

The Out-of-Sync Child: Recognizing and Coping with Sensory Integration Dysfunction, Carol Stock Kranowitz, Larry B. Silver (Foreword), Perigree, Penguin Group (2005)

Too Loud, Too Bright, Too Fast, Too Tight: What to Do If You Are Sensory Defensive in an Overstimulating World, Sharon Heller, Harper (2003)

SEXUAL ASSAULT

21st Century Complete Medical Guide to Sexual Assault, Rape, Teen Sexual Violence… Progressive Management Medical Health News, Author, Progressive Management (2004) (CD ROM)

Overcoming Childhood Sexual Trauma: A Guide to Breaking through the Wall of Fear for Practitioners and Survivors, Sheri Oz, Sarah-Jane Ogiers, Routledge (2006)

Sexual Assault of Children and Adolescents, Ann Wolbert Burgess, Lexington Books (1978)

The Trauma of Sexual Assault: Treatment, Prevention and Practice, Jenny Petrak, Barbara Hedge, Wiley (2002)

SEXUALLY TRANSMITTED DISEASES

Color Atlas and Synopsis Of Sexually Transmitted Diseases (2nd edn), H. Hunter Handsfield, M.D., McGraw-Hill Professional (2000)

Sexual Health Information for Teens: Health Tips about Sexual Development, Human Reproduction, and Sexually Transmitted Diseases, Deborah A. Stanley, Omnigraphics, Inc. (2003)

Staying Safe: A Teen's Guide to Sexually Transmitted Diseases, Miranda Hunter, William Hunter, Mason Crest Publishers (2004)

The Real Truth about Teens and Sex: From Hooking Up to Friends with Benefits——What Teens Are Thinking, and Doing, and Talking about, and How to Help Them Make Smart Choices, Sabrina Weill, Perigree Trade (2005)

What Every Parent Should Know about Teen Sex: The Secret STD Epidemic, Becky Ettinger, Xulon Press (2007)

SICKLE CELL ANEMIA

Comprehensive Handbook of Childhood Cancer in Sickle Cell Disease: A Biopsychosocial Approach, Ronald T. Brown, Oxford University Press, USA (2006)

Sickle Cell Anemia, Lizabeth Peak, Lucent Books (2007)

Sickle Cell Anemia: What Does It Mean to Have? (3d ed), Louise Spilbury, Heinemann Library (2005)

Understanding Sickle Cell Disease, Miriam Bloom, Ph.D., University Press of Mississippi (1995)

SPECIAL NEEDS—GENERAL

A Difference in the Family: Living With a Disabled Child (reprint edition), Helen Featherstone, Penguin (1981)

A Matter of Dignity: Changing the World of the Disabled, Andrew Potok, Bantam (2002)

Adopting the Hurt Child: Hope for Families with Special-Needs Kids: A Guide for Parents and Professionals (revised & updated edition), Gregory C. Keck, Regina M. Kupecky, Navpress Publishing Group (1998)

Children With Special Needs in Early Childhood Settings, Carol L. Paasche, Lola Gorrill, Bev Strom, Thomson Delmar Learning (2003)

Disability is Natural, Kathie Snow, Braveheart Press (2001)

Parenting Through Crisis: Helping Kids in Times of Loss, Grief and Change, Barbara Coloroso, Collins (2001)

Quirky Kids; Understanding and Helping Your Child Who Doesn't Fit In—When to Worry and When Not to Worry, Perri Klass, Eileen Costello, Ballantine Books (2004)

The Child With Special Needs: Encouraging Intellectual and Emotional Growth, Stanley I. Greenspan, et al., Perseus Books (1998)

The Early Intervention Dictionary: A MultiDisciplinary Guide to Terminology, Jeanine G. Coleman, Woodbine House (1993)

Uncommon Voyage: Parenting a Special Needs Child (2nd edn), Laura Shapiro Kramer, author, Seth Kramer, foreword, North Atlantic Books (2001)

Views From Our Shoes: Growing Up With a Brother or Sister With Special Needs, Donald J. Meyer, Woodbine House (1997)

SPECIAL NEEDS TRUSTS

Special Needs Trust Administration Manual: A Guide for Trustees, Barbara D. Jackins, Richard S. Blank, Peter M. Macy, Ken W. Shulman, Harriet H. Onello, People with Disabilities Press Series (2005)

Tax, Estate, and Lifetime Planning for Minors, Carmina Y. D'Aversa, American Bar Association (2006)

The Basics of Special Needs Planning: Protecting Your Clients Who Need the Most Protection (Audio CD Package), Harry S. Margolis, Vincent J. Russo, American Bar Association (2007)

Third-Party and Self-Created Trusts: Planning for the Elderly and Disabled Client (3rd edn), Clifton B. Kruse, Jr., American Bar Association (2002)

SPEECH AND LANGUAGE IMPAIRMENTS

Childhood Speech, Language and Listening Problems: What Every Parent Should Know (2nd edn), Patricia McAleer Hamaguchi, Wiley (2001)

Children with Specific Language Impairment, Laurence B. Leonard, The MIT Press (2000)

Preschool Language Disorders Resource Guide: Specific Language Impairment, Amy L. Weiss, Singular (2001)

Speech and Language Impairments in Children: Causes, Characteristics, Intervention and Outcome, Dorothy Bishop, Psychology Press (2001)

SPINA BIFIDA

Caring for the Child with Spina Bifida: Shriners Hospitals for Children, John F. Sarwak, M.D., American Academy of Orthopedic Surgeons (2002)

Children With Spina Bifida: A Parent's Guide, Marlene Lutkenhoff, Woodbine House (1999)

Living with Spina Bifida: A Guide for Families and Professionals, Adrian Sandler, M.D., The University Of North Carolina Press (2003)

Spinabilities: A Young Person's Guide to Spina Bifida, Marlene Lutkenhoff, Sonya G. Oppenheimer, Woodbine House (1997)

SUICIDE

Aftershock: Help, Hope, and Healing in the Wake of Suicide, Arrington Cox, David Candy, B & H Publishing Group (2003)

Let's Talk Facts About Teen Suicide: Healthy Minds, Healthy Lives, American Psychiatric Association, author, American Psychiatric Publishing, Inc. (2005)

Teen Suicide, Judith Peacock, LifeMatters (2000)

The Power to Prevent Suicide: A Guide for Teens Helping Teens, Richard E. Nelson, Ph.D., Free Spirit Publishing (1994)

When Nothing Matters Anymore: A Survival Guide for Depressed Teens, Bev Cobain, author, Peter S. Jensen, Foreword, Free Spirit Publishing (2007)

TERMINALLY ILL CHILDREN

Loss and Grief Recovery: Help Caring for Children with Disabilities, Chronic or Terminal Illness, Joyce Ashton, Dennis Ashton, Baywood Publishing Company (1996)

Supporting the Child and the Family in Pediatric Palliative Care, Erica Brown, author, Brian Warr, author, Sheila Shribman, Foreword, Jessica Kingsley Publishers (2007)

The Private Worlds of Dying Children, Myra Bluebond-Langner, Princeton University Press (1980)

When Children Die: Improving Palliative and End-Of-Life Care for Children and Their Families, Committee on Palliative and End of Life Care for Children and Their Families, author, Marilyn J. Field, editor, Richard E. Behrman, editor, National Academies Press (2003)

TRAUMA

An Adult's Guide to Childhood Trauma, Sharon Lewis, David Phillips Publishers (2000)

Childhood Trauma: Your Questions Answered, Ursula Markham, Element Books (1998)

Effects of Interventions for Childhood Trauma from Infancy through Adolescence: Pain Unspeakable, Sandra B. Hutchison, Routledge (2004)

Handbook for Treatment of Attachment-Trauma Problems in Children, Beverly James, Free Press (1994)

The Trauma Spectrum: Hidden Wounds and Human Resiliency, Robert C. Scaer, W.W. Norton & Co. (2005)

Too Scared to Cry: Psychic Trauma in Childhood (reprint edition), Lenore Terr, Basic Books (1992)

Trauma and Sexuality: The Effects of Childhood Sexual, Physical, and Emotional Abuse on Sexual Identity and Behavior, James A. Chu, M.D., editor, Elizabeth S. Bowman, M.D., editor, Informa Healthcare (2003)

Treating Trauma and Traumatic Grief in Children and Adolescents, Judith A. Cohen, Anthony P. Mannarino, Esther Deblinger, The Guilford Press (2006)

TRAUMATIC BRAIN INJURY

Children With Traumatic Brain Injury: A Parent's Guide, Lisa Schoenbrodt (editor), Woodbine House (2001)

Traumatic Brain Injury in Children and Adolescents: A Sourcebook for Teachers and Other School Personnel (2nd edn), Janet Tyler, Mary Mira, Pro-Ed (1999)

Traumatic Brain Injury in Children and Adolescents: Assessment and Intervention, Margaret Semrud-Clikeman, The Guilford Press (2001)

Traumatic Brain Injury Rehabilitation: Children and Adolescents (2nd edn), Mark Ylvisaker, Butterworth-Heinemann

Resources

The best thing you can do as the parent of a child with special needs is to educate yourself. Arm yourself with information, and you will get better results when advocating for your child. The internet is an invaluable resource where you can obtain information at any hour of the day or night. All websites were accessed in February 2010, but websites change frequently, new resources are created and existing websites change names or terminate. This information is fluid, but it should give you sufficient information to get started.

NATIONAL RESOURCES

There are various national information resources. I suggest the two following resources:

United Cerebral Palsy One Stop Resource Guide

Website: www.ucp.org

Don't let the name fool you. This directory contains valuable information on service providers, agencies and local chapters for *many* types of disabilities in addition to cerebral palsy. United Cerebral Palsy created this excellent directory because most of the people they serve have a disability in addition to cerebral palsy. It is a state-by-state directory of resources for persons with disabilities, including: abuse, aging, ADA (Americans with Disabilities Act), assistive technology, AIDS, Alzheimer's, Attention Deficit Disorder, autism, augmentative communication, brain injury, cerebral palsy, cystic fibrosis, developmental disabilities, disability organizations, domestic violence, Down syndrome, early intervention, Easter Seals, education, employment, epilepsy, federal agencies, federal government (including legislators), Goodwill, Habitat for Humanity, healthcare, housing, independent living, intellectual disability, learning disabilities, hearing impairments, legal, mental heath, multiple sclerosis, parent organizations, Prader-Willi, respite, sexual assault, speech and hearing, spina bifida, spinal cord injury, sports/recreation, state government information (including legislators), transition, transportation, veterans, and visual impairments, among others.

National Dissemination Center for Children with Disabilities (NICHCY)

NICHCY
P.O. Box 1492
Washington, DC 20013
Phone: (800) 695–0285 (Voice/TTY)
Fax: (202) 884–8441
Email: nichcy@aed.org
Website: www.nichcy.org

This site provides information on disabilities from birth through childhood, as well as on special education law and educational practices. This agency is also known as NICHCY, and provides information to help you find state chapters of disability organizations and parent groups, and to find state agencies that serve persons with disabilities. It compiles extensive information on websites of many agencies and organizations, states, governors, and U.S. senators.

NICHCY is an invaluable resource for authoritative information on specific disabilities and provides additional resources in print and video. The specific disabilities are: Attention Deficit Hyperactivity Disorder (ADHD), autism/pervasive developmental disorders, cerebral palsy, deafness/hearing loss, Down syndrome, emotional disturbance, epilepsy, intellectual disability, learning disabilities, reading and learning disabilities, severe and/or multiple disabilities, speech—language impairments, spina bifida, traumatic brain injury and visual impairments. NICHCY has extensive additional online information on ADHD, autism, and learning disabilities.

This is just a brief overview of the vast quantity of helpful materials to be found on the NICHCY website. The state resources alone are over 200 pages. Navigate throughout their immense website and get extremely useful information to advocate for your child.

STATE RESOURCES

Many state resources can be found in the United Cerebral Palsy One Stop Resource Guide and on the NICHCY website. In addition to those, I recommend checking the following resources:

State departments of education

Much of the law on the rights of disabled or special needs children arose in the area of education. State departments of education have valuable information on the rights of children with disabilities, which you can use to advocate for your child in his or her schooling, and to advocate for your child's rights in other areas, such as in the family courts. The state departments of education are:

ALABAMA STATE DEPARTMENT OF EDUCATION
5158 Gordon Person Building
P.O. Box 302101–2101
Montgomery, AL 36130–2101
Phone: (334) 242–9731

ALASKA DEPARTMENT OF EDUCATION
801 West 10th Street, Suite 200
Juneau, AK 99801–1894
Phone: (907) 465–8679

ARIZONA DEPARTMENT OF EDUCATION
1535 West Jefferson Street, Bin 32
Phoenix, AZ 85007
Phone: (602) 542–7466

ARKANSAS DEPARTMENT OF EDUCATION
4 Capitol Mall, Room 404A
Little Rock, AR 72201
Phone: (501) 682–4227

CALIFORNIA DEPARTMENT OF EDUCATION
1430 N Street, Suite 3600, 3rd Floor
Sacramento, CA 95814
Phone: (916) 327–0187

COLORADO DEPARTMENT OF EDUCATION
201 East Colfax Avenue
Denver, CO 80203
Phone: (303) 866–6838

CONNECTICUT STATE DEPARTMENT OF EDUCATION
165 Capitol Avenue, Room 355
Hartford, CT 06145
Phone: (860) 713–6871

DELAWARE DEPARTMENT OF EDUCATION
P.O. Box 1402
Dover, DE 19903
Phone: (302) 739–4663

DISTRICT OF COLUMBIA PUBLIC SCHOOLS
825 North Capitol Street, NE, 9th Floor
Washington, DC 20002–1994
Phone: (202) 576–7718

FLORIDA DEPARTMENT OF EDUCATION
325 West Gaines Street, Suite 852
Tallahassee, FL 32399–0400
Phone: (850) 245–0400

GEORGIA DEPARTMENT OF EDUCATION
205 Jessie Hill Jr. Drive, Suite 1954
Atlanta, GA 30334
Phone: (404) 657–7634

HAWAII DEPARTMENT OF EDUCATION
3633 Waialae Avenue, Building C, Rm. C210
Honolulu, HI 96816–3299
Phone: (808) 832–5880

IDAHO DEPARTMENT OF EDUCATION
650 West State Street
Boise, ID 83720–0027
Phone: (208) 332–6853

ILLINOIS STATE BOARD OF EDUCATION
100 North First Street
Springfield, IL 62777–0001
Phone: (217) 782–3950

INDIANA DEPARTMENT OF EDUCATION
State House, Room 229
Indianapolis, IN 46204–2798
Phone: (317) 232–0540

IOWA DEPARTMENT OF EDUCATION
Grimes State Office Building
Des Moines, IA 50319–0146
Phone: (515) 281–5286

KANSAS STATE DEPARTMENT OF EDUCATION
120 SE 10th Avenue
Topeka, KS 66612–1182
Phone: (785) 296–3204

KENTUCKY DEPARTMENT OF EDUCATION
17th Floor Capitol Plaza Tower, Room 1701
500 Mero Street
Frankfort, KY 40601
Phone: (502) 564–5279

LOUISIANA DEPARTMENT OF EDUCATION
P.O. Box 94064
Baton Rouge, LA 70804–9064
Phone: (225) 342–0091

MAINE DEPARTMENT OF EDUCATION
State House, Station 23
Augusta, ME 04333–0023
Phone: (207) 624–6790

MARYLAND DEPARTMENT OF EDUCATION
200 West Baltimore Street
Baltimore, MD 21201
Phone: (410) 767–0310

MASSACHUSETTS DEPARTMENT OF EDUCATION
350 Main Street, 3rd Floor
Malden, MA 02148
Phone: (781) 338–3532

MICHIGAN DEPARTMENT OF EDUCATION
P.O. Box 30008
Lansing, MI 48909
Phone: (517) 373–3921

MINNESOTA DEPARTMENT OF CHILDREN, FAMILIES AND LEARNING
1500 Highway 36W—N13
Roseville, MN 55113–4266
Phone: (651) 582–8253

MISSISSIPPI DEPARTMENT OF EDUCATION
P.O. Box 771
Jackson, MS 39205–3499
Phone: (601) 359–3499

MISSOURI DEPARTMENT OF EDUCATION
P.O. Box 480
Jefferson City, MO 65102–0480
Phone: (573) 526–6949

MONTANA OFFICE OF PUBLIC INSTRUCTION
P.O. Box 202501
Helena, MT 59620–2501
Phone: (406) 444–6712

NEBRASKA DEPARTMENT OF EDUCATION
P.O. Box 94987
301 Centennial Mall South
Lincoln, NE 68509–4987
Phone: (412) 471–2487

NEVADA DEPARTMENT OF EDUCATION
700 East Fifth Street
Carson City, NV 89701
Phone: (775) 687–9175

NEW HAMPSHIRE DEPARTMENT OF EDUCATION
State Office Park South
101 Pleasant Street
Concord, NH 03301
Phone: (603) 271–3876

NEW JERSEY DEPARTMENT OF EDUCATION
100 Riverview Plaza
Trenton, NJ 086625
Phone: (609) 292–8904

NEW MEXICO STATE DEPARTMENT OF EDUCATION
Education Building
613 Don Gaspar
Santa Fe, NM 87501–2786
Phone: (505) 827–6538

NEW YORK STATE EDUCATION DEPARTMENT
Education Building, Room 301
Albany, NY 1223
Phone: (518) 474–5213

NORTH CAROLINA DEPARTMENT OF PUBLIC INSTRUCTION
6334 Mail Service Center
Raleigh, NC 27699–6334
Phone: (919) 807–3754

NORTH DAKOTA DEPARTMENT OF PUBLIC INSTRUCTION
600 East Boulevard Avenue
Bismarck, ND 58505–0440
Phone: (701) 328–4886

OHIO DEPARTMENT OF EDUCATION
25 South Front Street, Mail Stop 708
Columbus, OH 43215–4183
Phone: (614) 466–4161

OKLAHOMA DEPARTMENT OF EDUCATION
2500 North Lincoln Boulevard
Oklahoma City, OK 73105
Phone: (405) 521–3812

OREGON DEPARTMENT OF EDUCATION
Public Service Building
255 Capitol Street, N.E.
Salem, OR 97310–0203
Phone: (503) 378–3600 Ext. 2634

PENNSYLVANIA DEPARTMENT OF EDUCATION
333 Market Street, 14th Floor
Harrisburg, PA 17126–0333
Phone: (717) 783–6752

RHODE ISLAND DEPARTMENT OF EDUCATION
Sheppard Building
255 Westminster Street
Providence, RI 02903
Phone: (401) 222–4600 Ext. 2241

SOUTH CAROLINA DEPARTMENT OF EDUCATION
1206 Ruttledge Building
1429 Senate Street
Columbia, SC 29201
Phone: (803) 734–8262

SOUTH DAKOTA DEPARTMENT OF EDUCATION AND CULTURAL AFFAIRS
700 Governors Drive
Pierre, SD 57501–2291
Phone: (605) 773–4748

TENNESSEE DEPARTMENT OF EDUCATION
Andrew Johnson Tower, 5th Floor
710 James Robertson Parkway
Nashville, TN 37243
Phone: (615) 532–6297

TEXAS EDUCATION AGENCY
171 North Congress Avenue
Austin, TX 78701–1494
Phone: (512) 475–3523

UTAH STATE OFFICE OF EDUCATION
250 East 500 South
P.O. Box 144200
Salt Lake City, UT 84114–4200
Phone: (801) 538–7802

VERMONT DEPARTMENT OF EDUCATION
120 State Street
Montpelier, VT 05620
Phone: (802) 828–0477

VIRGINIA DEPARTMENT OF EDUCATION
P.O. Box 2120
Richmond, VA 23218–2120
Phone: (804) 225–2025

WASHINGTON DEPARTMENT OF EDUCATION
600 Washington Street, SE
Olympia, WA 98502
Phone: (360) 725–6261

WEST VIRGINIA DEPARTMENT OF EDUCATION
1900 Kanawha Blvd. East
Building 6, Room 330
Charleston, WV 25305
Phone: (304) 558–7805

WISCONSIN DEPARTMENT OF PUBLIC INSTRUCTION
125 South Webster Street
P.O. Box 7841
Madison, WI 53707–7841
Phone: (608) 266–2803

WYOMING DEPARTMENT OF EDUCATION
Hathaway Building
2300 Capital Avenue, 2nd Floor
Cheyenne, WY 82002–0050
Phone: (307) 777–6245

State councils on developmental disabilities

These councils are funded through federal grants (Subtitle B of the Developmental Disabilities Assistance and Bill of Rights Act of 2000–DD Act). These agencies are valuable for people advocating for children with disabilities.

ALABAMA

Alabama State Council for Developmental Disabilities
RSA Union Building
100 North Union Street
P.O. Box 301410
Montgomery, AL 36130–1410
Phone: (334) 242–3973, (800) 846–3735 (Toll Free)
Fax: (334) 242–0797
Website: www.acdd.org

ALASKA

Governor's Council on Disabilities and Special Education
3601 C Street, Suite 740 (physical address)
P.O. Box 240249 (mailing address)
Anchorage, AK 99524–0249
Phone: (907) 269–8990
Fax: (907) 269–8995
Website: www.hss.state.ak.us/gcdse

ARIZONA

Governor's Council on Developmental Disabilities
3839 North 3rd Street, Suite 306
Phoenix, AZ 85012
Phone: (602) 277–4986, (866) 771–9378 (Toll Free), (602) 277–4949 (TTY)
Fax: (602) 277–4454
Email: gcdd@azdes.gov
Website: www.azgcdd.org

ARKANSAS

Governor's Developmental Disabilities Planning Council
Freeway Medical Tower
5800 West 10th Street, Suite 805
Little Rock, AR 72204
Phone: (501) 661–2589, (501) 661–2736 (TDD)
Fax: (501) 661–2399
Website: www.ddcouncil.org

CALIFORNIA

California State Council on Developmental Disabilities
1507 21st Street, Suite 210
Sacramento, CA 95814
Phone: (916) 322–8481, (916) 324–8420 (TDD)
Fax: (916) 443–4957
Website: www.scdd.ca.gov

COLORADO

Colorado Developmental Disabilities Council
3401 Quebec Street, Suite 6009
Denver, CO 80207
Phone: (720) 941–0176
Fax: (720) 941–8490
Website: www.coddc.org

CONNECTICUT

Connecticut Council on Developmental Disabilities
460 Capitol Avenue
Hartford, CT 06106–1308
Phone: (860) 418–6160, (800) 653–1134 (Toll Free), (860) 418–6172 (TTY)
Fax: (860) 418–6003
Email: Maggie.carr@po.state.ct.us
Website: www.state.ct.us/ctcdd

DELAWARE

State of Delaware Developmental Disabilities Council
Margaret M. O'Neill Building, 2nd Floor
410 Federal Street, Suite 2
Dover, DE 19901
Phone: (302) 739–3333, (800) 273–9500 (Toll Free out-of-state), (800) 464-HELP (Toll Free in-state)
Fax: (302) 739–2015
Website: http://ddc.delaware.gov

FLORIDA

Florida Developmental Disabilities
Council
124 Marriott Drive, Suite 203
Tallahassee, FL 32301–2981
Phone: (850) 488–4180, (800) 580–
7801 (Toll Free), (850) 488–0956 (TDD)
Fax: (850) 922–6702
Website: www.fddc.org

GEORGIA

Governor's Council on Developmental
Disabilities for Georgia
2 Peachtree St NW, Suite 8–210
Atlanta, GA 30303
Phone: (404) 657–2126, (404) 657–
2133 (TDD)
Fax: (404) 657–2132
Website: www.gcdd.org

HAWAII

Hawaii State Planning Council on
Developmental Disabilities
919 Ala Moana Blvd., Suite 113
Honolulu, HI 96814
Phone: (808) 586–8100
Fax: (808) 586–7543
Email: council@hiddc.org
Website: www.hiddc.org

IDAHO

Idaho State Council on Developmental Disabilities
802 W. Bannock St., Suite 308
Boise, ID 83702–0280
Phone: (208) 334–2178, (800) 544–
2433 (Toll Free, Idaho only), (208)
334–2179 (TDD)
Fax: (208) 334–3417
Website: www.state.id.us/icdd

ILLINOIS

Illinois Council on Developmental
Disabilities
100 West Randolph, Suite 10–600
Chicago, IL 60601
Phone: (217) 782–9696
Fax: (217) 524–5339
Website: www.state.il.us/agency/icdd

INDIANA

Governor's Planning Council for De-
velopmental Disabilities
150 West Market Street, Suite 628
Indianapolis, IN 46204
Phone: (317) 232–7770
Fax: (17) 232–3712
Website: www.in.gov/gpcpd

IOWA

Governor's Developmental Disabilities
Council
617 East Second Street
Des Moines, IA 50309
Phone: (515) 281–9083, (800) 452–
1936 (Toll Free)
Fax: (515) 281–9087
Website: http://idaction.com

KANSAS

Kansas Council on Developmental
Disabilities
Docking State Office Building
915 S. W. Harrison, Room 141
Topeka, KS 66612–1570
Phone: (785) 296–2608
Fax: (785) 296–2861
Website: www.kcdd.org

KENTUCKY

Kentucky Developmental Disabilities
Council
100 Fair Oaks Lane, 4th Floor
Frankfort, KY 40621 0001
Phone: (502) 564–7841, (877) 367–
5332 (Toll Free)
Fax: (502) 564–9826
Website: http://chfs.ky.gov/kcdd

LOUISIANA

Louisiana State Planning Council on
Developmental Disabilities
647 Main Street
Baton Rouge, LA 70802
Phone: (225) 342–6804
Fax: (225) 342–1970
Website: www.laddc.org

MAINE

Maine Developmental Disabilities
Council
139 State House Station
Augusta, ME 04333–0139
Phone: (207) 287–4213
Fax: (207) 287–8001
Website: www.MaineDDC.org

MARYLAND

Maryland Developmental Disabilities
Council
217 East Redwood Street, Suite 1300
Baltimore, MD 21202
Phone: (410) 767–3670
Fax: (410) 333–3686
Email: info@md-council.org
Website: www.md-council.org

MASSACHUSETTS

Massachusetts Developmental Dis-
abilities Council
1150 Hancock Street, 3rd Floor
Quincy, MA 02169
Phone: (617) 770–7676, (617) 770–
9499 (TDD)
Fax: (617–770–1987
Website: www.mass.gov/mddc

MICHIGAN

Michigan Developmental Disabilities
Council
Lewis Cass Building, 6th Floor
Lansing, MI 48913
Mailing Federal Express, UPS, etc. use
zip code 48933
Regular mail use zip code 48913
Phone: (517) 334–6123, (517) 334–
7354 (TDD)
Fax: (517) 334–7353
Website: www.michigan.gov/ddcouncil

MINNESOTA

Governor's Council on Developmental
Disabilities
Minnesota Department of Administration
370 Centennial Office Building
658 Cedar Street
St. Paul, MN 55155

Phone: (651) 296–4018, (877) 348–
0505 (Toll Free), (651) 296–9962
(TDD)
Fax: (651) 297–7200
Email: admin.dd@state.mn.us
Website: www.mnddc.org

MISSISSIPPI

Developmental Disabilities Council
1101 Robert E. Lee Building
239 North Lamar Street
Jackson, MS 39201
Phone: (601) 359–1270, (601) 359–
6230 (TDD)
Fax: (601) 359–6295
Website: www.cdd.ms.gov

MISSOURI

Missouri Council for Developmental
Disabilities
P.O. Box 687
1706 E. Elm Street
Jefferson City, MO 65102
Phone: (573) 751–8611, (800) 500–
7878 (Toll Free), (573) 751–8611
(TDD)
Fax: (573) 526–2755
Website: www.mpcdd.com

MONTANA

Montana DD Planning Council
P.O. Box 526
Helena, MT 59624
Phone: (406) 443–4332
Fax: (406) 443–4192
Website: www.mtcdd.org

NEBRASKA

Nebraska Planning Council on Devel-
opmental Disabilities
Department of Health and Human
Services
301 Centennial Mall, South
P.O. Box 95044
Lincoln, NE 68509–5044
Phone: (402) 471–2330, (402) 471–
9570 (TDD)
Fax: (402) 471–0383
Website: www.hhs.state.ne.us/ddplan-
ning

NEVADA

Office of Disability Services
Department of Human Resources
3656 Research Way, Suite 32
Carson City, NV 89706
Phone: (775) 687–4452, (775) 687–
3388 (TDD)
Fax: (775) 687–3292
Website: www.nevadaddcouncil.org

NEW HAMPSHIRE

New Hampshire DD Council
The Concord Center, Unit 315
10 Ferry Street
Concord, NH 03301–5004
Phone: (603) 271–3236, (800) 735–
2964 (Toll Free TDD)
Fax: (603) 271–1156
Email: nhddcncl@aol.com
Website: www.nhddc.com

NEW JERSEY

New Jersey DD Council
20 West State Street
P.O. Box 700
Trenton, NJ 08625–0700
Phone: (609) 292–3745
Fax: (609) 292–7114
Email: njddc@njddc.org
Website: www.njddc.org

NEW MEXICO

New Mexico DD Council
435 St. Michael's Drive, Building D
Santa Fe, NM 87505
Phone: (505) 827–7590
Fax: (505) 827–7589
Website: www.nmddpc.com

NEW YORK

New York State DD Council
155 Washington Avenue, 2nd Floor
Albany, NY 12210
Phone: (518) 486–7505, (800) 395–
3372 (Toll Free), (518) 486–7505
(TDD)
Fax: (518) 402–3505
Website: www.ddpc.state.ny.us

NORTH CAROLINA

North Carolina Council on Developmental Disabilities
3801 Lake Boone Trail, Suite 250
Raleigh, NC 27607
Phone: (919) 420–7901, (800) 357–
6916 (Toll Free)
Fax: (919) 420–7917
Website: www.nc-ddc.org

NORTH DAKOTA

State Council on Developmental Disabilities
North Dakota Department of Human Services
600 East Boulevard Avenue
Bismarck, ND 58505–0250
Phone: (701) 328–8953
Fax: (701) 328–8969
Website: www.ndcpd.org/uapdis/
home.html/index.shtml

OHIO

Ohio Developmental Disabilities
Planning Council
8 Long Street, 12th Floor
Columbia, OH 43215
Phone: (614) 466–5205, (614) 644–
5530 (TDD)
Fax: (614) 466–0298
Website: www.ohio.gov/ddc

OKLAHOMA

Street Address:
Oklahoma DD Council
2401 Northwest 23rd Street, Suite 74
Oklahoma City, OK 73107–2431

Mailing Address:
P.O. Box 25352
Oklahoma City, OK 73125
Phone: (405) 521–4966, (800) 836–
4470 (Toll Free), (405) 521–4984
(TDD)
Fax: (405) 521–4910
Website: www.okddc.org

OREGON

Oregon Council on Developmental
Disabilities
540 24th Place, NE
Salem, OR 97301–4517
Phone: (503) 945–9942, (800) 292–
4154 (Toll Free)
Fax: (503) 945–9947
Email: ocdd@ocdd.org
Website: www.ocdd.org

PENNSYLVANIA

Pennsylvania DD Council
569 Forum Building
Commonwealth Avenue
Harrisburg, PA 17120–0001
Phone: (717) 787–6057
Fax: (717) 772–0738
Website: www.paddc.org

PUERTO RICO

Puerto Rico DD Council
P.O. Box 9543
Santurce, PR 00908–0543
Phone: (787) 722–0595
Fax: (787) 721–3622
Email: prced@prtc.net

RHODE ISLAND

Rhode Island DD Council
400 Bald Hill Road, Suite 515
Warwick, RI 02886
Phone: (401) 737–1238
Fax: (401) 737–3395
Email: riddc@riddc.org
Website: www.riddc.org

SOUTH CAROLINA

South Carolina DD Council
1205 Pendleton Street, Room 453C
Columbia, SC 29201–3731
Phone: (803) 734–0465, (803) 734–
1147 (TDD)
Fax: (803) 734–0241
Website: www.scddc.state.sc.us

SOUTH DAKOTA

South Dakota Council on Develop-
mental Disabilities
Hillsview Plaza, East Hwy 34
c/o 500 East Capital
Pierre, SC 57501–5070
Phone: (605) 773–6369, (605) 773–
5990 (TDD)
Fax: (605) 773–5483
Website: www.state.sd.us/dhs/ddc

TENNESSEE

Tennessee Council on Developmental
Disabilities
Andrew Jackson Building
500 Deaderick Street, Suite 1310
Nashville, TN 37243–0228
Phone: (615) 532–6615, (615) 741–
4562 (TDD)
Fax: (615) 532–6964
Website: www.state.tn.us/cdd

TEXAS

Street Address:
Texas Council for DD
6201 East Oltorf St., Suite 600
Austin, TX 78741
Mailing Address:
Texas Council for DD
4900 North Lamar Blvd.
Austin, TX 78751–2399
Phone: (512) 437–5432, (800) 262–
0334 (Toll Free), (512) 437–5431
(TDD)
Fax: (512) 437–5434
Email: tcdd@tcdd.state.tx.us
Website: www.txddc.state.tx.us

UTAH

Utah Developmental Disabities Council
155 South 300 West, Suite 100
Salt Lake City, UT 84101
Phone: (801) 533–3965, (800) 333–
8824 (Toll Free)
Fax: (801) 325–3968
Website: www.gcpd.org

VERMONT

Vermont DD Council
103 South Main Street
Waterbury, VT 05671–0206
Phone: (802) 241–2612
Fax: (802) 241–2989
Website: www.ahs.state.vt.us/vtddc/

VIRGINIA

Virginia Board for People with
Disabilities
Ninth Street Office Building
202 North 9th Street, 9th Floor
Richmond, VA 23219
Phone: (804) 786–0016, (800)
846–4464 (Toll Free TDD), (800)
846–4464 (TDD)
Fax: (804) 786–1118
Website: www.vaboard.org

WASHINGTON, DC

D.C. Developmental Disabilities Council
64 New York Avenue, NE, Room 6161
Washington, DC 20002
Phone: (202) 671–4490, (202) 671–
4491 (TDD)
Website: http://dhs.dc.gov

WASHINGTON STATE

Washington State DD Council
P.O. Box 48314
906 Columbia Street, SW
Olympia, WA 98504–8314
Phone: (360) 725–2870, (800) 634–
4473 (TDD)
Fax: (360) 586–2424
Website: www.wa.gov/ddc/

WEST VIRGINIA

West Virginia DD Council
110 Stockton Street
Charleston, WV 25312–2521
Phone: (304) 558–0416, (304) 558–
2376 (TDD)
Fax: (304) 558–0941
Website: www.wvddc.org

WISCONSIN

Wisconsin Board for People with De-
velopmental Disabilities
201 W. Washington Ave., Suite 110
Madison, WI 52703–2796
Phone: (608) 266–7826
Fax: (608) 267–3906
Website: www.wcdd.org

WYOMING

Wyoming Council on DD
122 West 25th Street
Herschler Bldg., 1st Floor, West
Cheyenne, WY 82202
Phone: (307) 777–7230, (800) 438–
5791 (Toll Free, in-state only), (307)
777–7230 (TDD)
Fax: (307) 777–5690
Website: http://ddcouncil.state.wy.us

NATIONAL ASSOCIATION OF STATE COUNCILS ON DEVELOPMENTAL DISABILITIES

225 Reinekers Lane, Suite 650
Alexandria, VA 22314
Phone: (703) 739–4400
Fax: (703) 739–6030
Email: info@nacdd.org
Website: www.nacdd.org

ADDITIONAL AGENCIES AND ORGANIZATIONS

Clearinghouses

This is a list of clearinghouses that will provide a great deal of information on specific special needs. This information is provided by the National Dissemination Center for Children with Disabilities. After the list of clearinghouses is a list of organizations that can be of great assistance to people working with children with special needs.

AUTISM INFORMATION CENTER
Centers for Disease Control and Prevention
1600 Clifton Road
Atlanta, GA 30333
Phone: (800) CDC-INFO (232–4636)
Email: bddi@cdc.gov
Website: www.cdc.gov/ncbddd/autism/index.html

CANCER INFORMATION SERVICE
National Cancer Institute
Room 3036A, 6116 Executive Blvd., MSC8322
Bethesda, MD 20892–8322
Phone: (800) 422–6237 (Voice),
(800) 332–8615 (TTY)
Email: cancergovstaff@mail.nih.gov
Website: http://cancer.gov
Materials available in Spanish, Spanish speaker on staff

CENTER ON POSITIVE BEHAVIORAL INTERVENTIONS AND SUPPORTS
1761 Alder Street, 1235 University of Oregon
Eugene, OR 97403–5262
Phone: (541) 346–2505
Email: pbis@uoregon.edu
Website: www.pbis.org
Materials available in Spanish

CLEARINGHOUSE ON DISABILITY INFORMATION
Office of Special Education and Rehabilitative Services, Communication & Media Services
Room 3132, Switzer Building, 330 C Street S.W.
Washington, DC 20202–2524
Phone: (202) 205–8241 (Voice),
(202) 205–0136 (TTY)

ERIC CLEARINGHOUSE ON DISABILITIES AND GIFTED EDUCATION
Council for Exceptional Children (CEC)
(Project is no longer in operation, but a substantial website of disability-related materials is still available.)
Website: www.eric.ed.gov

ERIC SYSTEM
Educational Resources Information Center
Phone: (800) 538–3742
Website: http://eric.ed.gov

FETAL ALCOHOL SPECTRUM DISORDERS (FASD) CENTER FOR EXCELLENCE
Center for Substance Abuse Prevention
Substance Abuse and Mental Health Services Administration
2101 Gaither Road, Ste. 600
Rockville, MD 20850
Phone: (866) 786–7327
Email via the webform at: www.fascenter.samhsa.gov/about/contactUs/index.cfm
Website: http://www.fascenter.samhsa.gov/index.cfm

GENETIC AND RARE DISEASES INFORMATION CENTER
P.O. Box 8126, Gaithersburg, MD 20898–8126
Phone: (888) 205–2311 (Voice),
(888) 205–3223 (TTY)
Email: gardinfo@nig.gov
Website: http://rarediseases.info.nih.gov/GARD
Spanish speaker on staff

HEATH RESOURCE CENTER (NATIONAL CLEARINGHOUSE ON POSTSECONDARY EDUCATION FOR INDIVIDUALS WITH DISABILITIES)

The George Washington University
2121 K Street N.W., Suite 220
Washington, DC 20037
Phone: (800) 544–3284 (V/TTY),
(202) 973–0904
Email: askheath@heath.gwu.edu
Website: www.heath.gwu.edu

HRSA INFORMATION CENTER (FOR PUBLICATIONS AND RESOURCES ON HEALTH CARE SERVICES FOR LOW-INCOME, UNINSURED INDIVIDUALS AND THOSE WITH SPECIAL HEALTHCARE NEEDS)

Health Resources and Services Administration, U.S. Department of Health and Human Services
Parklawn Building, 5600 Fishers Lane
Rockville, MD 20857
Phone: (888) 275–4772
Email: ask@hrsa.gov
Website: www.ask.hrsa.gov
Publications available in Spanish,
Spanish speaker on staff

LAURENT CLERC NATIONAL DEAF EDUCATION CENTER AND CLEARINGHOUSE

KDES PAS-6, 800 Florida Avenue, NE
Washington, DC 20002–3695
Phone: (202) 651–5051 (Voice),
(202) 651–5052 (TTY)
Email: Clearinghouse.InfoToGo@
gallaudet.edu
Website: http://clerccenter.gallaudet.
edu/InfoToGo

NATIONAL CENTER FOR PREPAREDNESS, DETECTION AND CONTROL OF INFECTIOUS DISEASES (NCPCID)

Centers for Disease Control and Prevention
Mailstop C-14, 1600 Clifton Road
Atlanta, GA 30333
Phone: (800) 232-4636
Website: www.cdc.gov/ncpdcid

NATIONAL CENTER ON BIRTH DEFECTS AND DEVELOPMENTAL DISABILITIES

Department of Health and Human Services, Centers for Disease Control and Prevention
1600 Clifton Road
Atlanta, GA 30333
Phone: (404) 639–3534, (800) 311–3435
Email: bddi@cdc.gov
Website: www.cdc.gov/ncbddd/

NATIONAL CENTER ON SECONDARY EDUCATION AND TRANSITION

University of Minnesota, 6 Pattee Hall, 150 Pillsbury Drive S.E.
Minneapolis, MN 55455
Phone: (612) 624–2097
Email: ncset@umn.edu
Website: www.ncset.org

NATIONAL CLEARINGHOUSE FOR ALCOHOL AND DRUG INFORMATION (NCADI)

P.O. Box 2345
Rockville, MD 20847–2345
Phone: (800) 729–6686, (877) 767–8432 (español), (301) 468–2600,
(800) 487–4899 (TTY)
Email: info@health.org
Website: www.health.org
Materials available in Spanish, Spanish speaker on staff

NATIONAL CONSORTIUM ON DEAF-BLINDNESS

345 N. Monmouth Avenue
Monmouth, OR 97361
Phone: (800) 438–9376 (Voice),
(800) 854–7013 (TTY)
Email: info@nationaldb.org
Website: www.nationaldb.org
Materials available in Spanish

NATIONAL DIABETES INFORMATION CLEARINGHOUSE

One Information Way
Bethesda, MD 20892
Phone: (800) 860–8747, (301)
654–3327
Email: ndic@info.niddk.nih.gov, or
via webform at: http://diabetes.niddk.
nih.gov/about/contact.htm
Website: http://diabetes.niddk.nih.
gov/about/index.htm
Materials available in Spanish

NATIONAL DIGESTIVE DISEASES INFORMATION CLEARINGHOUSE

Two Information Way
Bethesda, MD 20892
Phone: (800) 891–5389, (301)
654–3810
Email: nddic@info.niddk.nih.gov,
or via webform at: http://digestive.
niddk.nih.gov/about/contact.htm
Website: http://digestive.niddk.nih.
gov/about/index.htm
Materials available in Spanish

NATIONAL HEALTH INFORMATION CENTER

P.O. Box 1133
Washington, DC 20013–1133
Phone: (800) 336–4797, (301)
565–4167
Email: info@nhic.org
Website: www.health.gov/nhic/
Materials available in Spanish, Spanish
speaker on staff

NATIONAL HEART, LUNG, AND BLOOD INSTITUTE INFORMATION CENTER

P.O. Box 30105
Bethesda, MD 20824–0105
Phone: (800) 575–9355, (301) 592–
8573, (240) 629–3255 (TTY)
Email: NHLBIinfo@rover.nhlbi.nih.
gov
Website: www.nhlbi.nih.gov
Spanish speaker on staff

NATIONAL INSTITUTE OF ALLERGY AND INFECTIOUS DISEASES (NIAID)

31 Center Drive, MSC 2520, Build-
ing 31, Room 7A-50
Bethesda, MD 20892–2520
Phone: (301) 496–2263
Website: www.niaid.nih.gov

NATIONAL INSTITUTE OF ARTHRITIS AND MUSCULOSKELETAL AND SKIN DISEASES

Information Clearinghouse, 1 AMS
Circle
Bethesda, MD 20892–3675
Phone: (877) 226–4267, (301) 495–
4484 (Voice), (301) 565–2966 (TTY)
Email: NIAMSinfo@mail.nih.gov
Website: www.niams.nih.gov
Materials available in Spanish, Spanish
speaker on staff

NATIONAL INSTITUTE OF NEUROLOGICAL DISORDERS & STROKE (NINDS)

NIH Neurological Institute, P.O. Box
5801
Bethesda, MD 20824
Phone: (800) 352–9424, (301) 496–
5751, (301) 468–5981(TTY)
Email via webform at: www.ninds.nih.
gov/contact_us.htm
Website: www.ninds.nih.gov
Materials available in Spanish, Spanish
speaker on staff

NATIONAL INSTITUTE ON DEAFNESS AND OTHER COMMUNICATION DISORDERS CLEARINGHOUSE

31 Center Drive, MCS 2320
Bethesda, MD 20892–3456
Phone: (800) 241–1044 (Voice),
(800) 241–1055 (TTY)
Email: nidcdinfo@nidcd.nih.gov
Website: www.nidcd.nih.gov
Materials available in Spanish, Spanish
speaker on staff

NATIONAL INSTITUTE ON MENTAL HEALTH (NIMH)

Public Inquiries, 6001 Executive
Boulevard, Room 8184, MSC 9663
Bethesda, MD 20892–9663
Phone: (866) 615–6464, (301) 443–
4513 (Voice), (301) 443–8431 (TTY)
Email: nimhinfo@nih.gov
Website: www.nimh.nih.gov/publicat/
index.cfm
Materials available in Spanish, Spanish
speaker on staff

NATIONAL KIDNEY AND UROLOGIC DISEASES INFORMATION CLEARINGHOUSE

Three Information Way
Bethesda, MD 20892
Phone: (800) 891–5390, (301)
654–3327
Email: nkudic@info.niddk.nih.gov, or
via webform at: http://kidney.niddk.
nih.gov/about/contact.htm
Website: http://kidney.niddk.nih.
gov/about/index.htm
Materials available in Spanish

NATIONAL LEAD INFORMATION CENTER

422 South Clinton Avenue
Rochester, NY 14620
Phone: (800) 424–5323
Email via website
Website: www.epa.gov/lead/nlic.htm
Materials available in Spanish, Spanish
speaker on staff

NATIONAL ORGANIZATION FOR RARE DISORDERS (NORD)

P.O. Box 1968
Danbury, CT 06813–1968
Phone: (800) 999–6673, (203) 744–
0100 (Voice), (203) 797–9590 (TTY)
Email: orphan@rarediseases.org
Website: www.rarediseases.org

NATIONAL REHABILITATION INFORMATION CENTER (NARIC)

4200 Forbes Boulevard, Suite 202
Lanham, MD 20706
Phone: (800) 346–2742, (301) 459–
5900, (301) 459–5984 (TTY)
Email: naricinfo@heitechservices.com
Website: www.naric.com

RESEARCH AND TRAINING CENTER ON FAMILY SUPPORT AND CHILDREN'S MENTAL HEALTH

Portland State University, P.O. Box 751
Portland, OR 97207–0751
Phone: (503) 725–4040 (Voice),
(503) 725–4165 (TTY)
Email: gordon1@pdx.edu
Website: www.rtc.pdx.edu/
Materials available in Spanish, Spanish
speaker on staff

RESEARCH AND TRAINING CENTER ON INDEPENDENT LIVING

University of Kansas
4089 Dole Building, 1000 Sunnyside
Ave.
Lawrence, KS 66045–7555
Phone: (785) 864–4095 (Voice),
(785) 864–0706 (TTY)
Email: rtcil@ku.edu
Website: www.rtcil.org
Materials available in Spanish

WEIGHT-CONTROL INFORMATION NETWORK (WIN)

1 WIN Way
Bethesda, MD 20892–3665
Phone: (202) 828–1025, (877) 946–4627
Email: win@info.niddk.nih.gov
Website: http://win.niddk.nih.gov/index.htm

Organizations

ALEXANDER GRAHAM BELL ASSOCIATION FOR THE DEAF AND HARD OF HEARING

3417 Volta Place N.W.
Washington, DC 20007
Phone: (866) 337–5220, (202) 337–5220 (Voice), (202) 337–5221 (TTY)
Email: parents@agbell.org
Website: www.agbell.org
Materials available in Spanish, Spanish speaker on staff

ALLIANCE FOR TECHNOLOGY ACCESS

1304 Southpoint Blvd., Suite 240
Petaluma, CA 94954
Phone: (707) 778–3011, (707) 778–3015 (TTY)
Email: atainfo@ataccess.org
Website: www.ataccess.org

AMERICAN ASSOCIATION OF KIDNEY PATIENTS (AAKP)

3505 Frontage Road, Suite 315
Tampa, FL 33607
Phone: (800) 749–2257, (813) 636–8100
Email: info@aakp.org
Website: www.aakp.org
Materials available in Spanish, Spanish speaker on staff

AMERICAN ASSOCIATION OF SUICIDOLOGY (TO FIND A SUPPORT GROUP)

5221 Wisconsin Avenue, N.W.
Washington, DC 20015
Phone: (800) 273–8255, (202) 237–2280
Email: info@suicidology.org
Website: www.suicidology.org

AMERICAN BRAIN TUMOR ASSOCIATION

2720 River Road
Des Moines IA 60018
Phone: (847) 827–9910, (800) 886–2282 (patient services)
Email: info@abta.org
Website: www.abta.org/
One publication in Spanish

AMERICAN COUNCIL OF THE BLIND

1155 15th Street N.W., Suite 1004
Washington, DC 20005
Phone: (800) 424–8666, (202) 467–5081
Email: info@acb.orWebsite: www.acb.org

AMERICAN DIABETES ASSOCIATION

1701 N. Beauregard Street
Alexandria, VA 22311
Phone: (800) 342–2383, (703) 549–1500
Email: AskADA@diabetes.org
Website: www.diabetes.org
Materials available in Spanish, Spanish speaker on staff

AMERICAN FOUNDATION FOR THE BLIND (AFB)

11 Penn Plaza, Suite 300
New York, NY 10001
Phone: (800) 232–5463, (212) 502–7662 (TTY)
Email: afbinfo@afb.net
Website: www.afb.org
Materials available in Spanish, Spanish speaker on staff

AMERICAN HEART ASSOCIATION, NATIONAL CENTER

7272 Greenville Avenue
Dallas, TX 75231
Phone: (800) 242–8721, (214) 373–6300
Email: inquire@amhrt.org
Website: www.americanheart.org
Materials available in Spanish

AMERICAN LIVER FOUNDATION
75 Maiden Lane, Suite 603
New York, NY 10038
Phone: (800) 465–4872, (888) 443–
7872, (212) 668–1000
Email: info@liverfoundation.org
Website: www.liverfoundation.org
Materials available in Spanish

AMERICAN LUNG ASSOCIATION
61 Broadway, 6th Floor
New York, NY 10006
Phone: (800) 586–4872, (212)
315–8700
Email via website
Website: www.lungusa.org/
Materials available in Spanish, Spanish
speaker on staff

AMERICAN OCCUPATIONAL THERAPY ASSOCIATION (AOTA)
4720 Montgomery Lane, P.O. Box
31220
Bethesda, MD 20824–1220
Phone: (301) 652–2682 (Voice),
(800) 377–8555 (TTY)
Website: www.aota.org

AMERICAN PHYSICAL THERAPY ASSOCIATION (APTA)
1111 North Fairfax Street
Alexandria, VA 22314
Phone: (800) 999–2782, (703) 684–
2782 (Voice), (703) 683–6748 (TTY)
Email: practice@apta.org
Website: www.apta.org
Materials available in Spanish, Spanish
speaker on staff

AMERICAN SOCIETY FOR DEAF CHILDREN
P.O. Box 3355
Gettysburg, PA 17325
Phone: (800) 942–2732, (717) 334–
7922 (Voice/TTY)
Email: asdc@deafchildren.org
Website: www.deafchildren.org

AMERICAN SPEECH-LANGUAGE-HEARING ASSOCIATION (ASHA)
10801 Rockville Pike
Rockville, MD 20852
Phone: (800) 638–8255, (301) 897–
5700 (TTY)
Email: actioncenter@asha.org
Website: www.asha.org
Materials available in Spanish, Spanish
speaker on staff

AMERICAN SYRINGOMYELIA AND CHIARI ALLIANCE PROJECT
P.O. Box 1586
Longview, TX 75606–1586
Phone: (800) 272–7282, (903)
236–7079
Email: info@asap.org
Website: www.asap.org

AMERICAN THERAPEUTIC RECREATION ASSOCIATION
629 North Main Street
Hattiesburg, MS 39401
Phone: 601 450 2872
Email: national@atra-online.com
Website: http://atra-online.com

ANGELMAN SYNDROME FOUNDATION
3015 E. New York Street, Suite
A2265
Aurora, IL 60504
Phone: (805) 432–6435, (630)
978–4245
Email: info@angelman.org
Website: www.angelman.org
Materials available in Spanish

ANXIETY DISORDERS ASSOCIATION OF AMERICA
8730 Georgia Avenue, Suite 600
Silver Spring, MD 20910
Phone: (240) 485–1001
Email: AnxDis@adaa.org
Website: www.adaa.org

APLASTIC ANEMIA & MDS INTERNATIONAL FOUNDATION, INC.

P.O. Box 613
Annapolis, MD 21404–0613
Phone: (800) 747–2820, (410) 867–0242
Email: help@aamds.org
Website: www.aamds.org
Materials available in Spanish, Spanish speaker on staff

THE ARC (FORMERLY THE ASSOCIATION FOR RETARDED CITIZENS OF THE U.S.)

1010 Wayne Avenue, Suite 650
Silver Spring, MD 20910
Phone: (301) 565–3842
Email: Info@thearc.org
Website: www.thearc.org

ARCH NATIONAL RESPITE NETWORK & RESOURCE CENTER

Chapel Hill Training-Outreach Project, 800 Eastowne Drive, Suite 105
Chapel Hill, NC 27514
Phone: (800) 773–5433 (National Respite Locator Service), (919) 490–5577
Website: www.archrespite.org

ARTHRITIS FOUNDATION

P.O. Box 7669
Atlanta, GA 30357
Phone: (800) 568–4045, (404) 872–7100
Email: help@arthritis.org
Website: www.arthritis.org
Materials available in Spanish, Spanish speaker on staff

ASTHMA AND ALLERGY FOUNDATION OF AMERICA

1233 20th Street, N.W., Suite 402
Washington, DC 20036
Phone: (800) 727–8462, (202) 466–7643
Email: info@aafa.org
Website: www.aafa.org/
Materials available in Spanish

AUTISM SOCIETY OF AMERICA

7910 Woodmont Avenue, Suite 300
Bethesda, MD 20814–3015
Phone: (800) 328–8476, (301) 657–0881
Email: info@autism-society.org
Website: www.autism-society.org
Materials available in Spanish

BEACH CENTER ON DISABILITY

The University of Kansas
Haworth Hall, Room 3136, 1200 Sunnyside Avenue
Lawrence, KS 66045–7534
Phone: (785) 864–7600, (785) 864–3434 (TTY)
Email: beachcenter@ku.edu
Website: www.beachcenter.org

BEST BUDDIES INTERNATIONAL, INC.

100 S.E. Second Street, Suite 1990
Miami, FL 33131
Phone: (800) 892–8339, (305) 374–2233
Email: info@bestbuddies.org
Website: www.bestbuddies.org

BLIND CHILDRENS CENTER

4120 Marathon Street
Los Angeles, CA 90029–0159
Phone: (323) 664–2153, (800) 222–3566
Email: info@blindchildrenscenter.org
Website: www.blindchildrenscenter.org
Materials available in Spanish, Spanish speaker on staff

BRAIN INJURY ASSOCIATION OF AMERICA

8201 Greensboro Dr., Suite 611
McLean, VA 22102
Phone: (703) 761–0750, (800) 444–6443
Email: FamilyHelpline@biausa.org
Website: www.biausa.org
Materials available in Spanish, Spanish speaker on staff

CADRE (CONSORTIUM FOR APPROPRIATE DISPUTE RESOLUTION IN SPECIAL EDUCATION)

Direction Service, Inc., P.O. Box 51360
Eugene, OR 97405–0906
Phone: (541) 686–5060, (541) 284–4740 (TTY), (800) 695–0285 (NICHCY)
Email: cadre@directionservice.org
Website: www.directionservice.org/cadre
Materials available in Spanish, Spanish speaker on staff

CENTER FOR EFFECTIVE COLLABORATION AND PRACTICE (CECP) (IMPROVING SERVICES FOR CHILDREN AND YOUTH WITH EMOTIONAL AND BEHAVIORAL PROBLEMS)

1000 Thomas Jefferson St., N.W., Suite 400
Washington, DC 20007
Phone: (888) 457–1551, (202) 944–5300, (877) 334–3499 (TTY)
Email: center@air.org
Website: http://cecp.air.org

CENTER FOR EVIDENCE BASED PRACTICE: YOUNG CHILDREN WITH CHALLENGING BEHAVIOR

(Technical Assistance Center on Social Emotional Intervention)
Louis de la Parte Florida Mental Health Institute
University of South Florida, 13301 Bruce B. Downs Blvd.
Tampa, FL 33612–3807
Phone: (813) 974–6111
Email: dunlap@fmhi.usf.edu
Website: http://challengingbehavior.org

CENTER FOR UNIVERSAL DESIGN

North Carolina State University, College of Design, Campus Box 8613
Raleigh, NC 27695–8613
Phone: (800) 647–6777, (919) 515–3082 (Voice/TTY)
Email: cud@ncsu.edu
Website: www.design.ncsu.edu/cud

CHILD AND ADOLESCENT BIPOLAR FOUNDATION

1000 Skokie Blvd., Suite 425
Wilmette, IL 60091
Phone: (847) 256–8525
Email: cabf@bpkids.org
Website: www.bpkids.org
Materials available in Spanish, Spanish speaker on staff

CHILDHOOD APRAXIA OF SPEECH ASSOCIATION OF NORTH AMERICA (CASANA)

123 Eisele Road
Cheswick, PA 15024
Phone: (412) 767–6589, (412) 343–7102
Email: helpdesk@apraxia-kids.org
Website: www.apraxia-kids.org

CHILDREN AND ADULTS WITH ATTENTION-DEFICIT/HYPERACTIVITY DISORDER (CHADD)

8181 Professional Place, Suite 150
Landover, MD 20785
Phone: (301) 306–7070, (800) 233–4050 (to request information packet)
Website: www.chadd.org
Materials available in Spanish, Spanish speaker on staff

CHILDREN'S CRANIOFACIAL ASSOCIATION

13140 Coit Road, Suite 307
Dallas, TX 75240
Phone: (800) 535–3643, (214) 570–9099
Email: contactCCA@ccakids.com
Website: www.ccakids.com

CHILDREN'S TUMOR FOUNDATION (FORMERLY NATIONAL NEUROFIBROMATOSIS FOUNDATION)

95 Pine Street 16th Floor
New York, NY 10005
Phone: (800) 323–7938, (212) 344–6633
Email: info@ctf.org
Website: www.ctf.org
Materials available in Spanish, Spanish speaker on staff

CHRONIC FATIGUE AND IMMUNE DYSFUNCTION SYNDROME ASSOCIATION (CFIDS)
P.O. Box 220398
Charlotte, NC 28222–0398
Phone: (800) 442–3437, (704) 365–2343
Email: cfids@cfids.org
Website: www.cfids.org

CLOSING THE GAP, INC. (FOR INFORMATION ON COMPUTER TECHNOLOGY IN SPECIAL EDUCATION AND REHABILITATION)
P.O. Box 68, 526 Main Street
Henderson, MN 56044
Phone: (507) 248–3294
Website: www.closingthegap.com

CONSORTIUM FOR APPROPRIATE DISPUTE RESOLUTION IN SPECIAL EDUCATION (SEE CADRE)

COUNCIL FOR EXCEPTIONAL CHILDREN (CEC)
1110 N. Glebe Road, Suite 300
Arlington, VA 22201–5704
Phone: (888) 232–7733, (866) 915–5000 (TTY), (703) 620–3660
Email: service@cec.sped.org
Website: www.cec.sped.org/

CRANIOFACIAL FOUNDATION OF AMERICA
975 East Third Street, Box 269
Chattanooga, TN 37403
Phone: (800) 418–3223, (423) 778–9192
Website: www.craniofacialfoundation.org
Materials available in Spanish, Spanish speaker on staff

CROHN'S & COLITIS FOUNDATION OF AMERICA
386 Park Avenue South, 17th Floor
New York, NY 10016
Phone: (800) 932–2423, (212) 685–3440
Email: info@ccfa.org
Website: www.ccfa.org
Materials available *online only* in Spanish, Spanish speaker on staff

CYSTIC FIBROSIS FOUNDATION
6931 Arlington Road
Bethesda, MD 20814
Phone: (800) 344–4823, (301) 951–4422
Email: info@cff.org
Website: www.cff.org
Materials available in Spanish, Spanish speaker on staff

DEPRESSION AND BIPOLAR SUPPORT ALLIANCE
730 N. Franklin Street, Suite 501
Chicago, IL 60610
Phone: (800) 326–3632, (312) 642–0049
Email: questions@dbsalliance.org
Website: www.dbsalliance.org
Materials available in Spanish, Spanish speaker on staff

DISABILITY STATISTICS CENTER
3333 California Street, Room 340, University of California at San Francisco
San Francisco, CA 94118
Phone: (415) 502–5210 (Voice), (415) 502–5216 (TTY)
Email: distats@itsa.ucsf.edu
Website: www.dsc.ucsf.edu

DISABLED SPORTS USA
451 Hungerford Drive, Suite 100
Rockville, MD 20850
Phone: (301) 217–0960 (Voice), (301) 217–0963 (TTY)
Email: Information@dsusa.org
Website: www.dsusa.org

EASTER SEALS—NATIONAL OFFICE
230 West Monroe Street, Suite 1800
Chicago, IL 60606
Phone: (800) 221-6827, (312) 726–6200 (Voice), (312) 726–4258 (TTY)
Email: info@easter-seals.org
Website: www.easter-seals.org
Materials available in Spanish, Spanish speaker on staff

**EPILEPSY FOUNDATION—
NATIONAL OFFICE**

4351 Garden City Drive, 5th Floor
Landover, MD 20785–4941
Phone: (800) 332–1000, (301)
459–3700
Email via website
Website: www.epilepsyfoundation.org
Materials available in Spanish, Spanish
speaker on staff

**FACES: THE NATIONAL
CRANIOFACIAL ASSOCIATION**

P.O. Box 11082
Chattanooga, TN 37401
Phone: (800) 332–2373, (423)
266–1632
Email: faces@faces-cranio.org
Website: www.faces-cranio.org

**FAMILY CENTER ON
TECHNOLOGY AND DISABILITY**

Academy for Educational Develop-
ment (AED)
1825 Connecticut Avenue, NW, 7th
Floor
Washington, DC 20009–5721
Phone: (202) 884–8068
Email: fctd@aed.org
Website: www.fctd.info

**FAMILY EMPOWERMENT
NETWORK: SUPPORT FOR
FAMILIES AFFECTED BY FAS/E**

772 S. Mills Street
Madison, WI 53715
Phone: (800) 462–5254, (608)
262–6590
Email: fen@fammed.wisc.edu
Website: http://pregnancyandalcohol.
org

**FAMILY RESOURCE CENTER ON
DISABILITIES**

20 East Jackson Boulevard, Room 300
Chicago, IL 60604
Phone: (800) 952–4199 (Voice/TTY,
Toll Free in IL only), (312) 939–3513
(Voice), (312) 939–3519 (TTY)
Website: www.frcd.org
Materials available in Spanish, Spanish
speaker on staff

**FAMILY VILLAGE (A GLOBAL
COMMUNITY OF DISABILITY-
RELATED RESOURCES)**

Waisman Center, University of
Wisconsin-Madison, 1500 Highland
Avenue
Madison, WI 53705–2280
Phone: (608) 263–5776 (Voice),
(608) 263–0802 (TTY)
Email: familyvillage@waisman.wisc.edu
Website: www.familyvillage.wisc.edu

**FAMILY VOICES (A NATIONAL
COALITION SPEAKING FOR
CHILDREN WITH SPECIAL
HEALTH CARE NEEDS)**

2340 Alamo SE, Suite 102
Albuquerque, NM 87106
Phone: (888) 835–5669, (505)
872–4774
Email: kidshealth@familyvoices.org
Website: www.familyvoices.org
Materials available in Spanish

**FEDERATION OF FAMILIES FOR
CHILDREN'S MENTAL HEALTH**

1101 King Street, Suite 420
Alexandria, VA 22314
Phone: (703) 684–7710
Email: ffcmh@ffcmh.com
Website: www.ffcmh.org
Materials available in Spanish

FIRST SIGNS, INC.

P.O. Box 358
Merrimac, MA 01860
Phone: (978) 346–4380
Email: info@firstsigns.org
Website: www.firstsigns.org

**FORWARD FACE (FOR CHILDREN
WITH CRANIOFACIAL
CONDITIONS)**

317 East 34th Street, Suite 901A
New York, NY 10016
Phone: (212) 684–5860
Email: info@forwardface.org
Website: www.forwardface.org

FOUNDATION FOR ICHTHYOSIS AND RELATED SKIN TYPES
1601 Valley Forge Road
Lansdale, PA 19446
Phone: (800) 545–3286, (215) 631–1411
Email: info@scalyskin.org
Website: www.scalyskin.org
Materials available in Spanish

GENETIC ALLIANCE
4301 Connecticut, N.W., Suite 404
Washington, DC 20008
Phone: (800) 336–4363, (202) 966–5557
Email: info@geneticalliance.org
Website: www.geneticalliance.org
Materials available in Spanish

HEAD START BUREAU
Administration on Children, Youth and Families
370 L'Enfant Promenade, S.W.
Washington, DC 20447
Website: www.acf.hhs.gov/programs/ohs

HEARING LOSS ASSOCIATION OF AMERICA
7910 Woodmont Ave., Suite 1200
Bethesda, MD 20814
Phone: (301) 657–2248, (301) 657–2249 (TTY)
Email: information@hearingloss.org
Website: www.hearingloss.org

HUMAN GROWTH FOUNDATION
997 Glen Cove Avenue, Suite 5
Glen Head, NY 11545
Phone: (800) 451–6434
Email: hgf1@hgfound.org
Website: www.hgfound.org
Materials available in Spanish

HUNTINGTON'S DISEASE SOCIETY OF AMERICA
158 West 29th Street, 7th Floor
New York, NY 10001–5300
Phone: (800) 345–4372, (212) 242–1968
Email: hdsainfo@hdsa.org
Website: www.hdsa.org
Materials available in Spanish

HYDROCEPHALUS ASSOCIATION
870 Market Street #705
San Francisco, CA 94102
Phone: (888) 598–3789, (415) 732–7040
Email: info@hydroassoc.org
Website: www.hydroassoc.org
Materials available in Spanish

IBM ACCESSIBILITY CENTER
11400 Burnet Road
Austin, TX 78758
Phone: (800) 426–4832 (Voice), (800) 426–4833 (TTY)
Email via website
Website: www-03.ibm.com/able

IMMUNE DEFICIENCY FOUNDATION
40 W. Chesapeake Avenue, Suite 308
Towson, MD 21204
Phone: (800) 296–4433
Email: idf@primaryimmune.org
Website: www.primaryimmune.org
Materials available in Spanish

INDEPENDENT LIVING RESEARCH UTILIZATION PROJECT
The Institute for Rehabilitation and Research, 2323 South Sheppard, Suite 1000
Houston, TX 77019
Phone: (713) 520–0232 (Voice/TTY)
Email: ilru@ilru.org
Website: www.ilru.org
Spanish speaker on staff

INTERNATIONAL DYSLEXIA ASSOCIATION (FORMERLY THE ORTON DYSLEXIA SOCIETY)
Chester Building #382, 8600 LaSalle Road
Baltimore, MD 21286–2044
Phone: (800) 222–3123, (410) 296–0232
Email: info@interdys.org
Website: www.interdys.org
Materials available in Spanish

INTERNATIONAL RESOURCE CENTER FOR DOWN SYNDROME

Keith Building, 1621 Euclid Avenue, Suite 802
Cleveland, OH 44115
Phone: (216) 621–5858, (800) 899–3039 (Toll Free in OH only)

INTERNATIONAL RETT SYNDROME ASSOCIATION

9121 Piscataway Rd.
Clinton, MD 20735–2561
Phone: (800) 818–7388, (301) 856–3334
Email: irsa@rettsyndrome.org
Website: www.rettsyndrome.org
Materials available in Spanish

INTERNET MENTAL HEALTH (WEBSITE ONLY)

Email: internetmentalhealth@telus.net
Website: www.mentalhealth.com

JOB ACCOMMODATION NETWORK (JAN)

West Virginia University, P.O. Box 6080
Morgantown, WV 26506–6080
Phone: (800) 526–7234 (Voice/TTY), (800) 232–9675 (Voice/TTY, information on the ADA)
Email: jan@jan.wvu.edu
Website: www.jan.wvu.edu
Materials available in Spanish, Spanish speaker on staff

KRISTIN BROOKS HOPE CENTER

2001 N. Beauregard St., 12th floor
Alexandria, VA 22311
Phone: (800) 784–2433 (Nat'l Hopeline Network), (703) 837–3364
Email: info@hopeline.com
Website: www.livewithdepression.org

LDONLINE (WEBSITE ON LEARNING DISABILITIES)

Website: www.ldonline.org
Spanish site:
www.ldonline.org/featuresespanol

LEARNING DISABILITIES ASSOCIATION OF AMERICA (LDA)

4156 Library Road
Pittsburgh, PA 15234
Phone: (412) 341–1515
Email: info@ldaamerica.org
Website: www.ldaamerica.org

LET'S FACE IT USA (FOR INFORMATION AND SUPPORT ON FACIAL DIFFERENCES)

University of Michigan, School of Dentistry/Dentistry Library
1011 N. University
Ann Arbor, MI 48109-1078
Email: faceit@umich.edu
Website: www.dent.umich.edu/faceit

LEUKEMIA & LYMPHOMA SOCIETY (FORMERLY LEUKEMIA SOCIETY OF AMERICA)

1311 Mamaroneck Ave.
White Plains, NY 10605
Phone: (800) 955–4572, (914) 949–5213
Email: infocenter@leukemia-lymphoma.org
Website: www.leukemia-lymphoma.org or www.leukemia.org
Materials available in Spanish, Spanish speaker on staff

LITTLE PEOPLE OF AMERICA— NATIONAL HEADQUARTERS

5289 NE Elam Young Parkway, Suite F-100
Hillsboro, OR 97124
Phone: (888) 572–2001
Email: info@lpaonline.org
Website: www.lpaonline.org
Spanish speaker on staff

LUPUS FOUNDATION OF AMERICA

2000 L Street NW, Suite 710
Washington, DC 20036
Phone: (800) 558–0121, (800) 558–0231 (español), (202) 349–1155
Email: info@lupus.org
Website: www.lupus.org
Materials available in Spanish, Spanish speaker on staff

MAGIC FOUNDATION (MAJOR ASPECTS OF GROWTH DISORDERS IN CHILDREN)
6645 W. North Avenue
Oak Park, IL 60302
Phone: (708) 383–0808
Email: mary@magicfoundation.org
Website: www.magicfoundation.org

MARCH OF DIMES BIRTH DEFECTS FOUNDATION
1275 Mamaroneck Avenue
White Plains, NY 10605
Phone: (914) 428–7100, (888) 663–4637
Email: askus@marchofdimes.com
Website: www.marchofdimes.com
Spanish site: www.nacersano.org
Materials available in Spanish, Spanish speaker on staff

MENTAL HEALTH AMERICA
2001 N. Beauregard, 12th Floor
Alexandria, VA 22311
Phone: (800) 969–6642, (703) 684–7722, (800) 433–5959 (TTY)
Email via website
Website: www.nmha.org
Materials available in Spanish, Spanish speaker on staff

MENTAL HELP NET (WEBSITE ONLY)
Website: http://mentalhelp.net

MUMS NATIONAL PARENT-TO-PARENT NETWORK
150 Custer Ct.
Green Bay, WI 54301–1243
Phone: (920) 336–5333, (877) 336–5333 (parents only)
Email: mums@netnet.net
Website: www.netnet.net/mums

MUSCULAR DYSTROPHY ASSOCIATION (MDA)
3300 East Sunrise Drive
Tucson, AZ 85718
Phone: (800) 572–1717, (520) 529–2000
Email: mda@mdausa.org
Website: www.mdausa.org

Website in Spanish: www.mdaenespanol.org
Materials available in Spanish, Spanish speaker on staff

NATIONAL ALLIANCE FOR THE MENTALLY ILL (NAMI)
Colonial Place Three, 2107 Wilson Blvd., Suite 300
Arlington, VA 22201–3042
Phone: (800) 950–6264, (703) 524–7600, (703) 516–7227 (TTY)
Email: info@nami.org
Website: www.nami.org
Materials available in Spanish

NATIONAL ASSOCIATION FOR THE DUALLY DIAGNOSED (NADD)
(mental illness and mental retardation)
132 Fair Street
Kingston, NY 12401
Phone: (800) 331–5362, (845) 331–4336
Email: info@thenadd.org
Website: www.thenadd.org

NATIONAL ASSOCIATION OF THE DEAF
814 Thayer Avenue, Suite 250
Silver Spring, MD 20910
Phone: (301) 587–1788, (301) 587–1789 (TTY)
Email: nadinfo@nad.org
Website: www.nad.org

NATIONAL ASSOCIATION OF HOSPITAL HOSPITALITY HOUSES
P.O. Box 18087, Asheville, NC 28814–0087
Phone: (800) 542–9730, (828) 253–1188
Email: helpinghomes@nahhh.org
Website: www.nahhh.org

NATIONAL ASSOCIATION OF PRIVATE SPECIAL EDUCATION CENTERS (NAPSEC)
1522 K Street N.W., Suite 1032
Washington, DC 20005
Phone: (202) 408–3338
Email: napsec@aol.com
Website: www.napsec.com

NATIONAL ATAXIA FOUNDATION
2600 Fernbrook Lane, Suite 119
Minneapolis, MN 55447
Phone: (763) 553–0020
Email: naf@ataxia.org
Website: www.ataxia.org
Materials available in Spanish

NATIONAL ATTENTION DEFICIT DISORDER ASSOCIATION
P.O. Box 543, Pottstown, PA 19464
Phone: (484) 944–2101
Email: mail@add.org
Website: www.add.org

NATIONAL BRAIN TUMOR SOCIETY
22 Battery Street, Suite 612
San Francisco, CA 94111
Phone: (800) 934–2873, (415) 834–9970
Email: nbtf@braintumor.org
Website: www.braintumor.org
Materials available in Spanish, Spanish speaker on staff

NATIONAL CENTER FOR LEARNING DISABILITIES (NCLD)
381 Park Avenue South, Suite 1401
New York, NY 10016
Phone: (212) 545–7510, (888) 575–7373
Email: help@getreadytoread.org
Websites: www.ld.org; www.getready-toread.org
Materials available in Spanish

NATIONAL CENTER FOR PTSD (POST-TRAUMATIC STRESS DISORDER)
U.S. Department of Veterans Affairs, 810 Vermont Avenue, NW
Washington, DC 20420
Phone: (802) 296-6300
Email: ncptsd@va.gov
Website: www.ptsd.va.gov

NATIONAL CENTER ON PHYSICAL ACTIVITY AND DISABILITY (NCPAD)
1640 W. Roosevelt Road
Chicago, IL 60608–6904
Phone: (800) 900–8086 (Voice/TTY)
Email: ncpad@uic.edu
Website: www.ncpad.org
Materials available in Spanish, Spanish speaker on staff

NATIONAL CHRONIC FATIGUE SYNDROME AND FIBROMYALGIA ASSOCIATION (NCFSFA)
P.O. Box 18426, Kansas City, MO 64133
Phone: (816) 313–2000
Email: information@ncfsfa.org
Website: www.ncfsfa.org

NATIONAL COUNCIL ON INDEPENDENT LIVING
1916 Wilson Boulevard, Suite 209
Arlington, VA 22201
Phone: (877) 525–3400 (Voice/TTY), (703) 525–3406, (703) 525–4153 (TTY)
Email: ncil@ncil.org
Website: www.ncil.org
Spanish speaker on staff

NATIONAL DISABILITY RIGHTS NETWORK (NDRN)
900 Second Street N.E., Suite 211
Washington, DC 20002
Phone: (202) 408–9514 (Voice), (202) 408–9521 (TTY)
Email: info@ndrn.org
Website: www.ndrn.org

NATIONAL DOWN SYNDROME CONGRESS
1370 Center Drive, Suite 102
Atlanta, GA 30338
Phone: (800) 232–6372, (770) 604–9500
Email: info@ndsccenter.org
Website: www.ndsccenter.org
Parent packet available in Spanish

NATIONAL DOWN SYNDROME SOCIETY

666 Broadway, 8th Floor
New York, NY 10012–2317
Phone: (800) 221–4602, (212)
460–9330
Email: info@ndss.org
Website: www.ndss.org
Materials available in Spanish, Spanish speaker on staff

NATIONAL EATING DISORDERS ASSOCIATION (FORMERLY EATING DISORDERS AWARENESS AND PREVENTION)

603 Stewart Street, Suite 803
Seattle, WA 98101
Phone: (800) 931–2237, (206)
382–3587
Email: info@NationalEatingDisorders.org
Website: www.nationaleatingdisorders.org
Materials available in Spanish

NATIONAL FEDERATION FOR THE BLIND

1800 Johnson Street
Baltimore, MD 21230
Phone: (410) 659–9314
Email: nfb@nfb.org
Website: www.nfb.org
Materials available in Spanish, Spanish speaker on staff

NATIONAL FRAGILE X FOUNDATION

P.O. Box 190488, San Francisco, CA
94119–0488
Phone: (800) 688–8765, (925)
938–9315
Email: NATLFX@FragileX.org
Website: www.fragilex.org
Materials available in Spanish

NATIONAL GAUCHER FOUNDATION

5410 Edson Lane, Suite 260
Rockville, MD 20852–3130
Phone: (800) 428–2437, (301)
816–1515
Email: ngf@gaucherdisease.org
Website: www.gaucherdisease.org

NATIONAL KIDNEY FOUNDATION

30 East 33rd Street
New York, NY 10016
Phone: (800) 622–9010, (212)
889–2210
Email: info@kidney.org
Website: www.kidney.org
Materials available in Spanish

NATIONAL LIBRARY SERVICE FOR THE BLIND & PHYSICALLY HANDICAPPED

The Library of Congress, 1291 Taylor Street N.W.
Washington, DC 20011
Phone: (800) 424–8567, (202) 707–5100 (Voice), (202) 707–0744 (TTY)
Email: nls@loc.gov
Website: www.loc.gov/nls
Materials available in Spanish, Spanish speaker on staff

NATIONAL LIMB LOSS INFORMATION CENTER

Amputee Coalition of America, 900 East Hill Avenue, Suite 285
Knoxville, TN 37915–2568
Phone: (888) 267–5669
Email: nllicinfo@amputee-coalition.org
Website: www.amputee-coalition.org/nllic_about.html
Materials available in Spanish

NATIONAL LYMPHEDEMA NETWORK

1611 Telegraph Avenue, Suite 1111
Oakland, CA 94612
Phone: (800) 541–3259, (510)
208–3200
Email: nln@lymphnet.org
Website: www.lymphnet.org

NATIONAL MENTAL HEALTH INFORMATION CENTER (FORMERLY THE KNOWLEDGE EXCHANGE NETWORK)

P.O. Box 42557, Washington, DC 20015
Phone: (800) 789–2647, (866) 889–2647 (TTY)
Website: www.mentalhealth.org
Materials available in Spanish, Spanish speaker on staff

NATIONAL MULTIPLE SCLEROSIS SOCIETY

733 Third Avenue
New York, NY 10017
Phone: (800) 344–4867
Email via website
Website: www.nationalmssociety.org
Materials available in Spanish, Spanish speaker on staff

NATIONAL ORGANIZATION FOR ALBINISM AND HYPOPIGMENTATION (NOAH)

P.O. Box 959, East Hampstead, NH 03826–0959
Phone: (800) 473–2310, (603) 887–2310
Email: webmaster@albinism.org
Website: www.albinism.org
Materials available in Spanish

NATIONAL ORGANIZATION ON DISABILITY (NOD)

910 16th Street N.W., Suite 600
Washington, DC 20006
Phone: (202) 293–5960 (Voice), (202) 293–5968 (TTY)
Email: ability@nod.org
Website: www.nod.org
Spanish speaker on staff

NATIONAL ORGANIZATION ON FETAL ALCOHOL SYNDROME (NOFAS)

900 17th St N.W., Suite 910, Washington, DC 20006
Phone: (800) 666–6327, (202) 785–4585
Email: information@nofas.org
Website: www.nofas.org
Materials available in Spanish, Spanish speaker on staff

NATIONAL PATIENT AIR TRANSPORT HOTLINE

c/o Mercy Medical Airlift, 4620 Haygood Road, Suite 1
Virginia Beach, VA 23445
Phone: (800) 296–1217, (757) 318–9174
Email: mercymedical@erols.com
Website: www.patienttravel.org

NATIONAL RESOURCE CENTER FOR FAMILY CENTERED PRACTICE

University of Iowa, 100 Oakdale Hall, W206 OH
Iowa City, IA 52242–5000
Phone: (319) 335-4965
Website: www.uiowa.edu/~nrcfcp
Materials available in Spanish, Spanish speaker on staff

NATIONAL RESOURCE CENTER FOR PARAPROFESSIONALS IN EDUCATION AND RELATED SERVICES

6526 Old Main Hill, Utah State University
Logan, UT 84322–6526
Phone: (435) 797–7272
Email: twallace@nrcpara.org
Website: www.nrcpara.org

NATIONAL RESOURCE CENTER ON SUPPORTED LIVING AND CHOICE

Syracuse University, Center on Human Policy, 805 S. Crouse Avenue
Syracuse, NY 13244–2280
Phone: (800) 894–0826, (315) 443–3851, (315) 443–4355 (TTY)
Email: thechp@sued.syr.edu
Website: http://thechp.syr.edu/nrc.html

NATIONAL REYE'S SYNDROME FOUNDATION
P.O. Box 829, Bryan, OH 43506
Phone: (800) 233–7393, (419) 636–2679
Email: nrsf@reyessyndrome.org
Website: www.reyessyndrome.org
Materials available in Spanish

NATIONAL SCOLIOSIS FOUNDATION
5 Cabot Place
Stoughton, MA 02072
Phone: (800) 673–6922, (781) 341–6333
Email: NSF@scoliosis.org
Website: www.scoliosis.org
Materials available in Spanish

NATIONAL SLEEP FOUNDATION
1522 K Street, N.W., Suite 500
Washington, DC 20005
Phone: (202) 347–3471
Email: nsf@sleepfoundation.org
Website: www.sleepfoundation.org
Materials available in Spanish

NATIONAL SPINAL CORD INJURY ASSOCIATION
6701 Democracy Blvd., Suite 300–9
Bethesda, MD 20817
Phone: (800) 962–9629, (301) 214–4006
Email: info@spinalcord.org
Website: www.spinalcord.org
Spanish speaker on staff

NATIONAL STUTTERING ASSOCIATION
119 W. 40th Street, 14th Floor
New York, NY 10018
Phone: (800) 937–8888
Email: info@westutter.org
Website: www.westutter.org

NATIONAL TAY-SACHS AND ALLIED DISEASES ASSOCIATION
2001 Beacon Street, Suite 204
Brighton, MA 02135
Phone: (800) 906–8723
Email: info@ntsad.org
Website: www.ntsad.org
Materials available in Spanish

NEUROFIBROMATOSIS, INC.
9320 Annapolis Road, Suite 300
Lanham, MD 20706–3123
Phone: (800) 942–6825, (301) 918–4600
Email: nfinfo@nfinc.org
Website: www.nfinc.org
Materials available in Spanish

NLD (NONVERBAL LEARNING DISORDER) ON THE WEB (WEBSITE ONLY)
Website: www.NLDontheweb.org

NONVERBAL LEARNING DISORDERS ASSOCIATION
2446 Albany Avenue
West Hartford, CT 06117
Phone: (800) 570–0217
Email: NLDA@nlda.org
Website: www.nlda.org

OBSESSIVE COMPULSIVE FOUNDATION, INC.
676 State Street
New Haven, CT 06511
Phone: (203) 401–2070
Email: info@ocfoundation.org
Website: www.ocfoundation.org
Materials available in Spanish, Spanish speaker on staff

OASIS@MAPP (ONLINE ASPERGER SYNDROME INFORMATION AND SUPPORT AND MAAP SERVICES FOR AUTISM AND ASPERGER SYNDROME) (WEBSITE ONLY)
Email: info@aspergersyndrome.org
Website: www.aspergersyndrome.org

OSTEOGENESIS IMPERFECTA FOUNDATION
804 Diamond Ave., Suite 210
Gaithersburg, MD 20878
Phone: (800) 981–2663, (301) 947–0083
Email: bonelink@oif.org
Website: www.oif.org
Materials available in Spanish

PARENTS HELPING PARENTS: THE PARENT-DIRECTED FAMILY RESOURCE CENTER FOR CHILDREN WITH SPECIAL NEEDS

3041 Olcott Street
Santa Clara, CA 95054
Phone: (408) 727–5775
Email: info@php.com
Website: www.php.com
Materials available in Spanish, Spanish speaker on staff

PARENTS OF GALACTOSEMIC CHILDREN

1519 Magnolia Bluff Dr.
Gautier, MS 39553
Email: president@galactosemia.org
Website: www.galactosemia.org

PARENT TO PARENT OF THE UNITED STATES (WEBSITE ONLY)

Website: www.p2pusa.org/index.html

PATHWAYS AWARENESS FOUNDATION

150 N. Michigan Avenue, Suite 2100
Chicago, IL 60601
Phone: (800) 955–2445
Email: friends@pathwaysawareness.org
Website: www.pathwaysawareness.org
Brochure and video available in Spanish

PRADER-WILLI SYNDROME ASSOCIATION

5700 Midnight Pass Road, Suite 6
Sarasota, FL 34242
Phone: (800) 926–4797, (941) 312–0400
Email: national@pwsausa.org
Website: www.pwsausa.org
Materials available in Spanish

RECORDING FOR THE BLIND AND DYSLEXIC

The Anne T. Macdonald Center, 20
Roszel Road
Princeton, NJ 08540
Phone: (800) 221–4792, (866) 732–3585
Email: custserv@rfbd.org
Website: www.rfbd.org

REGISTRY OF INTERPRETERS FOR THE DEAF

333 Commerce Street
Alexandria, VA 22314
Phone: (703) 838–0030, (703) 838–0459 (TTY)
Email: info@rid.org
Website: www.rid.org

RESNA (REHABILITATION ENGINEERING AND ASSISTIVE TECHNOLOGY SOCIETY OF NORTH AMERICA)

1700 N. Moore Street, Suite 1540
Arlington, VA 22209–1903
Phone: (703) 524–6686 (Voice), (703) 524–6639 (TTY)
Email: info@resna.org
Website: www.resna.org

SCHWAB LEARNING

1650 S. Amphlett Blvd., Suite 300
San Mateo, CA 94402
Phone: (800) 230–0988, (650) 655–2410
Email: webmaster@schwablearning.org
Website: www.schwablearning.org
Portion of website in Spanish

SCLERODERMA FOUNDATION

12 Kent Way, Suite 101
Byfield, MA 01922
Phone: (800) 722–4673, (978) 463–5843
Email: sfinfo@scleroderma.org
Website: www.scleroderma.org
Materials available in Spanish, can refer to Spanish speaker

SPECIAL OLYMPICS INTERNATIONAL

1133 19th Street N.W.
Washington, DC 20036
Phone: (800) 700–8585, (202) 628–3630
Email: info@specialolympics.org
Website: www.specialolympics.org
Materials available in Spanish and French, Spanish and French speaker on staff

SPINA BIFIDA ASSOCIATION OF AMERICA
4590 MacArthur Boulevard, N.W., Suite 250
Washington, D.C. 20007–4226
Phone: (800) 621–3141, (202) 944–3285
Email: sbaa@sbaa.org
Website: www.sbaa.org
Materials available in Spanish, Spanish speaker on staff

STUTTERING FOUNDATION
3100 Walnut Grove Road #603, P.O. Box 11749
Memphis, TN 38111
Phone: (800) 992–9392, (901) 452–7343
Email: stutter@stutteringhelp.org
Website: www.stutteringhelp.org
Materials available in Spanish

TASH (FORMERLY THE ASSOCIATION FOR PERSONS WITH SEVERE HANDICAPS)
29 W. Susquehanna Ave., Suite 210
Baltimore, MD 21204
Phone: (410) 828–8274 (Voice), (410) 828–1306 (TTY)
Email: info@tash.org
Website: www.tash.org

TECHNICAL ASSISTANCE ALLIANCE FOR PARENT CENTERS (THE ALLIANCE)
PACER Center, 8161 Normandale Blvd.
Minneapolis, MN 55437–1044
Phone: (888) 248–0822, (952) 838–9000, (952) 838–0190 (TTY)
Email: alliance@taalliance.org
Website: www.taalliance.org
Materials available in Spanish, Spanish speaker on staff

TOURETTE SYNDROME ASSOCIATION
42–40 Bell Boulevard
Bayside, NY 11361
Phone: (718) 224–2999
Email: ts@tsa-usa.org
Website: www.tsa-usa.org
Materials available in Spanish

TRACE R&D CENTER
1550 Engineering Drive, 2107 Engineering Hall
Madison, WI 53706
Phone: (608) 262–6966, (608) 263–5408 (TTY)
Email: info@trace.wisc.edu
Website: www.trace.wisc.edu

TUBEROUS SCLEROSIS ALLIANCE
801 Roeder Road, Suite 750
Silver Spring, MD 20910
Phone: (800) 225–6872, (301) 562–9890
Email: info@tsalliance.org
Website: www.tsalliance.org

UNITED CEREBRAL PALSY ASSOCIATION, INC.
1660 L Street N.W., Suite 700
Washington, DC 20036
Phone: (202) 776–0406, (800) 872–5827, (202) 973–7197 (TTY)
Email: national@ucp.org or webmaster@ucp.org
Website: www.ucp.org
Materials available in Spanish

UNITED LEUKODYSTROPHY FOUNDATION
2304 Highland Drive
Sycamore, IL 60178
Phone: (800) 728–5483
Email: ulf@tbcnet.com
Website: www.ulf.org
Materials available in Spanish

U.S. SOCIETY OF AUGMENTATIVE AND ALTERNATIVE COMMUNICATION (USSAAC)
P.O. Box 21418, Sarasota, FL 34276
Phone: (941) 925–8875
Email: USSAAC@msn.com
Website: www.ussaac.org

VESTIBULAR DISORDERS ASSOCIATION
P.O. Box 13305, Portland, OR 97213–0305
Phone: (800) 837–8428, (503) 229–7705
Email: veda@vestibular.org
Website: www.vestibular.org

**WILLIAMS SYNDROME
ASSOCIATION, INC.**

P.O. Box 297, Clawson, MI 48017–
0297
Phone: (800) 806–1871, (248)
244–2229
Email: info@williams-syndrome.org
Website: www.williams-syndrome.org
Materials available in Spanish

**WORLD ASSOCIATION OF
PERSONS WITH DISABILITIES**

4503 Sunnyview Drive, Suite 1121
P.O. Box 14111
Oklahoma City, OK 73135
Phone: (405) 672–4440
Email: thehub@wapd.org
Website: www.wapd.org

**ZERO TO THREE (NATIONAL
CENTER FOR INFANTS,
TODDLERS, AND FAMILIES)**

2000 M Street N.W., Suite 200
Washington, DC 20036
Phone: (800) 899–4301 (for publica-
tions), (202) 638–1144
Website: www.zerotothree.org
Materials available in Spanish

Glossary

504 Plan—a legally binding and enforceable document that states the disability which qualifies your child for reasonable accommodation such as taking necessary medication or having longer test-taking time, and provides a detailed plan for such reasonable accommodation. A 504 Plan does not involved specialized instruction, as in an Individualized Education Plan (IEP). It is not as involved as an IEP. See also *Individualized Education Plan*

Addiction—compulsive physiological need for and use of a habit-forming substance with particular physiological symptoms upon withdrawal from the use of those substances

ADHD/ADD—a condition which interferes with a person's ability to maintain attention and stay focused on meaningful tasks, control his impulses and regulate his activity level

Affidavit for Dissolution—a written statement of facts that is made under oath and notarized, that states all the facts necessary for a divorce to be granted without a formal hearing

AIDS/HIV (acquired immune deficiency syndrome)— disease of the human immune system caused by infection with HIV (human immunodeficiency virus) commonly transmitted in infected blood especially during illicit intravenous drug use and in bodily secretions during sexual intercourse

Alcohol abuse—continued excessive or compulsive use of alcohol

Alimony—spousal support, also known as maintenance

Allergies—extreme or pathological reaction (sneezing, difficulty breathing or skin rashes) to substances that do not cause the same reaction in the average individual

Answer—the response to a Petition

Asperger syndrome—a developmental disorder resembling autism, characterized by impaired social interaction, restricted interests and repetitive patterns of behavior, yet with normal language and cognitive development

Assets—property of value. This can include the house, real estate, vehicles, retirement accounts, bank accounts, household furnishings, cash, and other items of value

Asthma—chronic lung disorder with recurrent episodes of airway obstruction, labored breathing with wheezing coughing and a sense of chest constriction, often triggered by hyperreactivity to allergens or significant sudden change in air temperature

Attention Deficit Disorder—see *ADHD/ADD*

Attention Deficit Hyperactivity Disorder—see *ADHD/ADD*

Autism—considered a lifelong neurological disability, which usually appears during the first two or three years of life, severely impairs sensory processing, communication (both verbal and nonverbal), socialization, problem-solving, and development

Bipolar disorder—an illness which involves extreme mood swings that affect a person's perceptions, emotions, and behavior

Blindness and visual impairment—lack of or deficiency in sight

Cancer—a malignant tumor of potentially unlimited growth. It expands locally or systemically

Celiac disease—a chronic hereditary intestinal disorder; the inability to absorb gluten, which triggers an immune response

Cerebral palsy—a disability resulting from damage to the brain before, during or shortly after birth, which affects muscular coordination and speech

Child custody—see *Custody*

Child support—money one parent pays to the other parent to help meet the financial needs of a minor child

Chronic illness—a disease or illness that lasts a long time or recurs frequently and often slowly gets worse

Crohn's disease—an illness that includes diarrhea, cramping, appetite loss, weight loss, abscesses, and scarring

Custody—physical custody refers to where a child lives. Legal custody refers to the decision-making responsibility of the parent or parents

Cystic fibrosis—an illness with faulty digestion and breathing difficulty

Deafness and hearing impairment—lacking or deficient in the sense of hearing

Decree of Dissolution—divorce decree. The written order by the judge that grants the divorce and decides the issues raised in the case

Depression—a mood disorder marked by sadness, inactivity, difficulty thinking and concentrating, significant increase or decrease in appetite, significant increase or decrease in time spent sleeping, feelings of hopelessness, and sometimes suicidal thoughts or suicide attempts

Developmental disorders—a group of severe conditions caused by mental and/or physical impairments. These delays/impairments may include communication development, physical/motor development, cognitive development, social/emotional development, and/or adaptive/self-help development

Diabetes—an illness with insulin problems, excessive urine production, excessive amounts of sugar in the blood and urine, thirst, hunger, and weight loss

Diagnosis—the identification of a disease or disorder from its signs and symptoms

Disability—the inability to pursue an occupation, or the impairment in daily activities and/or education because of physical or mental impairment. See also specific disabilities in this glossary

Discovery—things lawyers do to get information on a lawsuit. Some types of discovery are depositions, interrogatories, requests for production of documents, requests for admissions, and subpoena duces tecum

Dissolution of marriage—the end of a marriage, also known as divorce

Divorce—the end of a marriage, also known as dissolution of marriage

Down syndrome—a congenital chromosomal condition that affects brain and body development and causes intellectual disability

Drug abuse—continued excessive or compulsive use of legal or illegal drugs

Drug addiction—compulsive physiological need for and use of a drug, legal or illegal, with particular physiological symptoms upon withdrawal from the drug

Dyslexia—a disorder or difficulty with the use and understanding of language. This can affect all aspects of the use of language including listening, speaking, reading, writing, and spelling

Eating disorders—psychological disorders affecting eating behavior, such as anorexia nervosa or bulimia

Emancipation—the age at which the child becomes a legal adult and the parents are no longer legally responsible for his care

Epilepsy—various disorders with abnormal brain electrical activity, usually with sudden brief episodes of altered or diminished consciousness, involuntary movements, or convulsions

Evidence—testimony and items that are relevant to the case, and offered to the court to prove or disprove allegations in the case. In the usual divorce case these may include the bank records and employment records. In a special needs case they may also include individualized education plans (IEPs), medical records, school records, therapy records, and treatment plans

Fetal alcohol syndrome—a condition caused by the mother's chronic alcohol consumption during pregnancy. The symptoms include mental retardation, growth retardation, facial abnormalities, and developmental delays

Fragile X syndrome—a condition caused by an abnormality of the X-chromosome. The symptoms include facial abnormalities, mental retardation, and impairment in communication, behavior, social and motor skills

Guardian-ad-Litem—the lawyer appointed by the court to represent the children when the court feels it is necessary. It may be necessary when there are issues of child abuse, neglect, abandonment, drug or alcohol abuse, or special needs. It may also be necessary when the parents are so contentious with each other that the court feels the children's needs are not being properly addressed by the parents

Hearing impairment—permanent or fluctuating impairment in hearing. Includes but is not limited to deafness

Heart disorders and disease—an abnormal condition of the heart or of the heart and circulation

HIV/AIDS—see *AIDS/HIV*

Hodgkin's disease—a malignant lymphoma with progressive enlargement of lymph nodes, spleen and liver, and progressive anemia

Individualized Education Plan (IEP)—an Individualized Education Plan is a legally binding and enforceable document that states your child's disability, the impact of your child's disability on the educational setting, the amount of special services your child will receive, and measurable goals for your child. To be used in cases which require specialized instruction, not just reasonable accommodation. More involved than a 504 Plan. See also *504 Plan*

Individuals with Disabilities Education Act of 2004—federal law which provides free and appropriate public education for all children with disabilities

Intellectual disability—significantly below average intellectual functioning, with an IQ of 70 or less, and resulting impairments in the ability to adapt

Kidney disease—an abnormal condition of the kidneys and/or renal system

Language disabilities—difficulty in communication skills, articulation, oral-motor skills, and the physical act of communicating a verbal message

Learning disabilities—any of various disorders that interfere with a person's ability to learn, including impaired verbal language function, reasoning, or academic skills

Legal custody—decision-making authority on the major issues concerning the child, such as medical care, religion, and education

Leukemia—an acute or chronic disease with abnormal increase in the white blood cell count

Lymphomas—usually malignant tumor of lymphoid tissue

Maintenance—spousal support, also called alimony

Medication—a substance used to treat disease or relieve pain

Mental disorder, mental illness—a mental or bodily condition with disorganization of personality, mind, and emotions, that causes serious impairment of normal psychological function

Mental retardation—see *Intellectual disability*

Migraine headaches—recurrent and usually severe headache on one side of the head, often accompanied by nausea and vomiting

Multiple sclerosis (MS)—a demyelinating disease marked by hardened tissue in the brain or spinal cord, often with partial or complete paralysis and with a jerking muscle tremor

Myeloma—a primary tumor of bone marrow, usually in several different bones at the same time

Neuromuscular disorders—disorders and anomalies of the nerves and muscles

Non-Hodgkin's lymphoma—various malignant lymphomas that are not Hodgkin's disease, but have malignant cells. Symptoms are enlarged lymph nodes, fever, night sweats, fatigue, and weight loss

Obesity—excessive accumulation and storage of fat in the body. In an adult it is a body mass index of 30 or more

Occupational therapy—the use of physical activity to maximize and maintain the ability of people who are limited by injury, illness, impairment, learning disability, developmental disability or mental illness

Orthopedic impairment—a deformity, disorder, or injury of the bones

PDL (Motion for Orders Pendente Lite)—temporary orders issued during a divorce

Pervasive developmental disorder—similar to autism, and often confused with autism. It is a less severe disorder than autism. PDD involves problems with social interaction, communication, and behavior and usually has some sensory involvement

Petition—the first document filed with the court to start a divorce case

Physical custody—refers to where your child lives

Physical therapy—therapy designed to improve a persons's physical abilities through activities to improve muscle control and motor coordination

Psychiatric/psychological issues—disorders relating to the mind

Seizures—convulsions, sensory disturbances, or loss of consciousness caused by abnormal electrical activity in the brain

Sensory integration disorder—impairment at a neurological level in how the brain perceives and processes sensory information. May cause impairment in emotions, attention, movement, relationships, or adaptive responses

Sexual abuse—to injure or damage a person in a sexual manner

Sexual assault—illegal sexual contact by forced contact without consent or on a person who is incapable of giving consent

Sexually transmitted diseases (STDs)—various diseases or infections that can be transmitted by direct sexual contact. Includes syphilis, chlamydia, genital herpes, and gonorrhea. Some STDs can be spread through nonsexual means, such as hepatitis B and AIDS

Sickle cell anemia—a chronic anemia with destruction of red blood cells and episodes of blocking of blood vessels. Sickle cells are abnormal red blood cells with a crescent shape

Special Needs Coordinator—a person who assists the court with special needs issues

Speech/language impairment—difficulty in communication skills, articulation, oral-motor skills, and the physical act of communicating a verbal message

Spina bifida—a congenital neural tube defect of the spinal column

Spousal support—money paid by a person to his or her former spouse, to support that former spouse financially. Also called alimony or maintenance

Stress—a physical, chemical, or emotional factor that causes bodily or mental tension

Substance abuse—compulsive physiological need for and use of a habit-forming substance, legal or illegal, with specific physiological symptoms upon withdrawal from the substance

Suicide—taking one's own life voluntarily and intentionally

Terminally ill person—a person who is in the final stages of a fatal disease, or is near death from an illness or medical condition

Therapy—treatment of a bodily, mental, or behavioral disorder

Trauma—a physical or psychological injury caused by an outside force

Traumatic brain injury—a sudden physical assault on the head that damages the brain

Treatment—to care for by medical or surgical means

Visual impairment—impairment to the vision, including but not limited to blindness

Index